EUROPEAN UNIVERSITIES IN THE AGE OF
REFORMATION AND COUNTER REFORMATION

European Universities in the Age of Reformation and Counter Reformation

Helga Robinson-Hammerstein
Editor

FOUR COURTS PRESS

Set in 10.5 on 12.5 point Ehrhardt for
FOUR COURTS PRESS
Fumbally Lane, Dublin 8
e-mail: info@four-courts-press.ie
and in North America
FOUR COURTS PRESS
c/o ISBS 5804 N.E. Hassalo Street, Portland, OR 97213.

© The various contributors and Four Courts Press 1998

A catalogue record for this title
is available from the British Library.

ISBN 1-85182-318-2

All rights reserved. No part of this publication may be reproduced, stored in or introduced into a retrieval system, or transmitted, in any form or by any means (electronic, mechanical, photocopying, recording or otherwise), without the prior permission of both the copyright owner and the publisher of this book.

Printed in Great Britain
by MPG Books Ltd, Bodmin, Cornwall.

Contents

PREFACE   VII

St Patrick's Cathedral and the university question
  in Ireland c.1547-1585   1
  James Murray

Archbishop Adam Loftus: The first provost of
  Trinity College, Dublin   34
  Helga Robinson-Hammerstein

Who went to Trinity? The early students of Dublin University   53
  Alan Ford

The libraries of Luke Challoner and James Ussher, 1595-1608   75
  Elizabethanne Boran

An early friendship network of James Ussher,
  archbishop of Armagh, 1626-1656   116
  Elizabethanne Boran

Aristotle and the English universities in the seventeenth century:
  A re-evaluation   135
  Mordechai Feingold

What is an early modern university?
  The conflict between Leiden and Amsterdam in 1631   149
  Willem Frijhoff

Educational politics in the Austrian lands and the foundation of
  the Jesuit university of Graz, 1585   169
  Gernot Heiss

The Jesuits and universities in Italy   187
  Gian Paolo Brizzi

INDEX   199

Preface

Some of the papers assembled in this collection had their origin in a conference generously sponsored by the then Dean of Arts (Humanities), Dr P.H. Kelly, to mark the four hundredth anniversary of the founding of Trinity College, Dublin in 1992. The occasion was also an opportunity to invite the members of the International Commission for the History of Universities who held their annual general meeting in this context. Other papers, notably those by Alan Ford, Mordechai Feingold and the second contribution by Elizabethanne Boran (on Ussher's friendship network), represent the natural follow-up to the initial reflections on the role of the early modern university. These papers were given as Trinity Term lectures to the postgraduate course (M.Phil.) in Reformation and Enlightenment Studies in 1995, 1996, 1997. James Murray's and my own paper were substantially revised in 1996.

The collection as a whole, therefore, reveals a continued preoccupation with the place of European universities in early modern politics and society. While there are two discrete sections, Irish and non-Irish contemporaneous university foundations and scholarly activities, there is one theme which runs through the collection. It is encapsulated in the word 'civility' which appears in almost all the papers and has planted intriguing clues throughout the volume. It seems clear that founders and promoters of universities thought of the institutions as purveyors of 'civility'. This was either openly announced or tacitly implied by the chief promoters of such plans.

The theme of 'civility' asserted itself in these papers without any premeditation on the part of the lecturers or organisers. Their assignment was merely to examine the experience of the European universities contemporary with the foundation of Trinity College, Dublin. It was only at the editorial stage that 'civility' was seen to be the *leitmotif* of their reflections.

These papers are in fact an initial attempt to define this crucial but very difficult term in the sixteenth and early seventeenth centuries. In the earlier sixteenth century Erasmus of Rotterdam had started the debate on the crucial role and content of *civilitas*. As Norbert Elias has pointed out in his *The Civilizing Process*[1] the concept of 'civility' originated in the short treatise of Erasmus of Rotterdam on the instruction of children, *De civilitate morum puerilium* (1530), which Elias suggests, 'clearly treated a theme that was ripe

---

1 Norbert Elias, *The Civilizing Process. The History of Manners and State Formation and Civilization.* Oxford 1994.

for discussion'. *Civilitas* was a commonplace word which, Elias argues, was given special sharpness in the 130 editions and the extraordinary number of translations of Erasmus's tract, so that henceforth it became fixed in the consciousness of people with that special sense it had received in the treatise: 'the civilizing of manners'. It marks a significant stage in social and convivial life (notably in the improvement of table manners, which was so important to Erasmus's own social vision). The didactic purpose of Erasmus's treatise was never forgotten thereafter. Although the focus of Erasmus's considerations was the education of young children, his ultimate purpose was the control of human passions, which he saw as the fundamental cause of social disorder. His treatise provided a starting-point with enormous potential for extension.

By the later sixteenth century we encounter a notion of 'civility' that has been greatly extended. The emphasis is now on the control of adult passions which is essential to the preservation of public peace. Statesmen and educators were now preoccupied with the inculcation of good faith through teaching at adolescent level. The word *civilitas* had, of course, always been connected with citizenship: 'civility' encouraged subjects to give effective support to civil government. Tudor Ireland presents the most striking instance of a government's awareness of the need for 'civility', by which royal officials meant a knowledge of the laws of the land and an understanding of the need for their observance. In addition, the English government was seeking to enlist the help of a university to further this process by educating an elite for church and state; all this was particularly marked in Tudor Ireland. Edmund Spenser's *A View of the Present State of Ireland*[2] refers to the condition of pacifying the country as 'reducing the people to perpetual civility'. 'Civility' obviously involved acceptance of dutiful, but also constructive obedience to the lawful sovereign. The Lord Deputy, Sir Henry Sidney, was the ideal champion of such a policy, although his attempts to implement it met with little success. The central problem in Ireland was the existence of two rival systems of law, the native Irish and that of the English government, Spenser's and Sidney's concept of 'civility' assumed that there was room only for their own system. Such a notion of 'civility' as conformity to a single legal and political system was in fact prevalent in all later sixteenth-century writings analysing the state of the nation and the curing of social ills.

What was to be the role of universities in this process? To Adam Loftus, the first provost of Trinity College, Dublin, the question of 'civility' was essentially one of language. He appeared to try to achieve 'civility' by overcoming a barbarous style, using the university to teach the historically contextualised grammatical languages, especially Ciceronian Latin. His aim was

---

2   Edmund Spenser, *A View of the Present State of Ireland*, (ed.) W.L. Renwick. Oxford 1970.

the inculcation of 'civility' in an elite through the art of speaking well and controlling the mind and thought-world. The educated elite must then lead and control the rest of the population. From Loftus's brief treatment of the civilizing process it is clear that for him 'civility' was the Christian humanist method of internalising grammar and analysing texts in their historical context. The place for such a process of 'civility' was ideally the *local* university. While it is commonly held that the Gaelic Irish were not to be included in this early seventeenth-century civilizing process, Alan Ford's paper tentatively suggests that Gaelic Irish students were not excluded from it in the early years of the operations of Trinity College, Dublin.

It is apparent that 'civility' moved from being a commonplace word without specific content to a term for a substantive programme of which much was expected. James Murray's contribution shows the programme in Ireland in its inchoate and often jeopardized state. Gernot Heiss deals with the seminal purpose of 'civility' in education in an institutionalised form. 'Civility' exercised a 'debarbarising effect' when the individual student of Christian humanism learned rational thinking, discipline and self control. A comparison with Gian Paolo Brizzi's paper demonstrates that there was indeed no difference between Protestant and Catholic (Jesuit) institutions in the curriculum of 'civility'. Gernot Heiss studying the preoccupation of early seventeenth-century governments with the inculcation of 'civility' in society, detects a loss of confidence in traditional courtly culture and a growing reliance on the more substantial intellectual culture of the universities. Willem Frijhoff deals with a slightly later period, in which the intention of inculcating 'civility' was becoming more closely linked to civic culture. The term was now being coloured by the notion of usefulness. It is certainly worth remembering that already at the end of the sixteenth century Sir Humphrey Gilbert's foundation in London, Gresham College, stresses what must have become the dominant feature of 'civility' in England by the mid-seventeenth century: the direct usefulness, the immediate applicability of what was being studied.

What precisely was to be achieved when setting 'civility' as the target in higher education and how were teachers to achieve it? It seems very likely that a specific course of learning, studying certain books and becoming proficient in the analysis of live issues was recognised as necessary. In the case of Ireland the books brought together by Luke Challoner and James Ussher even in their private libraries offer us a glimpse of the process of choosing appropriate texts. Mordechai Feingold's paper, moving to the English university scene, suggests that the civilising process in Oxford may have been far more 'liberal' and tolerant of diversity of opinion and insight than hitherto admitted. Future research will doubtless concentrate on the content and mechanics of inculcating 'civility'. It is more than likely that university life as an exemplary community existence enjoyed the approval of intellectuals as a shaper of civility in the later sixteenth and early seventeenth centuries. In these model communities of students friendship networks were created which subsequently promoted the solidarity of those former university friends, now pillars of state and church. This process extended beyond single universities, as is shown by the ramifications of James Ussher's friendship network, explored by Elizabethanne Boran.

The publication of these papers affords an opportunity to thank very warmly those who have supported this venture. The important role of Dr P.H. Kelly has already been mentioned above. The publication was made possible by financial support from the Academic Development Fund, for which the Provost of Trinity College, Dublin deserves special thanks. I should like also to acknowledge the hard work and dedication of postgraduate helpers. Special thanks are due to Mark James Lilley who translated the article by Gian Paolo Brizzi and assisted in the translation of that of Gernot Heiss. He also undertook some difficult tasks normally reserved for co-editors, such as the preparation of the index. Paul O'Connor carried out the extensive duties of copy-editor. To both these research students I owe a great debt of gratitude. All the contributors deserve my special thanks for their unstinting cooperation, unfailing patience and display of 'civility'.

Helga Robinson-Hammerstein
Dublin, 24 July 1997

St Patrick's Cathedral and the university question in Ireland c.1547-1585

James Murray

On 4 June 1585 the most ambitious of Tudor Ireland's reforming viceroys, Sir John Perrot, was dealt a crushing blow in his efforts to secure a lasting remedy for the kingdom's political, religious and social ills. At the hands of Lord Chancellor Loftus, archbishop of Dublin, and in the presence of their fellow Irish councillors Sir Lucas Dillon, Sir Edward Waterhouse and Bishop Jones of Meath, the deputy received letters signed by the queen which confirmed that the English government would allow him to proceed no further with one of his pet projects: the foundation of an Irish university out of the resources of the metropolitan cathedral of St Patrick, Dublin.[1] For Perrot, the sinking of the scheme was both humiliating and bewildering. It was humiliating because it undermined his authority in relation to Archbishop Loftus, the man who had resisted the project from its inception, with the result that his standing amongst the local political community was seriously weakened.[2] It was bewildering because it represented a major *volteface* in government policy. Although Perrot had clearly signalled at the outset of his deputyship that he wished to establish an Irish university as part of his reform programme, it was not he but the English Privy Council who had insisted that St Patrick's cathedral might 'be made to serve' this purpose.[3]

---

1 S.P. 63/117/11, Archbishop Adam Loftus to Lord Burghley, 7 June 1585.
2 According to Perrot the quashing of the scheme was 'blown abroad' in Dublin as the archbishop's 'conquest' of the lord deputy, see Perrot to Burghley, n.d., c. June 1585, Bodleian Library, Perrot MS 1, ff 107v-108v. Perrot's response to this was publicly to attack Loftus's conduct as a senior official in church and state, including his nepotistic bestowal of cathedral prebends on his kinsmen and his alledged profiteering from his position as lord chancellor and leader of the Commission for Ecclesiastical Causes, see Perrot to Walsingham, 5 June 1585, Bodleian Library, Perrot MS 1, ff 113v-114v; the letter is calendared in C. McNeill (ed.), 'The Perrot Papers: the Letter-book of Lord Deputy Perrot between 9 July 1585 and 26 May 1586' in *Analecta Hibernica* 12, 1943, pp. 23-24.
3 Victor Treadwell, 'Sir John Perrot and the Irish Parliament' in *Proceedings of the Royal Irish Academy* 85 C, 1985, p. 272; S.P. 63/107/39, later copy and extract of the Privy Council's 'Memorial' to Perrot, 19 January 1584; the full text of the 'Memorial' is printed in J. Lodge (ed.) *Desiderata Curiosa Hibernica*, vol. 1, pp. 28-35.

Historians, no less than Perrot himself, have been at a loss ever since to explain the regime's contradictory dictates. Indeed they have invariably sidestepped the problem by treating the abandonment of Perrot's project as a function of the deputy's inability to compete with Archbishop Loftus when it came to mobilizing support for his cause amongst the queen's most trusted councillors. In this scenario the irascible and bullish deputy was simply outplayed in the game of court politics by a more astute, experienced and politic adversary who wooed and won the decisive backing of the lord treasurer of England, Sir William Cecil, Lord Burghley, on behalf of his cathedral. While there is no doubt that factional intrigue played its part in determining the fate of 'Perrot's college', such an analysis provides only a partial explanation of the government's inconsistency and the ultimate failure of the project. It does not, for example, explain why the regime initially promoted the scheme; nor, subsequently, why the lord deputy became its most zealous adherent. Moreover, such an analysis does not easily comprehend the fact that the quashing of Perrot's scheme had already been foreshadowed: the implementation of a similarly conceived initiative had met with a similarly unhappy ending in the 1560s.[4]

Both these schemes, in fact, were but separate manifestations of a single policy which dominated the Tudor regime's efforts to establish an Irish university throughout much of Elizabeth's reign. Derived from an earlier proposal put forward by George Browne, Dublin's first reformation archbishop, the policy was founded upon the notion that the exploitation of the property and revenues of St Patrick's Cathedral provided the most advantageous means of endowing the new academy. Despite its recurring attractiveness to the regime, however, the thinking behind this policy was inherently flawed. Blinded by the self-evident truth of the central proposition, its formulators were guilty of two basic oversights. In the first place, no allowance was made for the fact that the implementation of the policy would inevitably disrupt the life of the local institutional church. Secondly, little cognizance was taken of the opposition that this was likely to arouse from within the same quarter. More so than any other prevailing factors, it was these conceptual flaws which ultimately scuppered Perrot's university scheme, and its precursor of the 1560s. To appreciate this more fully, it is necessary to examine in some

---

4   See for example E.C.S., *The government of Ireland under the honourable, just and wise governor Sir John Perrot Knight ... beginning 1584 and ending 1588*. London 1626, pp. 72-74; Sir James Perrot, *The Chronicle of Ireland 1584-1608*, edited by H. Wood. Dublin 1933, pp. 48-49; Hiram Morgan, *Tyrone's Rebellion. The Outbreak of the Nine Years War in Tudor Ireland*. Woodbridge 1993, p. 32. Accounts of Perrot's efforts to erect a college which recognize the connection between it, Browne's proposal and the 1560s scheme will be found in Richard Bagwell, *Ireland under the Tudors*. London 1885-1890, vol. 3, pp. 131-135 and H. Hammerstein, 'Erzbischof Adam Loftus und die elisabethanische Reformationspolitik in Irland', Dr Phil. Diss, Marburg (Lahn), 1976, pp. 172-204.

detail the intellectual origins of the official policy, and the manner and circumstances in which it was applied by the Elizabethans.

I ARCHBISHOP BROWNE'S SCHEME

The idea of endowing a college with the property and revenues of St Patrick's Cathedral was first expounded by Archbishop Browne in a 'Device' or petition to King Edward VI, written in the winter of 1547-1548.[5] There is something anomalous about the archbishop's proposal, however, because nobody – apart from the cathedral clergy – stood to lose as much from the cathedral's rededication as he. For centuries the cathedral had been situated beside his main Dublin residence, the Palace of St Sepulchre, in the southern suburbs of the city. The precincts of the cathedral and the palace formed an administrative complex – in effect, the nerve-centre of the diocese – which was demarcated by the stretch of city wall between St Nicholas's Gate and the Pole Gate and the three medieval streets of St Bride, St Kevin and St Patrick. It was from here that his ordinary and secular jurisdictions were supervised and executed.[6] The cathedral was concerned solely with the execution of the archbishop's ordinary jurisdiction, the process of spiritual government; and its main function was to provide financial support for the archbishop's officials in the form of prebendal livings. Thus the archdeacon of Dublin, the officer responsible for maintaining moral discipline throughout the diocesan heartland, was beneficed there as a canon and one of the six dignitaries of the cathedral. So, too, was his partner, the official-principal, who, as the archbishop's principal legist, presided over the latter's consistory court where he judged suits brought at the instance of parties, and dispatched much of the see's record business such as the granting of probate on wills. Apart from this function, the cathedral made one other significant contribution to local episcopal government. The see's consistorial business was actually dispatched within its body. Sessions were held *in loco consistorii* by the west wall of the north aisle during term time.[7]

---

5 S.P. 61/1/10: printed in extenso in E.P. Shirley (ed.), *Original Letters and Papers in illustration of the History of the Church of Ireland during the Reigns of Edward VI, Mary & Elizabeth*. London 1851, pp. 5-10.

6 C. McNeill, 'The secular jurisdiction of the early archbishops of Dublin' in *Journal of the Royal Society of Antiquaries in Ireland* 45, 1915, pp. 81-108; H. Wood (ed.), *Court Book of the Liberty of St Sepulchre within the Jurisdiction of the archbishop of Dublin 1586-1590*. Dublin 1930, pp. vii – xiii.

7 C. McNeill (ed.), *Calendar of Archbishop Alen's register, c.1172-1534*. Dublin 1950, p. 297; Representative Church Body Library, Dublin Diocesan Registry collection, MS 4, pp. 36-40; Marsh's Library, MS Z4.2.19, pp. 1-126; H.F. Berry, *Register of Wills and*

Given the importance of the cathedral's role in local episcopal government, Archbishop Browne's promotion of a scheme which effectively sanctioned its destruction, calls for some explanation. The apparent incongruity, however, has gone largely unnoticed by historians. This is due to the fact that Browne's 'Device' has been examined only within the context of his efforts – as a favourer of learning and as a dutiful civil servant – to further the Protestant reformation, rather than as a text prepared by an archbishop on an issue which had major implications for the administration of his diocese. As a result, the petition has been variously portrayed as the 'great' and 'enlightened' vision of a Protestant patriarch; and as the somewhat desultory attempt of a scrupulously obedient cleric to highlight his reformist credentials before the new, religiously radical regime of Edward VI.[8] While elements of both these interpretations are certainly plausible, they have been highlighted at the expense of what was arguably Browne's major preoccupation in his 'Device'. Far from sanctioning the destruction of his cathedral for the greater good of Irish education, and far from being the work of one bent solely on winning the new king's recognition, Browne's 'Device' is a retrospective and pointed critique of what was, by then, the officially approved and already accomplished dissolution of St Patricks' Cathedral.

St Patrick's Cathedral was surrendered into the hands of Henry VIII's commissioners by its dean and chapter on 8 January 1547, about a year prior to the penning of Browne's university proposal.[9] The suppression of St Patrick's, a secular cathedral, was unparalleled within the Tudor dominions during the reformation. In England, the only cathedrals which met with a similar fate were the monastic cathedrals of Coventry and Bath, both of which were regarded as superfluous because their bishops already possessed seats in the secular co-cathedrals of Lichfield and Wells.[10] The medieval inheritance of the see of Dublin – two cathedral churches in close proximity to each other, one regular, the other secular – meant that it too was ripe for a similar trimming at the outset of the Henrician Reformation. In the late 1530s and early 1540s, however, it was St Patrick's sister cathedral, Christ Church, which seemed the most likely to be suppressed because of the Henrician regime's antipathy towards the monastic life, and because of its

---

Inventories of the Diocese of Dublin in the time of Archbishops Tregury and Walton 1457-1483. Dublin 1898; V. Jackson, *The Monuments in St. Patrick's Cathedral, Dublin.* Dublin 1987, p 2.

8 J.P. Mahaffy, *An Epoch in Irish History.* London 1903, p. 57; Brendan Bradshaw, 'George Browne, First Reformation Archbishop of Dublin, 1536-1554' in *Journal of Ecclesiastical History* 21, 1970, pp. 316-318.

9 J. Morrin (ed.), *Calendar of the Patent and Close Rolls of Chancery in Ireland of the reigns of Henry VIII, Edward VI, Mary and Elizabeth.* Dublin 1861-2, vol. 1, p. 132.

10 S.E. Lehmberg, *The Reformation of Cathedrals.* Princeton 1988, p. 82.

poorer endowment which was reckoned to be only IR£260 net. In contrast, St Patrick's Cathedral, with an annual income of nearly IR£1,400 gross in the 1540s, was considered by the Irish administration to be 'well endowed and meet to be preserved and maintained'.[11]

What altered this situation, and determined that in the matter of the reformation of cathedrals, the see of Dublin diverged from the pattern established on the mainland, was the impact of a unique conjunction of domestic political factors and the onset of the final phase of Henry VIII's policy of expropriating English ecclesiastical property. The first of the local political factors directly concerned the fate of Christ Church. Although it lived under the threat of suppression between 1539 and 1543, the institution survived in an altered secular state, a cathedral of the new foundation, because it was able to call upon the support of the mayor and aldermen of Dublin. Being the oldest and most venerable of the two Dublin cathedrals, and the only major religious institution located within the old city walls, the civic elite argued vehemently against its suppression as they believed it would denude and devalue the city's ordered urban landscape, and ultimately threaten its English identity. Their lobbying on behalf of the cathedral was successful on more than one occasion during these years and, as a result, the plan to suppress it was finally abandoned in January 1544.[12]

Had Christ Church been dissolved it is unlikely that St Patrick's would have met with a similar fate. Yet the abandonment by the crown of its plans for the elder cathedral, did not in itself lead to the suppression of St Patrick's. On the contrary, the crown continued to exhibit signs of its traditional favour to the cathedral when, later in the same year, Henry VIII granted its dean and canons a licence exempting them from personal attendance at their benefices in other dioceses.[13] It was, in fact, the emergence of a new development in the crown's attack on the possessions of the English church – the dissolution of the English secular colleges – which proved to be the more significant catalyst in bringing about St Patrick's demise. Although the bulk of the English colleges were dissolved between 1547 and 1549, it has been estimated that about 25 per cent were brought down through 'voluntary' surrender during the final two years of Henry's reign. The effect of this upon St Patrick's was twofold. Because the majority of the surrenders resulted from the promptings of royal servants and courtiers

---

11 *State Papers, Henry VIII.* London 1830-52, vol. 3, pp. 414-6; W. Monck Mason, *The history and antiquities of St. Patrick's Cathedral, Dublin.* Dublin 1820, pp. 28-99, *passim.*
12 Representative Church Body Library, Christ Church Cathedral muniments, Registrum Novum, vol. 3, pp. 1104-21; *State Papers, Henry VIII*, vol 2, pp. 544-6; see also vol. 3, pp. 130-1, 414-6, 468, 484, 489-90.
13 See Newport B. White (ed.), *The 'Dignitas Decani' of St Patrick's Cathedral Dublin.* Dublin 1957, pp. 128-132.

and the descendants of the founders of colleges, all of whom were intent on enriching themselves with valuable college properties, they both encouraged, and acted as procedural models for, a privately initiated attack upon the Dublin cathedral, especially as the latter had a similar collegial constitution.[14] However, while acknowledging that the English surrenders exerted a considerable influence on the genesis of this attack, it is also clear that the circumstances surrounding its suppression had a particular local colouring. The policy of dissolving the English colleges provided, in effect, the opportunity for those who sought the cathedral's suppression. For the underlying motive we must look at the manner in which Henry VIII's deputy, Sir Anthony St Leger, conducted crown government in Ireland during his first period in office.

A crucial element of the deputy's mode of government was his construction of a following among the various constituents of the Irish administration and the community of the English Pale through the lavish dispersal of crown property upon potential or actual recruits. The terms by which St Leger let crown property to his supporters involved much financial malpractice, so much so that between 1540 and 1547 his administration built up considerable debts.[15] St Patrick's Cathedral, the richest ecclesiastical institution on the island, presented itself as an obviously exploitable source to aid in reducing these debts, and as a means of ensuring that the deputy's support base was maintained, especially as the crown's monastic property was, by then, a much diminished resource. Thus, having been recalled to England in the spring of 1546 to resolve a dispute with the earl of Ormond and aware, no doubt, of the success of his fellow courtiers in securing new ecclesiastical spoils in the shape of the secular colleges, the lord deputy used his visit to instigate the dissolution of the cathedral; a process which in its initial prompting by St Leger and the manner of its subsequent execution clearly followed the pattern of the contemporaneous dissolutions on the mainland.[16]

The process of dissolution began in earnest in the following autumn. In early October St Leger secured Henry VIII's support for the plan, and spoke

---

14 On the English dissolution see J.J. Scarisbrick, 'Henry VIII and the dissolution of the secular colleges' in Claire Cross, David Loades and J.J. Scarisbrick (eds.), *Law and Government under the Tudors. Essays presented to Sir Geoffrey Elton on his retirement.* Cambridge 1988, pp. 51-66.

15 Ciaran Brady, *The Chief Governors. The rise and fall of reform government in Tudor Ireland, 1536-1588.* Cambridge 1994, pp. 13 ff.; S.G. Ellis, *Tudor Ireland. Crown, Community and the Conflict of Cultures 1470-1603.* London 1985, pp. 145-147.

16 The connection of St Leger's initiative with the attack against the English secular colleges is reinforced by his simultaneous involvement in the suppression of Holy Cross Abbey, Thurles, a former Cistercian monastery which had been converted into a secular college at the height of the campaign against the religious orders; see Brendan Bradshaw, *The Dissolution of the Religious Orders in Ireland under Henry VIII.* Cambridge 1974, pp. 124-125.

with the chancellor of the court of augmentations about current administrative practices for the swift and efficient suppression of a religious house and the distribution of pensions to its inmates. On 8 November letters subscribed by the English Privy Council were issued under the king's secret stamp to Archbishop Browne and the dean and chapter of St Patrick's informing them of its imminent suppression. On the same day St Leger and other commissioners – with the notable omission of Browne, who had previously served on all other royal commissions concerning ecclesiastical matters – were appointed to receive its surrender.[17] Although the king commanded that the 'thing' was 'to pass immediately without delay', the dissolution was not secured until exactly two months later, on 8 January 1547, because the cathedral canons put up some resistance. It appears that the consent of the precentor, the treasurer and archdeacons, and fifteen of the prebendaries was withheld until they had suffered the chastening experience of forcible imprisonment at the hands of their dean, Edward Basnet.[18] The surrender obtained, St Leger and his fellow commissioners moved on to the surveying of the cathedral's property which took place on the 27 January, the day before Henry VIII died, and again on 13 May 1547, after the accession of Edward VI and the granting of a new commission. Finally, throughout the summer and autumn of 1547, the cathedral clergy were pensioned off, during which time St Leger also oversaw the disposal of the bulk of their property to his supporters on 21-year leasehold terms.[19]

Although St Patrick's was refounded under the aegis of Mary Tudor on Lady Day 1555,[20] its dissolution during the final months of Henry VIII's life was a seminal event as far as the conception of future schemes for the foundation of a university in Ireland was concerned. It provided the main stimulus for the writing of Archbishop Browne's 'Device', a text that set out in detail the principle and manner in which the resources of the dissolved cathedral might be redirected to endow a college, and which provided thereafter a written authority for those who thought that this was the most desirable way to proceed with the establishment of a local university. Yet the evident concern for Irish educational matters shown by the archbishop in his 'Device' was not the only preoccupation of his proposal to Edward VI. A close reading of the text reveals that he was equally, if not more, concerned with the immediate problems which the cathedral's abolition posed for the govern-

17 S.P. 1/225, f 125r. Browne's exclusion from the commission is significant. It indicates that he was neither a party to St Leger's plans, nor that he was expected to support the initiative.
18 S.P. 1/225, f 125r; William Monck Mason (as note 11), p. 150.
19 William Monck Mason (as note 11), pp. 28-99 *passim*, 151-4, lxv; M.C. Griffith, (ed.), *Calendar of Inquisitions formerly in the office of the Chief Remembrancer of the Exchequer prepared from the MSS of the Irish Record Commission*. Dublin 1991, pp. 113-7.
20 William Monck Mason (as note 11), pp. 155-160.

ment of his see. For at different points, even in the detailed provisions laid down for the establishment of the college, he interpolated a number of suggestions which, collectively, show not only his basic antipathy to the act of suppression and the manner in which it was executed, but also his determination to counteract the worst effects of the attendant administrative disruption. Indeed, given the likelihood that Browne's idea of using the cathedral for educational purposes owed much to the crown's decision in March 1547 to endow a grammar school in the cathedral precincts,[21] it is arguable that this sub-text was the most personal element in the petition; and that the university proposal was only a strategem to make his critique of recent crown policy, and his desired objectives, more palatable to the new king.

Whether this was the case or not, there is no denying that the 'Device' portrays the archbishop as an episcopal governor deeply concerned with preserving the traditional administrative structures of his diocese. The biggest casualty of the cathedral's fall was the administration of ecclesiastical discipline, because the office of the see's most important overseer and corrector of morals, the archdeacon of Dublin, was done away with when his appendant freehold benefice disappeared with the cathedral. Faced with this problem, the archbishop included in his 'Device' a direct appeal for the restoration of 'two archdeacons of Dublin' because 'there is no bishop in Christendom without an archdeacon, but only Dublin, an so the said archbishop the worse able to supply his charge'.[22] However, potential difficulties concerning the conduct of the see's record and instance business also resulted from the dissolution. Although the other major diocesan offices were not tied to the cathedral establishment in the same direct manner as the archdeaconry, they, too, were similarly affected by it. The archbishop's customary practice of supporting the combined offices of official-principal and vicar-general through the bestowal of cathedral prebends was now at a virtual end. The practice would cease once the final residue of pensioned ex-prebendaries died out. Alternative means of support would eventually have to be found, particularly as the fees generated by instance suits and the issuing of licences were insufficient to finance this side of the see's administrative work.[23] And there was still one final discomforting feature of the dissolution which Archbishop Browne had to consider. What would become of his consistory court? Would it have to move elsewhere, away from its former and favourable location close to the archbishop's own residence? And, if not, how would it

---

21 William Monck Mason (as note 11), p. 153.
22 E.P. Shirley, *Original Letters* (as note 5), p. 9.
23 On this point see the comment of Archbishop Alen, Browne's immediate predecessor in the see of Dublin, concerning the lack of business processed by the consistory in the 1530s. According to Alen this was due to the poverty of his clients; see in Representative Church Body Library, Dublin, Dublin Diocesan Registry Collection, MS 4, p. 39.

cope with having the generally inimical common lawyers so close to hand, an imminent eventuality from March 1547 when Edward VI sanctioned the relocation of the four courts of judicature to a certain portion of the dissolved church of St Patrick.[24]

It was to counteract problems such as these that Browne interwove into his text his most subtly executed, but also most far-reaching, suggestion. He proposed, in effect, that St Patrick's should be refounded under another name and in a different guise, and that it should retain its traditional role as the administrative hub of the diocese. This was to be achieved by removing the dean and chapter of Christ Church to the precincts of the dissolved cathedral where they would perform divine service for the new college in the old cathedral church; a church which was to be renamed the church of Holy Trinity, Christ Church's more formal title. It was not to be their sole function, however. Browne also recommended that the same dean and chapter should 'be incorporated by such name as shall please the king's majesty, with honest livings to them appointed', and that they should have a 'common seal to assist the archbishop for the time being, in common matters as the king's laws shall permit'.[25] A church with a chapter and a common seal which assisted an archbishop in common matters – for which read, administrative matters – would have functioned in the manner of a cathedral no matter what King Edward chose to call it. Thus Browne was attempting to resurrect his cathedral under the disguise of an incorporated university church, which was to have the ancillary function of assisting the local diocesan in governing his see. Far from being an innovatory scheme, then, Browne's plan for the erection of a university in Dublin resembled previous attempts, dating from the fourteenth and fifteenth centuries, to establish a university in conjunction with, but not at the expense of, the suburban cathedral church.[26]

Browne's attempt to save his cathedral as an incorporated university church indicates that he did not support the official decision to suppress it. This attitude was also evident in the detailed provisions he laid down for the college establishment, provisions which reveal a real distaste on the archbishop's part for the motives which underpinned the cathedral's dissolution and for the man who instigated it, Sir Anthony St Leger. In particular, he lamented the fact that the cathedral's parochial benefices had been frittered away by St Leger and not made to serve a worthier cause such as the financing of a university, even though the deputy had declared that it was the

---

24 William Monck Mason (as note 11), p 153. On the competition afforded by the common law courts to the ecclesiastical courts in Ireland see S.G. Ellis, *Reform and Revival. English Government in Ireland, 1470-1534*. Woodbridge 1986, pp. 107, 128-9, 133.
25 E.P. Shirley, *Original Letters* (as note 5), p. 10.
26 J. Watt, *The Church in Medieval Ireland*. Dublin 1972, pp. 127-9; McNeill, *Alen's Register* (as note 7), p. 260.

king's pleasure 'that the ... church should be converted to a better use ... which much the rather provoked the dean and fellows there to condescend to the surender thereof'.[27] Clearly, the archbishop did not take the view that the deputy's need to pay off his debts and to maintain his patronage network was a 'better use'. For Browne, St Leger's instigation of the suppression without the episcopal consent, coupled with his illegal detention of most of the cathedral's plate, jewels and ornaments, and his involvement in similarly motivated initiatives to procure the archbishop's palace of St Sepulchre and some of the see lands, revealed him as a scheming and acquisitive politician.[28] It was thus the initial cause of the intense hatred which he felt for St Leger, a hatred which manifested itself soon after when, in the early 1550s, he launched a vigorous campaign to discredit him before the king and the English Privy Council. Not surprisingly, one of the charges levelled by Browne against St Leger was that his governorship was characterised by an unprecedented squandering of the crown's resources, and by a general level of corruption which enabled him to become 'wonderous rich'.[29]

The quick alienation of the benefices and resources of St Patrick's meant that the erection of Browne's proposed college – with its master and 'seniors', its four lectureships, an unspecified number of readers, and a student body of 200 individuals – would require, if it was to take immediate effect, investment from non-cathedral resources. He petitioned the king, therefore, to sanction the appropriation to the college of six valuable rectories lying outside the diocese of Dublin. He also recommended that the archdeacon of Meath and the restored archdeacons of Dublin should support additional lecturers, and that all of the Irish chantries should be suppressed to provide supplementary income. What he really desired, however, was that the former cathedral prebends – as a group the richest concentration of ecclesiastical benefices on the island – would be devoted to the university. Thus he directed his final appeal to the king, their current proprietor, imploring him to unite 'the benefices late appending to the said church to the said university', the revenues of which were traditionally paid in corn and now 'demised in money to the king's majesty's use'. If this was granted, and Browne stated that he, as archbishop of Dublin, and the mayor of Dublin, would be prepared to pay a fixed rent to the crown in recompense, then the master and students would be able 'to have corn at a reasonable price for their better maintenance'.[30]

---

27 E.P. Shirley, *Original Papers* (as note 5), p. 13.
28 William Monck Mason (as note 11), p. 152; Public Record Office, S.P. 61/3/45, S.P.10/4/27; National Archives of Ireland, Ferguson MSS, vol. v, pp. 21-4.
29 S.P. 61/3/45; W.K. Jordan (ed.), *The Chronicle and Political Papers of King Edward VI*. London 1966, p. 102 & p. 119.
30 E.P. Shirley, *Original Letters* (as note 5), pp. 6-14.

It was this final proposal – the funding of a university from the cathedral's appropriated livings – which was to prove the most influential in the longer term, for it was the most eagerly embraced by the Elizabethan proponents of the university. Browne, however, put it forward more in hope than in the expectation that it would be implemented. The fact that the property was already legally alienated, and that the services of St Leger as lord deputy were retained by the new king, determined that the scheme would not be adopted by the Edwardian regime. In essence, then, the archbishop's proposal was a rearguard action against secularization, a forlorn attempt to recover an ecclesiastical resource and reinvest it in an undertaking which would continue to benefit the church. Had St Patrick's not been dissolved, it is inconceivable that Browne would have recommended such a course of action. His 'Device' clearly reveals that he disagreed fundamentally with the policy because it posed insuperable problems for the day to day government of his diocese. It is ironic, therefore, that the document served as a blueprint for the subsequent schemes to found a university in Ireland, given that the advocates of these schemes had no such qualms about destroying the administrative machinery of the see of Dublin.

II THE SECOND ATTEMPT

The enactment of the Elizabethan religious settlement by the Irish parliament in 1560 provided the spur for the revival of plans to found a university in Ireland. Although nothing concrete had materialized by the time parliament sat, both the perceived need for a university to create a reformed ministry, and the intention of establising it, were clearly a part of official thinking. Thus the act for the restoration to the crown of the 'ancient jurisdiction over the State Ecclesiastical and Spiritual' allowed for its foundation by stipulating that any 'persons ... promoted or preferred to any degree learning, *in any university that hereafter shall be within this ... realm*' would be obliged to take the oath of supremacy.[31] A specific proposal for the university, however, was not put together until the autumn of 1563, when, on 20 October, instructions were issued by the queen to her special commissioners for Ireland, Sir Thomas Wroth and Sir Nicholas Arnold, commanding them, among other things, to survey the precincts and possessions of St Patrick's Cathedral with a view to converting it into a university. The instructions also reveal the identities of the two men who were responsible for the proposal. These were Sir William Cecil, the queen's secretary, who, as part of his brief of over-

---

31 *Statutes at Large passed in the Parliaments held in Ireland 1310-1800*. 20 vols. London 1786-1801, vol. 1, 1786, p. 281 (author's italics).

seeing the crown's Irish policy, drafted the commissioners' instructions; and Hugh Brady, a native born Protestant and graduate of Oxford, who was appointed bishop of Meath the day after they were issued. The commissioners were specifically advised to confer with Brady on the matter of the university.[32]

The initial planning for the college by Cecil and Brady was carried out at some point between the spring of 1561 and the issuing of the instructions to the commissioners over two years later. During this time Brady was the resident rector of the parish of All Hallows in Honey Lane, London, a post which, in geographical terms, gave him easy access to the queen's secretary.[33] Brady's entry into Cecil's service, however, would have depended upon more than the mere proximity of his parochial cure to the seat of Tudor government. A formal introduction or commendation would also have been a prerequisite, the source of which is likely to have been his ordinary Edmund Grindal, the bishop of London, who was not only a protégé, close adviser and personal friend of the queen's secretary, but also Brady's first benefactor in England. In February 1561 the Bishop recommended him to the patrons of All Hallows, the grocers' company of London, as one fit 'for the function of the same parsonage'. It seems natural, therefore, that when Cecil disclosed his intention of proceeding with the establishment of a college in Ireland, Grindal would have alerted him to the existence of the parson of All Hallows; for here was a man whose Irish background, graduate status and Protestant sympathies marked him out as an ideal sounding board for the development and testing of the secretary's plan.[34]

The planning process was simple in its conception and execution. Armed with Browne's 'Device', Cecil and Brady adopted the archbishop's core idea of using the revenues of St Patrick's Cathedral to endow the new college.[35] They also produced a 'plat' for the erection of a college at Dublin, which, again, appears to have been based upon the supposition that virtually all the revenues of St Patrick's would be used to endow the new establishment. In essence, the 'plat' was a costed account of the future college's requirements

---

32 J.S. Brewer and W. Bullen (eds.), *Calendar of the Carew Manuscripts ... 1515-1624*. London 1867-73, vol. 1, pp 359-60; J. Morrin (as note 9), pp. 484-5.
33 G. Hennessy, *Novum Repertorium Ecclesiasticum Parochiale Londinense*. London 1898, p. 77; Public Record Office, E 334/7, f 109v; Guildhall Library London, MS 9537/2, f 32r.
34 Guildhall Library London, MS 11588/1, f 46v.
35 The one surviving copy of Browne's 'Device' is endorsed by Cecil, Public Record Office, London, S.P. 61/1/10. Although it was bound up with the State Papers Ireland Edward VI in the nineteenth century, this version may be a later office copy of the early 1560s. Cecil's awareness of the document, however, is likely to have stemmed from the earlier period when he served as Edward's principal secretary between 1550 and the king's death in 1553.

and proposed that it should have a principal or provost; two preachers; readers in divinity, logic and philosophy; twelve fellows (one of whom was to act as college bursar); twelve bachelors; forty scholars; an appendant grammar school with a master and usher; and a variety of domestic servants. All told, it was estimated that the running costs of this establishment, including outlay on staff and expenditure upon provisions, would amount to £1,270 12s. per annum, a sum which was almost equal to the value of St Patrick's total endowment when it was suppressed in 1547.[36] Yet while the influence of Browne's 'Device' is discernible within the first Elizabethan scheme for a university in Ireland, it is also clear that the latter was conceived in an entirely different context. Browne's 'Device' was written against the background of the Henrician attack on the Church's wealth, and was a defiant, though politic, gesture against the secularization of his own see's resources. Between the penning of his proposal and its adoption by Cecil and Brady, however, two crucial developments occurred which determined that the later scheme was animated by new concerns that made the projected dissolution of St Patrick's an ideologically desirable act in itself.

The first of these was the refoundation of St Patrick's by Mary Tudor as an act of Catholic restoration. Not only did the cathedral become a symbol of Catholicism as a result, but it also came to be perceived as an agent for the same restoration; for the cathedral resumed its traditional administrative role in the diocese of Dublin, a function which was quickly dedicated to the task of achieving Catholic uniformity. In the wake of the enactment of the Elizabethan settlement, the survival of such an institution with many of its Marian personnel intact was a highly suspect and questionable prospect; and it gave added ammunition to Protestant activists who sought its abolition for the 'godly' purpose of founding a university in Ireland.

The second development of the post-Edwardian period was the emergence of a radical English Protestant mentality, a mentality which grew in part out of the experience of continental exile which befell a small but influential coterie of English Protestant emigrés during the Marian period. One implication of this was the emergence of a vociferous demand for a more radical programme of Protestant liturgical reform, a demand which, if not espoused by Queen Elizabeth, was supported by enough influential politicians to facilitate the public airing of criticisms of institutions like the secular cathedral which seemed to harbour an attachment to outmoded and quasi-Catholic liturgical practices.[37] Thinking of this also added some weight to the call for the dissolution of St Patrick's Cathedral and the redirection of its revenues to the projected university. Thus, from being a relatively straightforward

36 E.P. Shirley, *Original Letters* (as note 5), pp. 126-128; this document is endorsed by Cecil.
37 S.E. Lehmberg (as note 10), pp. 268-271.

question in the reigns of Henry VIII and Edward VI about how best to use spiritual revenues – for the administration of a single diocese, for the support of crown government or for the training of a local ministry – the question of St Patrick's Cathedral and the projected university evolved into a complex debate suffused with new ideological nuances. Despite this, the original question remained at the heart of the argument, while its ultimate resolution would prove to be the deciding factor in determining the fate of the cathedral.

When the news broke in the winter of 1563-1564 that the government intended to proceed with the dissolution of the cathedral it immediately caused some disquiet. Sir Thomas Cusack, a former lord chancelor, cautioned Cecil that the proposed alteration be suspended until the political disorders of the moment were redressed. Cusack's caution, however, was probably influenced more by a meeting with one of the cathedral clergy at Chester than by any fear that the implementation of the university scheme would deflect the reforming energies away from Ireland's poltical problems. It is likely that the unnamed cleric's response to the plan was a negative one – indeed he was probably in England to plead the cathedral's case – and that this betokened to Cusack the potential indigenous resentment that the plan might invoke, during what was still an early and delicate stage in the implementation of the Elizabethan religious settlement. This, it is arguable, was Cusack's real fear. In what appears as a cunning move, therefore, he appointed the cleric as his letter bearer to the court, crediting him as an 'honest man' who was to be given credence in all that is said, and one who 'should declare unto your honour the doings of those things in Ireland', including no doubt local misgivings about the university scheme. Thus, if Cusack was personally reluctant to become the voice of protest himself, he did not shun the opportunity of ensuring that that same voice got a proper hearing.[38]

The implementation of the scheme was not, in any case, given immediate priority by the English Privy Council. Although Wroth and Arnold duly completed their survey of the cathedral soon after their arrival in Dublin in February 1564, the Council appear not to have examined their findings until the spring or early summer of 1566.[39] In the interim the most prominent ecclesiastics in Ireland entered into a regular correspondence with English politicians either to ensure that there would be no slackening of resolve to see the enterprise through or to attempt to discourage its implementation altogether. Those for the university scheme included Bishop Brady of Meath and the then archbishop of Armagh, Adam Loftus, the two most vocal

38 S.P. 63/10/12, Cusack to Cecil, 2 February 1564.
39 According to Arnold the survey was brought over to the English Privy Council by Wroth, presumably on his recall by the Queen in October 1564, see E.P. Shirley, *Original Letters* (as note 5), pp. 235-236, also pp. 208, 258-259.

Protestant ecclesiastics in Ireland.[40] Against them stood the archbishop of Dublin and lord chancellor of Ireland, the religious conservative Hugh Curwen, who had overseen the restoration of catholicism in Ireland under his Queen Mary.[41] While it would be wrong to ignore the fact that Brady's and Loftus's support for the scheme was animated both by the current Protestant thinking on the role of education in the training of a preaching ministry, and by the Renaissance notion that education was a civilizing influence in society, their arguments for the university consolidated around what to them was one obvious and pertinent fact: the dissolution of St Patrick's was an essential undertaking because the cathedral was an emblem of the religious conservatism that plagued the diocese of Dublin in the early years of Elizabeth's reign. This insular perspective did not reduce the intellectual force of their argument, however. By extending their attack on St Patrick's to include the conservative Archbishop Curwen, they were effectively attempting to extinguish the old Catholic order which had survived in Dublin because Curwen and many of his cathedral clergy had been prepared to take the oath of supremacy in 1560. For Brady and Loftus, therefore, the prosecution of the university scheme was wholly and unambiguously identified with the successful progress of the Protestant reformation in the English Pale. Failure to prosecute the scheme would impede the progress of the same, not just because it would hamper the reformation of the ministry, but because it would lead to the preservation of a conservative, time-serving and obstructive element in what was strategically the most important diocese in Ireland.

The most eloquent exposition of this theme emanated from Bishop Brady in a letter written to Cecil in January 1565, which expressed his deeply felt anxiety at the slow progress the university scheme was making.[42] Interestingly, he spent little time justifying the need for, or the benefits to be derived from, educating Ireland's 'tender youth'. This was taken as read. His main concern was to inform the queen's secretary of the urgent need to rid the Irish Church of the cathedral of St Patrick. For Brady, it performed no useful function. On the contrary, it maintained a body of clergy who through their wilful resistance to the spirit of the reformed religion – 'they say themselves they be old bottles, and cannot away with this new wine' – were ham-

---

40 For studies of the careers of Brady and Loftus see H. Coburn Walshe, 'Enforcing the Elizabethan Settlement: the vicissitudes of Hugh Brady, bishop of Meath, 1563-84' in *Irish Historical Studies* 26, 1989, pp. 352-376; Helga Hammerstein (as note 4); Loftus and Brady also solicited and secured the support of the earl of Leicester, see A. Kendall, *Robert Dudley earl of Leicester*. London 1980, p. 67.
41 The best notice of Curwen's career is in A.B. Emden, *A Biographical Register of the University of Oxford A.D. 1501-1540*. Oxford 1974, pp. 137-138.
42 E.P. Shirley, *Original Letters* (as note 5), p. 162.

pering its progress. As 'a sort of dumb dogs', they were neither capable of teaching nor preaching to their flocks. Yet as 'disguised dissemblers', as practitioners of a survivalist Catholic faith within the reformed church, all of them – from Archbishop Curwen to the humblest petty canon – were 'living enemies to the truth, and all setters forth therof'. For these reasons, the suppression of the cathedral could not be subjected to any further delay.

Where Bishop Brady urged upon Cecil the absolute necessity of converting the cathedral into a university by a rhetorically powerful description of the ills inherent therein, his ally in the cause, Archbishop Loftus of Armagh, offered the secretary a practical means of moving the project forward. In the same month that Brady addressed his appeal to Cecil, Loftus acquired the deanery of St Patrick's *in commendam*. Thus, when he wrote to the secretary in the following October he was able to put forward a plan to execute the scheme, involving the use of his insider's position as the senior dignitary in St Patrick's. Loftus's main recommendation to Cecil was that Archbishop Curwen, the 'old bishop', should be translated to an English see because he was 'a man ... as unwilling to this as to further any other our business'. In his stead a new archbishop was to be appointed who would work with Dean Loftus in securing, as joint ordinaries of the cathedral, the replacement by resignation or deprivation of all the cathedral clergy who opposed the university scheme. The intention thereafter was that they would then proceed to pack the cathedral with 'favourers of the matter', from which there would follow 'the full resignation in to her highness's hands of the bishop, the dean and the chapter, to do withall what her gracious will shall be'.[43]

It is clear from the foregoing that both Brady and Loftus hoped to use the implementation of the university scheme as a vehicle for destroying the Dublin diocesan establishment as it was then constituted. They sought the removal of the conservative Archbishop Curwen, and the suppression of his cathedral church which they believed harboured a crypto-Catholic clergy. There is considerable evidence, in fact, that their analysis of the situation in Dublin was correct, as can be seen from the religious dispositions of the cathedral dignitaries Thomas Creef and Robert Wellesley, who, as official-principal and archdeacon of Dublin respectively, served as Curwen's leading diocesan officials at the time the university question arose. Creef began his cathedral career in the 1520s as a vicar choral. Thereafter, he steadily rose up the ranks acquiring the prebend of Saggard in the mid-1530s, which he held until the suppression of the cathedral in 1547; and the precentorship which he obtained in 1555 when the cathedral was re-erected by Queen

---

43 H.J. Lawlor, *The Fasti of St Patrick's*. Dundalk 1930, p. 45; E.P. Shirley, *Original Letters* (as note 5), p. 226; S.P. 63/15/12.

Mary. His conservatism is sufficiently well attested to in the fact that Curwen chose him as his leading legist during the era of Catholic restoration. It is also evident in the testimony of the latter's predecessor in the see, George Browne. In the 1530s, Creef had been a steward of Archbishop Browne but was sacked 'for his popishness', an orientation which was manifested soon after, when on a visit to England he went on a pilgrimage to Canterbury and Walsingham.[44] This conservative streak remained with Creef throughout his long career in the cathedral, although he subscribed to all of the Tudor religious settlements. In the early 1570s, by which time Adam Loftus had succeeded to the archbishopric of Dublin, he led the campaign to restore the chapter's right freely to elect their dean. In reporting the matter to Lord Burghley in April 1574, the archbishop pinpointed Creef's religious conservatism as the motivation behind his campaign, describing him as 'a man of this country['s] birth, well spent in years and corrupt in religion'.[45]

Robert Wellesley, the archdeacon of Dublin, was a man whose credentials, as well as the circumstances of his appointment, also mark him out as a member of the 'gainsayers and dissemblers' so disliked by Loftus and Brady. Like Creef, he acquired his cathedral dignity as a crown nominee when St Patrick's was restored by Mary Tudor in 1555. More so than Creef, however, his appointment was symbolic of the revival of the old order; for, as the former prior of Conall in Kildare, he was one of a number of ex-monastic heads who were given prebends in the restored cathedral. Wellesley did not disappoint the crown's expectations. Soon after, he was appointed vicar-general of Dublin by the custodians of the spiritualities, the deans of Christ Church and St Patrick's, and immediatey instituted disciplinary proceedings against married clergy in the diocese, including a fellow canon, the English pluralist Richard Johnson.[46]

The existence of men like Creef and Wellesley in St Patrick's, particularly as they were responsible for administering the see of Dublin, was disturbing in the extreme for Protestants like Loftus and Brady. As the existing diocesan authorities were charged with enforcing a number of important provisions from the statutes comprising the Elizabethan religious settlement, it meant that the fate of Protestantism in Dublin was in the hands of crypto-Catholics. Not surprisingly, their efforts on behalf of the new religious dispensation were negligible, a state of affairs which became public knowl-

---

44 H.J. Lawlor (as note 43), pp. 56, 164, 212; S.P. 60/7/27, George Browne to Cromwell, 27 July 1538. Apart from being his patron, Archbishop Curwen also chose Creef to witness his will on 20 November 1564.
45 S.P. 63/45/81, Loftus to Burghley, 23 April 1574 (printed *in extenso* in M.V. Ronan, *The Reformation in Ireland under Elizabeth 1558-1580*. London 1930, p. 453).
46 Newport B. White, *'Registrum Diocesis Dublinensis': A Sixteenth Century Dublin Precedent Book*. Dublin 1959, pp. 77-78; William Monck Mason (as note 11), pp. 156-158.

edge after a visitation of the English Pale was undertaken by the crown's ecclesiastical commissioners in the spring of 1565. According to Archbishop Loftus, who headed the commission, they found many grave offences against the crown's religious laws being committed in the heartland of English Ireland – including continual 'frequenting of the mass' – a situation which in Dublin must have been encouraged by the diocesan administration's lack of readiness to enforce the state's religious dictates.[47]

These highly visible failings presented the old archbishop of Dublin, Hugh Curwen, with enormous difficulties in his endeavours to construct an argument which would successfully defend his cathedral from renewed and probably final dissolution. One approach that was definitely out of bounds was a defence – like that of his predecessor, George Browne – based on the central position of the cathedral in the administrative framework of his diocese; for it was in its administrative role that the cathedral's flaws were at their most glaring. Indeed, the exposure of these flaws by Brady and Loftus appeared, by the autumn of 1565, to have brought St Patrick's to the very brink of extinction. In a set of instructions issued by the English Privy Council for the incoming lord deputy, Sir Henry Sidney, and the Irish Council, Curwen was forbidden to make any further appointments to prebends becoming vacant thereafter; and was ordered to examine in conjunction with Loftus and Brady, the best means of reforming the cathedral for 'the public benefit of learning in that realm'.[48] There was, as it had always been envisaged, only one such means of reformation – the transferral of the bulk of the cathedral's revenues to the new university – and, in April 1566, the archbishop responded by informing the Privy Council that he and the other bishops had treated with the existing prebendaries in the intervening months, and that the latter had agreed to give up whatever portion of their livings was thought necessary for the support of the new academy.[49]

Given the gravity of the situation, Curwen's defence strategy appears at first sight as an unfocussed amalgam of specious and cogent arguments for staying the dissolution. This eclecticism, however, probably owes much to the fact that the arguments were put together in committee by the archbishop and his cathedral prebendaries; and that the fullest surviving version of the same – a letter to the earl of Pembroke written in June 1564 – may also have been its earliest exposition.[50] The specious arguments put forward by Curwen included the proposition that a university would be of little use to

---

47 S.P. 63/13/42, Loftus to the queen, 17 May 1565; also in E.P. Shirley, *Original Letters* (as note 5), pp. 194-197.
48 S.P. 63/14/2, also E.P. Shirley, *Original Letters* (as note 5), pp. 206-209.
49 S.P. 63/17/8, Irish Council to the English Privy Council, 13 April 1566, also E.P. Shirley, *Original Letters* (as note 5), pp. 233-237.
50 S.P. 63/11/13, also E.P. Shirley, *Original Letters* (as note 5), pp. 151-153.

Ireland as there were very few adequately endowed ecclesiatical benefices in the country to accommodate prospective graduates. This unduly pessimistic prognosis was accompanied by the exaggerated suggestion – made perhaps at the insistence of xenophobic English-Irish members of his cathedral chapter – that the university would inevitably be infiltrated by Gaelic students who, learning the secrets of the Englishry while based in Dublin, would advertise the Irish rebels of the same with all the attendant dangers that this would entail for the English Pale.

The more weighty arguments in favour of the cathedral's preservation were concerned with the patronage and constitution of its prebendal livings. These livings made up virtually the entire complement of ecclesiastical benefices in the archbishop of Dublin's gift. Without them, Curwen argued, he would be unable to have 'one learned man to preach god's word in his diocese'. Although he had signally failed hitherto to do much in the way of appointing learned and 'godly' preachers, the argument was of a more general application; for, as his use of the third person deliberately indicated, any attempt to meddle with the fund of the archiepiscopal advowsons would have major repercussions beyond the period of his conservatively inclined episcopate. Future, more overtly Protestant archbishops of Dublin would face the same difficulty. Without any advowsons they, too, would be unable to play any part in the appointment of 'godly' preachers in their diocese.

It was another argument in Curwen's defence strategy, however, which ultimately proved to be the most telling. The archbishop informed the earl of Pembroke that the cathedral prebends were parochial cures whose main source of revenue was the predial tithes of corn. He went on to argue that such source of revenue would be a very unstable foundation upon which to build the college because it would be subject to the vagaries of inflation and deflation. More importantly, he argued that it would be inappropriate to bestow these parochial cures upon young scholars as they were intended for older and wiser men who, theoretically, would play some pastoral role within the parishes which donated the tithes. This was the crucial point in St Patrick's favour. Unlike the secular cathedrals, whose prebendal livings were financed almost exclusively by landed property or temporalities,[51] the endowment of the cathedral of St Patrick consisted almost entirely of parochial benefices whose income was derived from tithes or spiritualities, and whose incumbents bore the responsibility for maintaining the *cura animarum*. For Curwen, this was the quintessential characteristic of his cathedral and the cornerstone of all the arguments he advanced to save it. The archbishop let no opportunity pass whereby he might reiterate it, including the Irish

---

51 S.E. Lehmberg (as note 10), pp. 165-6; R. O'Day, *The English Clergy. The Emergence and Consolidation of a Profession 1558-1642*. Leicester 1979, pp 148-52.

Council's letter of April 1566, the point at which he resignedly informed the English Privy Council that his clergy were willing to accept the inevitability of the cathedral's demise.[52] His tactic was fully justified on this occasion, however. Belatedly and unexpectedly, his argument had the desired effect. By 10 June 1566, it had become apparent that Sir William Cecil, the orchestrator of the university project, was pepared to relinquish it. He was now against, as Archbishop Loftus regretfully acknowledged, 'the conversion of the tithes, contrary to the institution, from the use of their pastors'.[53]

Cecil's new sensitivity about appropriating the livings of St Patrick's was a remarkable turnabout, particularly when it is viewed against the forceful and persuasive argument for suppression advanced by Loftus and Brady. Even Loftus's counterblast against the supposed impropriety of appropriating the prebendaries' tithes – according to the archbishop the way these parishes were served left their inhabitants 'much fleeced and nothing at all fed' – had little effect. How, then, do we explain it? Given the fact that Cecil had been aware from the outset, through Browne's 'Device', that the cathedral's resources were mainly tithe-based, it seems likely that in reaching his decision he was subjected to a persuasive pressure other than Curwen's correspondence. The most likely source, although not directly connected to the progress of the university scheme, would have been the emerging critique of lay impropriations. At the time Cecil revived the scheme, public criticism about the way monastic tithes had been diverted since Henry VIII's day from the church to lay impropriators was gathering strength among forward Protestants. In England, it had found expression in a key paper put before the 1563 Convocation of the Canterbury clergy.[54] In Ireland, it was given voice by the queen's council who, in their letter of 15 April 1566, declared that the widescale impropriation of tithes was one of the main obstacles hindering the progress of reformed religion throughout the island. It was possible to construe the diversion of the tithes of St Patrick's prebendal livings towards the foundation of a university as a similar act of secular plunder. The implications of such an act – the laicization of the rectorial tithes of 57 Dublin parishes (i.e., 33 per cent) – would have been particularly vivid after the results of Wroth and Arnold's survey were finally examined and digested in the late spring or early summer of 1566.[55] Thus, although he undoubtedly favoured the university enterprise, the secretary's fear of falling prey to the charge of sanctioning even more lay encroachment upon spiritual resources lay at the root of his decision to abandon the project.

52 S.P. 63/17/8, also E.P. Shirley, *Original Letters* (as note 5), p. 236.
53 S.P. 63/18/13, Archbishop Loftus to Cecil, 10 June 1566, also E.P. Shirley, *Original Letters* (as note 5), pp. 157-159.
54 W.P. Haugaard, *Elizabeth and the English Reformation*. Cambridge 1968, pp. 178-179.
55 E.P. Shirley, *Original Letters* (as note 5), pp. 234-235.

There was a greater a sense of irony, therefore, in the circumstances which brought about the university scheme's demise, than in those which surrounded its conception. Initially, the scheme was inspired by the writings of a man who would have disagreed with the fundamental premise upon which it was built, the destruction of St Patrick's Cathedral. Now, it was abandoned because of the influence of the thinking of men who would have sympathised deeply with the views of its main proponents, Hugh Brady and Adam Loftus. Indeed, Loftus himself was one of the signatories to the Irish council's letter which condemned impropriations. Although he could not have foreseen it, it was this defence of the clergy's traditional proprietorial interest in parochial tithes, a stance which was becoming increasingly appealing to radically minded Protestant clergy on both sides of the Irish sea, that ultimately secured a future for the 'popish' cathedral of St Patrick.

III THE THIRD ATTEMPT

The failure of the first Elizabethan scheme for a university was a major blow to the Protestant reform party in Ireland. The achievement of two of its avowed objectives – the destruction of the conservative clerical elite in Dublin, and the creation of a Protestant seminary to train the Church of Ireland's ministry – were delayed as a result. Despite this, an opportunity soon emerged to restore the flagging momentum of the movement when the aged and sickly archbishop of Dublin, Hugh Curwen, left Ireland in the late autumn or winter of 1567 to take up residence in England as the newly appointed bishop of Oxford. Although Curwen's long sought after translation had been resolved upon by the queen before the university scheme was abandoned, the timing of its execution and the spate of personnel changes that were ushered in in its wake, boosted the morale and political strength of the reform faction and encouraged it to pursue its aims with renewed vigour.[56]

The most important of these personnel changes concerned the replacement of Curwen in his dual capacity as archbishop of Dublin and lord chancellor of Ireland. Adam Loftus, the unambiguously Protestant archbishop of Armagh, was nominated in his stead to bring sound religious leadership to the strategically important diocese of Dublin, a task which the new incumbent regarded as vital to the progress of Protestantism 'because thereof will the rest in a manner depend'.[57] In the Court of Chancery, Curwen was replaced by Dr Robert Weston, the dean of the Arches, an eminent civil lawyer and an exemplar of Protestant virtue and piety. Weston was also

---

56 E.P. Shirley, *Original Letters* (as note 5), pp. 142-5, 240-1, 300-3.
57 E.P. Shirley, *Original Letters* (as note 5), pp. 174-6, 300-3.

granted the deanery of St Patrick's Cathedral as a sinecure by the queen. Although he was not in orders, the new lord chancellor took his spiritual charge seriously and signalled his devotion to the principles of 'godly' religion by endowing a number of perpetual vicarages on his prebendal livings.[58] Taken together with the already ensconced bishop of Meath, Hugh Brady, and the Protestant lord deputy, Sir Henry Sidney, the promotion of Loftus and Weston created, in theory, the strongest and most powerfully placed reforming nexus in Irish officialdom since the beginning of the Reformation. It promised great things for the cause of 'true religion' on the island. As Sidney remarked when hailing Loftus's appointment to Dublin, '*nunc venit hora ecclesiam reformandi*'.[59] Despite this avowal, however, the time was not as propitious for reform as the lord deputy had so confidently predicted. The quest to bridge the gap between the ideals of religious reform and the development and execution of relevant policies so as to make the ideals a reality was to remain fraught with difficulties. Nowhere were these difficulties more clearly visible than in the lord deputy's ill-fated attempt to revive the government's moribund university policy in the parliament of 1569-1571.

The erection of a university never figured in the legislative programme of the 1569-1571 parliament. In the autumn session of 1569, however, the lords and commons made a 'motion ... for the founding of an university'. It is clear from Edmund Campion's account of these proceedings that Lord Deputy Sidney was the prime mover behind the discussions which gave rise to the parliamentary motion. Sidney's enthusiasm for and strong advocacy of the cause – it was backed up by a pledge to donate £20 in lands and £100 in money for the university's endowment – probably stemmed from the fact that the principle commanded general support throughout the political community at large. According to Lord Chancellor Weston it was 'well liked universally of all here'.[60] This support comprehended the important reforming constituency of the English Pale; a grouping which included such diverse adherents as Rowland White, James Stanihurst and John Ussher, and which regarded the provision of education as an important element in reducing Ireland to good order and civility.[61] For Sidney, therefore, it provided an opportunity of instituting a policy which would have the virtue of satisfying the aspirations of various interest groups – political reformers and religious

---

58 Bodleian, Perrot MS 1, f 104r..
59 E.P. Shirley, *Original Letters* (as note 5), pp. 293-294.
60 S.P. 63/30/29, Weston to Cecil 12 March 1570; Edmund Campion, *Two bokes of the histories of Ireland*, ed. A.F. Vossen. Assen 1963, pp. 94-5, 145-6.
61 On White see N. Canny, 'Rowland White's "Discorse touching Ireland", *c*.1569', in *Irish Historical Studies*, 20, 1976-7, pp. 439-65, here especially 460-1; on James Stanihurst see C. Lennon, *Richard Stanihurst the Dubliner 1547-1618*. Dublin 1981, pp. 19-34 *passim*; on Ussher and his proposal to found a university from the profits of the Staple after the par-

reformers alike – and of binding them together for the general good of the Irish commonwealth.⁶²

Paradoxically, it was precisely this general level of support commanded by the principle of establishing a university that ultimately brought about the demise of Sidney's scheme. This was because the different groups and individuals who supported the principle held divergent and incompatible views concerning the university's future aims and development. Although these views were not openly articulated – on the contrary, the parliamentary motion gave the appearance of a unity which Lord Deputy Sidney hoped to harness – the suspicion that they existed led to division of opinion in parliament concerning the most appropriate manner of funding the projected college. And it was upon this division of opinion that the scheme eventually floundered. Sidney hoped to endow the university through an assortment of private donations of money and land on the model of his own proffer and, according to a letter of the Irish Privy Council of 4 March 1570, the scheme was 'so well liked' that it 'hath provoked many good men to offer very liberally to help it forward'. Yet in a letter written only eight days later, Lord Chancellor Weston contradicted this view by informing Cecil that without the queen's financial support 'our bareness and poverty in this realm is not able to support such a work of charge'.⁶³ Here was the division of opinion over funding in its starkest terms. What did it signify?

In reality, the division of opinion had nothing to do with finance. The point at issue was the question of who would exercise ideological control over the university. When recounting the doings of the autumn session of parliament to Cecil in March 1570, Weston drew a careful distinction between the emergence of the motion for a university, and the simultaneous work that he and the bishops had undertaken on the drafting of reformist bills for the erection of free schools, for curbing clerical non-residence and for reparing ruined churches and chapels. The chancellor, in fact, was distancing himself ever so slightly from the motion, the implication being that he and the bishops played no active part in bringing it forward. On the contrary, with the active encouragement of their speaker, James Stanihurst, the motion appears to have emanated from the commons. Nevertheless, Weston and the bishops had to, and genuinely did, support the principle underlying the motion, for

---

liamentary scheme failed in 1570 see J.T. Gilbert, *History of the City of Dublin*. Dublin 1834-9 (3 vols.), vol 1, pp 383-5, and V. Treadwell, 'The Irish Parliament of 1569-71' in *Proceedings of the Royal Irish Academy* 65, C, 1966-1967, pp. 55-89.

62 On the reforming milieu generally at the time see Nicholas Canny, *The formation of the Old English Elite in Ireland*. Dublin 1975.
63 Acts of the Privy Council, Ireland, 1556-1571, pp. 246-247; S.P. 63/30/29, Weston to Cecil, 12 March 1570.

these were the men who had only recently campaigned for the establishment of a university in St Patrick's. What they did not, nor were bound to, agree to was Sidney's idea of endowing the college through private donations, for this would have meant that power and influence over the shaping of the university's religious orientation would devolve upon the donors, not all of whom – including Speaker Stanihurst – could be counted upon to give full and unqualified support to the Protestant cause.[64] Hence Weston's insistence that 'the device, direction and foundation of ... so godly a deed' should reside with the queen alone and that it should 'consecrate to perpetual memory her majesty's godly zeal to true religion and learning'. If the foundation and direction of the college were to reside elsewhere – with trimming or even papistically inclined laymen – then such a consecration to true religion would not be guaranteed. It is evident that the lord deputy did not share this view. In contrast to Weston and the bishops, his greatest anxiety was that if parliament failed at this juncture to get the university up and running, then the general goodwill to establish the new foundation would become dissipated and ultimately lead to nothing. Sidney was also more tolerant on religious matters than the bishops, and may have felt that his munificence and his willingness to include the local community in the work of creating an indigenous seat of learning would do more to convert papists and religious trimmers to Protestantism, than the establishment of the exclusivist institution that the hierachy had in mind.

Faced with the deputy's determined enthusiasm, the opponents of a privately funded university attacked the scheme on the grounds that it would lead necessarily to the creation of a poor and niggardly institution. They contended that a sufficient sum would not 'arise to make a muster of colleges', that the university would be 'a feble and raw foundation' and that the projected location of the college would 'be not all so commodious'. His exasperated counter-argument – 'that time must ripen a weak beginning, that other universities began with less' – made little impression upon the doubters. Weston and the bishops brought the entire project to an impasse.[65] In doing so, it is likely that they had the support of other groupings in parliament who had their own private fears about the implications of the scheme. These may have included those who would have been fearful that the deputy's call for private donations might evolve into the enactment of legislation involving the imposition of direct taxation on behalf of the university. The parliament was particularly notable for the techiness and deep suspicion with which it viewed the government's economic motives on a whole range of issues, including bills for the abolition of coign and livery and the regulation of Irish trade. The

64 Campion (as note 60), pp. 144-6; Colm Lennon (as note 61), pp. 28, 30-31, 87.
65 S.P. 63/27/48, Weston to Cecil, 18 March 1569.

opposition may even have included, as Sidney later intimated, some active 'papists' who, unlike the chancellor and the bishops, did not believe that they would have any influence on the university's religious orientation rather, that it would become a wellspring for breeding Protestant evangelists in Ireland. Whatever the case, no agreement on the means for funding the university was achievable in parliament and a compromise solution was adopted to bring the squabbling to an end. This was the Irish Council's letter of 4 March 1570 to the English Privy Council, which highlighted, *à la* Sidney, native enthusiasm for the project and the willingness of the local community to contribute towards its funding. Side by side with this, however, the letter also contained the Weston viewpoint: the English Council were petitioned to solicit the queen 'to devise, order and direct' the establishment of the university and to 'further it with her most bounteous liberality'.[66] It was a risky strategy which failed to pay off. The parsimonious queen's unwillingness to sponsor and finance the university led to its disappearance from the order of business transacted in the subsequent sessions of the parliament.

IV THE PERROT SCHEME

The failure of Sidney's university initiative in 1570, coming so soon after the failure of the Cecil-Brady scheme, severely blighted the regime's enthusiasm for proceeding with the establishment of an Irish university. And, despite the revelations which emerged in the intervening years that the all too evident inadequacies of the Church of Ireland's clergy stemmed from their lack of a good, Protestant education; and the continued belief among would-be reformers of Ireland that an indigenous university was a necessary prerequisite for bringing civility into the country; fourteen years were to pass before the regime regained sufficient confidence and motivation to try again. Even at this juncture, the winter of 1583-1584, it was external pressure, rather than a spontaneous gesture on the part of the English Privy Council, which helped put the foundation of an Irish university back upon the political agenda. In a series of tough negotiations conducted between the incoming lord deputy, Sir John Perrot, and the Council, to determine the final content of an ambitiously conceived vice-regal reform programme, it was Perrot who broached the possibility of including the foundation of a university as a policy objective.[67] Initially, however, even he did not rank the

---

66 Acts of the Privy Council, Ireland, 1556-1571, pp. 246-247.
67 S.P. 63/110/34, Robert Draper, Parson of Trim to Burghley, 15 May 1584; S.P. 63/108/87, 'Necessary Considerations for the Causes of Ireland' (item 17), n.d., *c*.1583; on the negotiations generally see Hiram Morgan (as note 4), p. 30.

university question among the major issues to be addressed by his new government, with the result that it did not figure very prominently in his deliberations with the Council. Indeed, in December 1583, it was completely excluded from the first batch of instructions which were issued to him on his appointment as deputy.[68]

That Perrot was ultimately enjoined to pursue the foundation of an Irish university afresh, was due in large measure to the renewed interest which his initial suggestion aroused in Lord Treasurer Burghley. Burghley, of course, was the man who had sought in the 1560s to make Archbishop Browne's earlier university proposal a reality. Now, in the 1580s, he clearly saw in Perrot's pro-university stance an opportunity to revive a policy the implementation of which he still evidently hankered after. By the time the final content of Perrot's reform programme was resolved upon, in December 1583, his thoughts had fully crystallized. In a working paper entitled 'The heads of the instructions for the lord deputy of Ireland' Burghley added in his own hand one further objective: that the new deputy should 'certify the state of St Patrick's, and how it might be a college of learning'.[69] Soon after, he secured his fellow councillors' support for the scheme who, in a supplementary 'memorial' issued to Perrot on 19 January 1584, commanded him to consider how St Patrick's and its revenues might serve the erection of a college 'as heretofore hath been intended'.[70]

In hindsight, the sanctioning of the revived university scheme by Burghley and the Privy Council is inexplicable, given that the arguments which had led to the cathedral's reprieve the first time round were still applicable in the 1580s. Viewed from the vantage point which Burghley then occupied, however, there were still some convincing arguments for proceeding in this manner. In the first place, there was a patent need for a university and, as Sidney's ill-fated parliamentary initiative had so graphically illustrated, there were few easy alternatives to the St Patrick's option. More importantly, there were good grounds for assuming that local opposition to the scheme would neither be as pronounced nor as influential as it had been in the 1560s. The current occupant of the archbishopric of Dublin, Adam Loftus, had been one of the most vocal supporters of the earlier attempt to implement the scheme, and Burghley probably counted upon receiving his continued support, presuming that he would use his office to facilitate the smooth transformation of cathedral into college, in much the same way as he had proposed to use his position as dean of St Patrick's to achieve the same ends in the 1560s.

---

68 *Desiderata Curiosa* (as note 3), vol. 1, pp. 35-49.
69 S.P. 63/106/43.
70 *Desiderata Curiosa* (as note 3), vol. 1, p. 28.

The most overriding consideration behind Burghley's decision to revive the old university scheme, however, was the internal logic of the scheme itself. As in the 1560s, the lord treasurer was driven on by an inspirational, but largely false, belief that the crown's underlying intention had always been to use Dublin's supernumerary cathedral for the godly purpose of erecting a college. Based upon an apocryphal notion ultimately attributable to Archbishop Browne's 'Device', this belief had achieved mythical status by the 1580s, positing that it was King Edward VI who had originally taken surrender of St Patrick's and that, had he lived longer, he would have proceeded to convert it into a university.[71] The St Patrick's scheme, therefore, was not merely an accessible policy option, which had been held on file in the offices of the monarch's secretaries for close on forty years, but a piece of unfinished business pertaining to Edward VI's reformation of the Tudor churches. Thus, for the lord treasurer, a man whose spiritual outlook had been shaped in the crucible of King Edward's court, there was a deeply compelling, almost moral, imperative to see it through to its conclusion.

It seems likely that Burghley also used the existence of this appealing Protestant *mythos* to convert Perrot to the belief that St Patrick's was the best means of funding the erection of the college; for, initially, at least, the deputy had favoured endowing it with some of the recently escheated lands of the Desmond and Baltinglas rebels, to be supplemented by a series of money and labour fines to be imposed upon those rebels 'thought fit to be pardoned'.[72] It is unlikely, however, that he bargained for Perrot's response. As a former Edwardian courtier himself, the new lord deputy was profoundly affected by the *mythos*. It fired his imagination and determined that he brought to the task of founding the university a sense of mission which exceeded even the zeal evinced by the most ardent supporters of the project in the 1560s, Hugh Brady and Adam Loftus. Like them, he believed that the dissolution of St Patrick's was much more than just a means of securing the erection of a college. For Perrot, it was nothing less than a means of purifying the Irish church of the remnants of its 'popish' past, a task which cried out for fulfilment so that the memory of the Protestant boy king would be properly honoured.[73]

---

71 Bodleian, Perrot MS 1, ff 93v-94r, Perrot to the queen, 18 June 1585. In reality, it was Henry VIII who had taken the original surrender. The idea that the crown wanted to convert it into a university may have been born out of Archbishop Browne's recollection of an allegedly dishonest ploy by Henry's lord deputy, Sir Anthony St Leger, to win the accedence of the dean and chapter to the surrender. According to Browne, St Leger had maintained that Henry VIII intended to put the cathedral to a godly use which moved its clergy tosubmit to the royal will. It was the archbishop himself, however, who had suggested in his later petition to Edward VI that this godly purpose might be the foundation of a university.
72 British Library, Harleian MS 3292, ff 10rv; S.P. 63/108/87.
73 Bodleian Library, Oxford: Perrot MS 1, ff 95v-96r & 111r.

Perrot's radical Protestant vision of his mission was implicit in his blueprint for the new university, copies of which were dispatched to Burghley and the queen's secretary Sir Francis Walsingham, on 21 August 1584.[74] Although these communications were concerned ostensibly with the intended structure and organisation of the college, they also contained a subtext which reveals the nature and depth of the lord deputy's ideological commitment to the project. Perrot effectively re-endorsed the Privy Council's plan on the grounds that it would rid Dublin of the excesses of its medieval ecclesiastical heritage; for here 'in this little city' there were two 'great', 'richly-endowed' cathedrals 'too near together for any good they do'. And to leave his political masters in no doubt that there were compelling relgious reasons for following their instructions, he commended the scheme further because it would contribute to the abolition of one of the main foci of religious idolatory within the local church. The mere fact that St Patrick's Cathedral was dedicated to Ireland's patron saint meant necessarily that it was held 'in more superstitious reputation than the other dedicated to the name of Christ' and was thus 'fitter to be suppressed than continued'. In Perrot's eyes, therefore, the work which the Council had committed to him was not merely the foundation of a university, but the right to execute an act of Protestant iconoclasm. Thus he eagerly looked forward to the appealing prospects of Christ being allowed to 'devour' St Patrick and his followers, and of his own government stripping the Irish church of a hateful secular cathedral which served no other purpose than to maintain absentee prebendaries and unimpressive vicars choral, 'a sort of idle singing men that cannot aptly pronounce an English word or readily read the lesson appointed for public prayers'.

Burghley's successful conversion of Perrot to being in favour of the old university policy soon created unanticipated difficulties for its successful implementation. Far from being a boon to the scheme, Perrot's passionate espousal of the cause cut across the lord treasurer's carefully designed plan to pre-empt and counteract prospective opposition to it. Burghley was keenly aware that the scheme had foundered in the 1560s because its opponents had persuasively contended that the tithe-based revenues of St Patrick's could not be justifiably diverted towards the outwardly secular ends of establishing a college, given that there was such a high level of lay impropriations throughout the Irish church generally. To minimize the impact of the inevitable restatement of this argument, therefore, Burghley and the Council had also enjoined Perrot to consider how parliament might introduce a tax upon the lessees of impropriated parsonages to provide further financial aid

---

74 Bodleian Library, Oxford: Perrot MS 1, ff 24v-25v; S.P. 63/111/73.
75 *Desiderata Curiosa* (as note 3), vol. 1, pp. 28-29.

to the incipient college. In effect, his aim was to spread the burden of responsibility for financing the college among both lay and ecclesiastical proprietors of tithes. All would be forced to contribute to the noble aim of 'training up the youth in that realm in the knowledge of god and other good learning', a disarming tactic which was designed to prevent local churchmen from taking the moral high ground through the claim that they were the exclusive victims of the government's plans.[75]

The zealous Perrot, however, would not countenance this approach. For him, his conviction that St Patrick's Cathedral was a redundant 'popish' remnant of the medieval church – it 'serveth to little use then for singing men to meet together twice a day to sing badly, rather of custom than of devotion'[76] – and that Edward VI had sanctioned its dissolution in order to establish a Protestant academy, was sufficient reason for proceeding with the plan as he believed it was orginally conceived, that is, without the inclusion of a sop designed to appease self-interested clergymen. Indeed, Perrot was convinced that there would be no need for additional financial resources to support the college. St Patrick's alone would suffice. Out of annual revenues reckoned by Perrot to be worth 4,000 marks sterling he believed he would establish not one but two universities, with the added bonuses that he would also use the church as a site for the Irish courts, and the canons' houses within the cathedral close as an 'Inn of Court to bestow the judges in'. Thus, despite the Council's recommendation, he planned to press ahead with the scheme by the passing of an act concerned solely with the dissolution of St Patrick's and the 'commission of it to these good uses'.[77]

Perrot's insistence on maintaining the pristine purity of Edward VI's plan had a more profound impact on the fate of the scheme, however, than the subversion of Burghley's politic manoeuvres. His increasingly obsessive desire to destroy the cathedral and the language in which he expressed it ultimately brought the scheme into disrepute. Although his pronouncements on the cathedral were unexceptional to the extent that they conformed to the type of criticism that any radical Protestant would have levelled against an English secular cathedral in the sixteenth century, the fact that they emanated from one who occupied a position of high authority in the Elizabethan regime, and that they were uttered in the post-Grindalian age of the Elizabethan regime, made them appear as the opinion of a subversive. In short, Perrot's views were interpretable as 'precisian' values and were thus politically unacceptable. Surprisingly, the man who identified this and

76 Bodleian Library, Oxford: Perrot MS 1, f 110v, Perrot to the earl of Leicester, 10 June 1585.
77 See note 74 above.
78 On Loftus's religious convictions see article by H. Robinson-Hammerstein which follows below.

successfully exploited it on behalf of St Patrick's Cathedral was once the holder of similar views himself, the erstwhile puritan and supporter of the university scheme, the lord chancellor and archbishop of Dublin, Adam Loftus.[78]

By the time Perrot embarked upon his mission to convert St Patrick's Cathedral into a university in the early autumn of 1584, Adam Loftus was completing his seventeenth year as archbishop of Dublin. His experiences during this period had brought about a great change in his views about the cathedral: he had become convinced that it was an indispensable appendage to his archbishopric. Like Archbishop Browne, he now appreciated the importance of its administrative role in the diocese. Like Archbishop Curwen, he had come to value it as the major fund of archiepiscopal patronage. He was determined, therefore, to ruin Perrot's plans for the cathedral, no matter what damage might be inflicted upon his relationship with the queen's notoriously irascible deputy. Thus, from October 1584 until June 1585, when the cathedral's reprieve was finally confirmed by the queen, he oversaw a vigorous campaign to stave off this threat through regular correspondence with the leading English Privy Councillors, and through the dispatch of emissaries from among his clergy to lobby the same Councillor's at court.[79]

The arguments Loftus employed were virtually a rerun of those advanced by his predecessor, Hugh Curwen, in the 1560s, when he himself had sought the suppression of the cathedral. He stressed both the inadvisability of dispensing with the fund of archiepiscopal advowsons which would be better employed in advancing Protestant preachers to well endowed livings; and the impropriety of using parochial cures to finance an institution which would have no direct pastoral benefit for the parishoners who paid their ecclesiastical dues to finance the livings. Arguments of this type had saved St Patrick's in the 1560s and were of no less force in the mid-1580s. Indeed, in some ways the cathedral's position was now even stronger. Most of the old conservative prebendaries, like Creef and Wellesley, who in the earlier period had tarnished its reputation in the eyes of Protestants, had died; and Loftus had replaced them with men of impeccable reformist credentials like himself. These included their successors in the offices of official-principal and archdeacon of Dublin, the Cambridge graduates Dr Robert Conway and Henry Ussher MA. Ussher, in fact, was one of the growing body of actual

---

79 See, for example, Loftus to Walsingham, 4 October 1584 and 21 March 1585, S.P. 63/115/4 and S.P. 63/115/32; Loftus to Burghley, 7 October 1584 and 18 March 1585, S.P. 63/112/5 and S.P. 63/115/27; Loftus's emissaries were Archdeacon Ussher and Richard Bancroft, prebendary of Mulhuddert. They visited the Court in the winter of 1584 and in the spring of 1585 respectively; Perrot to Walsingham, 16 November 1584, S.P. 63/112/72.

or prospective graduate preachers holding cathedral prebends, all of whom reflected Loftus's avowed aim of reconstructing St Patrick's along Protestant lines.[80] The archbishop was not confident, however, that these selling points were sufficient in themselves to win him the support of the English Privy Council against the deputy. To secure this victory, he chose to take advantage of Perrot's greatest political weakness – his uncompromising religious principles – by aligning himself and his cathedral with the increasingly powerful anti-Puritan wing of the Elizabethan establishment.

Loftus's move to the 'right' is evident in the stress which his cathedral prebendaries laid upon tradition in justifying the continued existence of their church. In their preamble to a petition presented to the English Privy Council by Archdeacon Ussher in December 1584, they confidently anounced that their church was a 'body politic' founded 'about four hundred years now last past' by the queen's 'most noble progentior King John'. The cathedral's structures and functions, they continued, were shared 'with other like worthy foundations within her majesty's noble realm of England'. Its destruction, therefore, could not be countenanced because it would deface the worthy memory of the queen's progenitors, as well as being quite unjust and against reason, given the fact that it was of 'an order of bodies politics used and allowed in this land, agreeable to her majesty's laws'. In other words, the prebendaries were electing to combat Perrot's attack on their cathedral on the grounds that such an act would be a threat to the established ecclesiastical order as enshrined in the queen's religious settlement, a settlement which maintained many continuities with the medieval past. In this scenario, the deputy was, by implication, a dangerous innovator and not to be trusted, while the clergy of St Patrick's were the upholders of traditional law and order.[81] This was the kind of argument which would have appealed to the conservatively minded queen. It was also designed to appeal to the man who ultimately proved to be Loftus's and the cathedral prebendaries' most influential ally, the queen's vice-chamberlain, Sir Christopher Hatton, the 'rising-star' of Elizabethan government who, like the monarch, was a favourer of tradition and a known hater of precisian values.[82]

Loftus's courting of Hatton was an astute piece of political opportunism, given that it was commonly known that the vice-chamberlain was an avowed enemy of the deputy, and that he would be only too willing to join with any

---

80 For a list of graduates and prospective graduates holding prebends in the cathedral at this time see Loftus's book 'A true note of the livings of St Patrick's church and of all and singular the dignities, prebends and ministers thereof, how and in what sort they are possessed and by whom and how qualified', 4 August 1585, S.P. 63/118/45(1).
81 P.R.O., SP 63/113, no 56.
82 E. St John Brooks, *Sir Christopher Hatton: Queen Elizabeth's Favourite*. London 1946; repr. 1978, pp. 197-219.

cause that sought to undermine Perrot's credibility. However, Loftus would not have been able to exploit this advantage so effectively had he not had so near to hand a direct line of communication to the vice-chamberlain. The medium in question was Richard Bancroft, prebendary of Mulhuddart in St Patrick's Cathedral, the future bishop of London, archbishop of Canterbury and scourge of Puritans, who, at this juncture, was Sir Christopher Hatton's household chaplain.[83] Bancroft was especially suitable for the task of lobbying his master on behalf of St Patrick's as he was a man who was both emotionally and financially beholden to the cathedral and, as a consequence, personally committed to its survival. Not only had he held the well endowed prebend of Mulhuddart for most of the preceding two decades, a prebend which served to support his post-graduate career at university, but he was also the maternal great-nephew of Hugh Curwen, the former archbishop of Dublin and defender of St Patrick's in the 1560s. It was Curwen, in fact, who had paid for Bancroft's undergraduate education at Christ's College, Cambridge, and who had presented him to his prebend in St Patrick's.[84]

Bancroft is known to have fed Hatton with information on the conflict between Loftus and Perrot and there can be little doubt that it was accompanied by the gloss that the deputy's designs upon St Patrick's were inspired by patently transparent Puritan inclinations. Nor can there be much doubt, given Hatton's feelings about Perrot and his religious preferences, that he was prevailed upon by his chaplain to give his backing to Archbishop Loftus. The intervention of Bancroft and his procurement of Hatton's support for St Patrick's were to prove decisive. It gave Loftus the political leverage he needed to pressurize Burghley into abandoning the scheme. The turning point came in the spring of 1585. Loftus dispatched Bancroft to negotiate directly with the lord treasurer in March of that year. Emboldened by the support of Hatton, the archbishop and his envoy aggressively staked out their position. Loftus's letter, which Bancroft delivered to Burghley, contained an ultimatum: he threatened to resign unless the lord treasurer procured from the queen 'private letters' forbidding any talk of the dissolution of St Patrick's in Perrot's forthcoming parliament.[85] In the face of this poltical pressure, the consensus-seeking politician in Burghley capitulated. In April or May 1585, he wrote to Perrot to inform him in uncompromising terms that he could never allow the alteration of St Patrick's 'to any other public use whatsoever'. To save face, he declared that his decision was based on the promptings

83 E. St John Brooks (as note 82), pp. 333-334.
84 S.B. Babbage, *Puritanism and Richard Bancroft*. London 1962, pp. 7-8.
85 Correspondence on the matter is transcribed into Hatton's letter book. At least one of the letters (Loftus to Burghley, 18 March 1585) came into Hatton's hands via Bancroft as he was the bearer, see H. Nicolas, *Memoirs of the life and times of Sir Christopher Hatton K.G.* London 1847, pp. 357-359.

of conscience. As on the previous occasion when he abandoned the university scheme, the tithe issue was singled out as the sticking point. In a solemn tone, the hypocrisy of which was not lost upon Perrot, he told the deputy that there was 'none so great an error in this our Church of England' than the conversion of parsonages with cure of souls to 'private uses'. By the end of May, Loftus had his letters of reprieve from the queen.[86]

The failure of the 1580s scheme marked the final abandonment of the Elizabethan regime's long commitment to the notion of converting St Patrick's Cathedral into a university. The policy failed because its core idea was fundamentally flawed. For a variety of reasons – the misreading of Browne's 'Device', the unfamiliarity of the main policy formulators with the local church in Dublin, and the existence of a conscious bias against the secular cathedral among some reformers – the proponents of the university scheme failed to appreciate the importance of the cathedral within the local ecclesiastical fabric and, as a consequence, failed to make any provision for dealing with the political fall-out that accompanied each successive attempt to implement the policy. The conceptual flaw in the policy had major implications which extended beyond the internal affairs of the Church of Ireland. While politicians and divines debated the efficacy or otherwise of converting the cathedral into a university, Bishop Brady's 'tender youth' sought an education on the continent, in universities and colleges where they were nourished on the doctrines and tenets of post-Tridentine Catholicism. Thus when a university was finally founded in 1592 it had much, perhaps too much, ground to make up in the battle to prevent what Queen Elizabeth described as the infection of her Irish subjects in the universities of France, Italy and Spain with 'popery and other ill qualities'.[87] In conclusion, the protracted gestation of the university was a crucial factor in determining the ultimately unsuccessful outcome of the Protestant reformation in Ireland, if for no other reason than that the Church of Ireland entered the seventeenth century with a largely unreformed ministry.[88]

---

86   S.P. 63/112/68.
87   J. Morrin (as note 9), vol 2, p. 227; H. Hammerstein, 'Aspects of the Continental Education of Irish Students in the reign of Queen Elizabeth I', in *Historical Studies* 8, 1971, pp. 137-53.
88   A. Ford, *The Protestant Reformation in Ireland, 1590-1641*. Second Edition. Dublin 1997, pp. 31-47. On the crucial role played by the provision of university education in the reformation of the ministry in England see O'Day, (as note 51), pp. 127-43.

Archbishop Adam Loftus:
The first provost of Trinity College, Dublin

Helga Robinson-Hammerstein

Most people familiar with Irish history of the early modern period who see the title of this essay are very probably influenced by J.P. Mahaffy's verdict on Adam Loftus's role in the founding of the College. Mahaffy published his history of Trinity College at the beginning of the twentieth century, but he is still the opinion-leader in this matter.[1] Mahaffy's observations on Loftus range widely through a whole catalogue of vituperative negatives. Here are some examples: 'Loftus, far from being the founder of Trinity College, as he is represented in Taylor's and Stubbs' histories, was rather the chief obstacle that delayed its foundation till the golden opportunity had been lost.'[2] Mahaffy was referring to Loftus's quarrel with Sir John Perrot about the transformation of St Patrick's Cathedral into an Irish university in the 1580s.[3] On Loftus's role in the eventual establishment of Trinity College on the present site, Mahaffy commented as follows: 'Archbishop Loftus helped by making speeches, and gave the dignity of his name to the College by *posing* as its first Provost, but he neither actually governed the society nor contributed more than a decent thank offering (£100) for the profits he had retained in S. Patrick's'.[4]

Mahaffy thus not only peremptorily dismissed Loftus's entitlement to be regarded as anything more than the nominal first provost of Trinity College, Dublin, he also ultimately denied that Loftus had exercised any influence on

---

1 J.P. Mahaffy, *An Epoch in Irish History: Trinity College, Dublin, its Foundation and Early Fortunes, 1591-1660*. London 1903; reprint: Port Washington, London 1970.
2 J.P. Mahaffy (as note 1), p. 30; the earlier histories mentioned here are: W.B.S. Taylor, *History of the University of Dublin*. London 1845 and J.W. Stubbs, *The History of the University of Dublin* ... Dublin 1889.
3 On this quarrel and its context see most conveniently: Ciaran Brady, *The Chief Governors. The Rise and Fall of Reform Government in Tudor Ireland, 1536-1588*. Cambridge 1994, pp. 291-300; in greater detail, my doctoral dissertation: 'Erzbischof Adam Loftus und die elisabethanische Reformationspolitik.' Marburg 1976, pp. 172-204; see also Victor Treadwell, 'Sir John Perrot and the Irish Parliament of 1585-6' in *Proceedings of the Royal Irish Academy* 85, C, 1985, pp. 259-308 and James Murray in this collection above.
4 My emphasis, J.P. Mahaffy (as note 1), pp. 60-61.

the Dublin corporation in persuading its members to offer the site: 'His influence was very strong negatively, in resisting another scheme; he deserves no further credit in the matter.'[5]

Mahaffy's judgement seems unassailable, since it was obviously derived from a close reading of the primary sources, a selection of which he allowed to speak for themselves. However, that is precisely part of the problem: such sources cannot really speak for themselves, they need to be comparatively and contextually interpreted, and one must be aware that they often contradict each other. Furthermore, Mahaffy's moralising tone is no longer favoured by modern historians.

Let us take the pronouncements of two of Loftus's contemporaries which may be of direct relevance to our evaluation of Loftus's problems, experiences and intentions as the first provost of Trinity College, Dublin; the pronouncements concern Loftus's vision of politics and his religious persuasion. The first of these contemporaries is the pamphleteer Barnaby Rich, who called himself a 'soldier of the pen'. He supplemented his Irish military pension by informing on the leading officials in Ireland. The queen's privy councillors paid a great deal of attention to such reports when it suited them. Rich accused Adam Loftus, the Irish lord chancellor and archbishop of Dublin, of tolerating that 'detested Jesuitical generation of the pope's riff raff, who are the cause of the Dublin citizens' pervasive addiction to popery'.[6] In a satirical fable of 1593, Rich drew the following pen-portrait of Loftus:

> I could tell you the tale of an ass, who, leaving the place where he was first foaled, fortuned to stray into a strange forest, and finding the beasts of that desert to be but simple ... this paltry ass ... found means to wrap himself in a lion's skin, and then with proud looks and *lofty* countenance, ranging among the herds, he would stretch out his filthy throat, bellowing and braying (as nature taught him) with so hideous and horrible a noise, that the poor beasts that were within his hearing began already to tremble and shake for fear ... in the end he became

---

5   J.P. Mahaffy (as note 1), p. 61.
6   Barnaby Rich seems to have considered himself an agent especially against Adam Loftus, but the latter did retain the trust of the English Privy Council throughout. Rich to Burghley, 20 May 1591, S.P. 63/150,12; S.P. 63/158/51. On Rich's services more generally: T.M. Cranfill and D.H. Bruce, *Barnaby Rich*. Austin Texas 1953, pp. 41-78. Rich was in close contact with two members of the Irish Ecclesiastical Commission, Robert Legge and Robert Pypho. This provided him with an opportunity to 'dig around'. In 1592 in his *Adventures of Brusanus*, he represented Loftus as 'Gloriosus', a haughty fool. See also: Barnaby Rich, *The Original Why the Lord Chancellor and his Brother of Meath first conceived displeasure against me*. London 1592, reprinted in E.M. Hinton (ed.), *Ireland through Tudor Eyes*. Philadelphia 1936, pp. 86-88.

a notable sheepbiter, worrying and devouring whole flocks of sheep, that happened within his precincts and jurisdiction.[7]

According to Rich as a contemporary witness, Loftus performed his ecclesiastical and secular duties and assignments in Ireland by resorting to trickery, deception and intimidation, untroubled by any scruples of conscience.

The second contemporary witness is Meredith Hanmer, a cleric and historian, not a government agent. For purposes of private assessment he drew up a list of those whom he suspected of upholding Puritanism in Ireland.[8] Adam Loftus is not only at the top of that list, but as archbishop of Dublin he is represented as the man who attracted other Puritans to serve under him. Hanmer, therefore, placed Loftus firmly on the 'radical wing' of Anglicanism in Ireland, among those Anglicans who were looking for a real or 'second reformation' and who were, like their continental peers, most strongly drawn to the teaching of John Calvin.[9]

My question here is not, who is right: Rich or Hanmer? Rather, what do these accounts and others like them, since these are by no means unique, tell us about Elizabethan political society, about the 'political nation' in Ireland, about conditions under which government officials like Loftus had to operate. More specifically, I am interested in what they tell us about the circumstances in which Trinity College, Dublin was established and most importantly, what role the College was intended to play in Elizabethan Irish politics.

So, what can we find out about the attitudes, vision of politics, the commitment to university education of the man who was nominated in the English queen's Charter of March 1592 as the first provost of Trinity

---

7   Barnaby Rich, *Greenes News both from Heaven and Hell*. 1593; later on Rich devoted the same persistent attention to the college and its students in *A Catholike conference between Syr Tady MacMareall a popist priest of Waterford, and Patrick Pleine a young student in Trinity College by Dublin*. Dublin 1612.

8   Notes on puritans, papists or schismatics S.P. 63/214/36 = Cal. S.P. Ireland Addenda 1565-1654, p. 680; written around 1600, but retrospective, as far as the Puritan appointments were concerned. I am grateful to Alan Ford for drawing my attention to this reference; my interpretation of the evidence, however, differs somewhat from his. See Alan Ford, 'The Church of Ireland, 1558-1634: a puritan church?' in A. Ford, J. McGuire & K. Milne (eds.), *As by Law Established. The Church of Ireland since the Reformation*. Dublin 1995, pp. 52-68, here p. 56.

9   Heinz Schilling (ed.), *Die reformierte Konfessionalisierung in Deutschland. Das Problem der 'Zweiten Reformation'*. Gütersloh 1986 (= Schriften des Vereins für Reformationgeschichte 195). There especially pp. 387-438 the editor's 'Die "Zweite Reformation" als Kategorie der Geschichtswissenschaft'. See also: Heinz Schilling, 'Between the territorial state and urban liberty: Lutheranism and Calvinism in the County of Lippe' in R. Po-chia Hsia (ed.), *The German People and the Reformation*. Ithaca, NY 1988, pp. 263-283.

College, Dublin? The following facts are incontrovertible. He had come to Ireland in May 1560 as the private chaplain of the lord deputy, the earl of Sussex. A Yorkshireman, educated at Cambridge (probably at Trinity College), a protégé of the queen's leading minister, William Cecil, a learned man with staunchly Protestant credentials, Loftus was given the most prestigious ecclesiastical offices in rapid succession: he was made dean of St Patrick's (1561), archbishop of Armagh and primate of All Ireland (1563) and archbishop of Dublin (1567); the latter was the ecclesiastical appointment which he retained until his death in 1605.[10] However, is it not strange that he was satisfied to settle for the lesser post of archbishop of Dublin when he had held the much more prestigious post of archbishop of Armagh and primate of All Ireland? The answer, of course, lies in the troubled history of the archdiocese of Armagh; the title may have been higher, but the post was rather less influential. Loftus certainly recommended himself as a fervent preacher, eager to release those in Ireland who, as he put it later, were destined to be saved from the darkness of idolatry into the full light of the gospel. These are standard expressions of the missionary energies of all those who were no mere office holders anywhere at the time. The vocabulary is unambiguously associated with the second reformation. In 1567 the lord deputy, Sir Henry Sidney, hailed Loftus's accession to the archsee of Dublin as announcing 'the hour of reformation' which had now come.[11]

I am inclined to argue that for the English government as well as for Loftus in Ireland, the founding of a local university was the absolutely indispensable cornerstone of such a reformation. All other measures of reform – and reform was an interlocking complex structure – would come to grief or would not even get off the ground, if such a foundation could not be brought about. A university in Ireland had been on the agenda of Tudor policy makers since the reign of Henry VII. Such an observation should not suggest, however, that the ruler and his closest group of advisors and counsellors were always able to act as the supreme policy-makers and that there was in actual fact a coherent policy plan. In theory such a plan undoubtedly existed, but the historical reality made it even less probable for theory to match reality than anywhere else in Europe. If anything was done in the matter of a university policy it was likely to be left to highly motivated individuals who were prepared to do the government's job. In this respect, the Tudor government

10 See my doctoral dissertation (as note 3), pp. 63ff. The Charter is a parchment, 732 x 570 mm, with the Great Seal of Ireland appended, impression in dark brown wax: Dublin, Trinity College Manuscripts Department MUN/D/15; see my comments and partial transcript in J.M.M. Hermans & M. Nelissen (eds.), *Charters of Foundation and Early Documents of the Universities in the Coimbra Group*. Groningen 1994, pp. 60-61, 88-90.

11 S.P. 63/4/76; S.P. 63/4/83; Sir Henry Sidney's letter is reprinted in E.P. Shirley (ed.), *Original Letters and Papers of the Church of Ireland* ... London 1851, No. CIX.

could rely on its loyal, capable and foward-thinking intellectuals of a practical bent. It is indeed no exaggeration to maintain that a local university in Ireland was considered the crucial instrument to promote the 'territorialisation', the actual control of the state, to overcome opposition of the feudal lords, to inculcate a constructive ethos among a law-abiding elite who had been persuaded that their best chance lay with their support of the ordered state. However, while the need for a local university was theoretically never denied, government officials may have considered its execution a matter of detail. The university in and for Ireland was throughout the Tudor period conceived as an instrument to 'introduce civility'. Ultimately this meant bringing an elite into line with good manners and acceptable conduct, or what counted for such among the policy-makers in England. The Tudor government was, therefore, never prepared to acknowledge the prevailing conditions in Ireland, primarily the rule offered by the chieftains, as a form of order; but what the Tudor government policy was actually trying to do was to replace one concept of order with another, namely the centralised Tudor monarchy. The latter was justified as suitable for the whole country and as holding the promise of a more peaceful development in coexistence. All this was certainly a tacit assumption long before the reformation of religion made such a scheme even more urgently necessary; and an Irish university was crucial at all stages. There was only one occasion when a university as an academic institution of high calibre was rejected by a leading official.[12]

There were comprehensive reforming plans for Tudor Ireland, especially under Queen Elizabeth; they were only intermittently pursued. This lack of consistency occurred because all English government officials in Ireland sooner or later learned that local conditions could not be changed over night. Furthermore, the conditions were hardly ever favourable to the systematic implementation of any policy designed in England, where the theorists were unaware of or could not really take on board the actual situation in Ireland. It seems to have happened quite often that government officials holding high positions of prestige in Ireland were not listened to, instead their credibility and effectiveness were undermined by listening to spies, although most English recipients of spy reports must have known exactly what to credit and what not. Not only did government officials in Ireland find themselves improvising at all times, the need to improvise also meant that they were compromising their own positions, and they were well aware that they might eventually even be held personally responsible for misdirecting the government when they were actually carrying out the governments policies. Government officials in Ireland did find their work frequently hampered by

---

12 See my 'Royal Policy and Civic Pride: Founding a University' in David Scott (ed.), *Treasures of the Mind. Trinity College Dublin Centenary Exhibition.* London 1992, pp. 1-6; see also James Murray above.

the adverse effect of informers, like Barnaby Rich, reporting against them to the English Privy Council. But naming these informers and exposing them as troublemakers did not help their case either. To cope with this dilemma, the government officials in Ireland were forced to devote most of their energies to scheming and developing complex survival strategies rather than being able to persuade the Irish that the Tudor government was interested in their welfare and that they were likely to be much better off as loyal subjects of the English crown.[13]

Adam Loftus proved a supreme adept at the art of survival in Ireland. In addition to his ecclesiastical appointments which yielded far too little in material terms, he was given high secular posts. There was, of course, no contradiction in this, because both secular and ecclesiastical appointments were supposed to be operating smoothly to the same basic norms. In fact, the situation in Ireland in the second half of the sixteenth century was such that it required the combination of secular and ecclesiastical posts, since the one was bound to be ineffectual without the other. Adam Loftus was made one of the two lords justices on several occasions. The lords justices were charged with running the country during the absence of the lord deputy. From August 1581 Loftus was also appointed lord chancellor of Ireland, a position he filled – relatively unhampered by various accusations of misconduct – until his death in 1605.[14] An additional feature of his survival strategy was the constant and unwavering support and patronage of William Cecil, Lord Burghley, which he was indeed fortunate enough to retain until the latter's death in 1598. Most important, however, I should like to suggest, was the support derived from the existence of a Puritan friendship network which had formed around Queen Elizabeth's secretary of state, Sir Francis Walsingham, in London.[15] I am inclined to think that that was Loftus's actual lifeline, although nothing could be taken for granted in this world of courtly life and government positions.

In Ireland Adam Loftus did indeed survive politically and exercised his influence effectively; he did so largely through developing a highly success-

---

13 Ciaran Brady, *The Chief Governors* (as note 3); Wallace MacCaffrey, 'Place and patronage in Elizabethan politics' in S.T. Bindoff et al. (eds.), *Elizabethan Government and Society*. London 1961, pp. 95-117; Pam Wright, 'A change in direction' in David Starkey et al. (eds.), *The English Court from the Wars of the Roses to the Civil War*. London 1987, pp. 147-172; see also Colm Lennon, *Sixteenth Century Ireland. The Incomplete Conquest*. Dublin 1994, p. 315 ff.

14 The most authentic portrait of Adam Loftus, in the senior common room, TCD, shows him as lord chanecellor of Ireland. He was cleared of accusations: S.P. 63/48/19 & 30; S.P. 63/144/34.

15 Loftus to Walsingham S.P. 63/124/53; on Sir Francis Walsingham's role as sponsor of 'Puritans' see Patrick Collinson, *The Elizabethan Puritan Movement*. London 1967, pp. 198-200.

ful networking strategy of his own. He established himself at the centre of a substantial circle made up of many of the leading Anglo-Irish families, in Dublin, in the Pale and further afield by forging lasting kinship ties through a broadly dependable marriage policy.[16] Marriage alliances might be considered of dubious value, but this is where the married clergy of the Anglican church had a distinct advantage over the Catholic clergy, as it turned out. In Loftus's case the marriages were always alliances of carefully assessed interest. What made this possible for him was the following highly gratifying fact: he had been supremely successful at fulfilling God's commandment to be fruitful and multiply. He had had twenty children, twelve of whom survived into adulthood, and only one of these did not marry. Such abundance of offspring was not only to be accounted evidence of divine election in a general sense; it was a specific talent, he might say, given to him by God to employ in his survival strategy. Four sons and seven daughters made highly advantageous marriages which provided the necessary, psychologically reassuring, protective support structures for the activities of their prolific father. There was also no disadvantage in having so many daughters, because as female offspring of the archbishop and leading official in Ireland, they did not require as much of a crippling dowry as daughters of lesser officials in search of well-to-do husbands. When Adam Loftus was accused of misappropriating funds and ecclesiastical benefices in the construction of his enviable network, he succeeded in clearing his name without difficulty. The accusations were revealed as part of a smear campaign and they ultimately helped him to fortify his position even more. He was able to prove to the satisfaction of his friends in England and his supporters among the members of the English Privy Council that his secular posts had quite legitimately yielded the required resources; implying that the sums required were also far lower than those suggested by his 'slanderers'. While other English Protestant clergy refused to settle in Ireland with their families – the rich pickings were all concentrated in the hands of the archbishop-chancellor – Loftus had made a virtue of necessity and by doing so rendered himself relatively unassaible.[17]

I have represented Adam Loftus as a survivor, because he saw opportunities and used them as God-given 'talents' which also confirmed his sense of election. If this was the case, Loftus would most certainly have to be con-

---

16 Loftus married Jane Purdon, eldest daughter of Adam Purdon of Lurgan Race, Co. Louth. She died July 1595. She bore him twenty children. Their daughter Isabella was the first wife of William Ussher, son and heir of John Ussher. See entry *DNB* [Robert Dunlop].

17 In addition, the relations of Loftus's wife played a re-enforcing role in the network, see S.P. 63/144/34, 14 May 1589, there Loftus is said to be sorely needed in Ireland where he is also well connected through the marriages of his children to the landed gentry of the country; see my doctoral dissertation (as note 3), pp. 199-204; TCD Manuscript T.1.8: A Collection of Genealogical and Historical Papers related principally to Archbishop Adam Loftus.

sidered a thorough-going Puritan. But is such an interpretation sustainable in the light of the conventional view that Loftus was an unprincipled, avaricious, time-serving creature of the English government? Can he really be credited with a sincere, sensitively functioning religious conscience? How Puritan was Loftus? (It should be noted that some historians tend to refer to 'Puritanism' already in connection with the early Elizabethan period, anticipating by more than a decade the first appearance of the term in primary sources.)

I am certainly inclined to think that Loftus's Puritanism was at the heart of his survival strategy. I am also convinced that his Puritanism helps to explain what was the true motive of his actions delaying the early foundation of an Irish university by resisting the conversion of St Patrick's Cathedral as well as, eventually, promoting the establishment of Trinity College, Dublin and giving it a distinctly Puritan orientation. While it would be impossible to prove that the Puritan ethos lay like bedrock under his actions and decisions, one can without much difficulty make out some features of a coherent Puritan predisposition in his approach to public affairs.

The first thing to note – as Patrick Collinson has urged – is the fact that the reformation of religion was not merely some legislative and administrative transaction tidily concluded by the religious settlement of 1559 in England and 1560 in Ireland once and for all.[18] The reformation of religion involved a profound cultural revolution which individuals and groups were constantly at pains to refine in order to arrive at a *purer*, more authentic practice of the Faith. One can draw up a catalogue of typically Puritan convictions and attitudes, but – as Alan Ford has rightly warned – one must be careful not to apply the list inappropriately.[19] There are many notable characteristics which may be absent from the spiritual formation of some perfectly genuine Puritans, while others may feature more prominently. The actual compound of elements was dictated by circumstances; and historical reality determined the practice. In fact the touchstone of Puritanism – the exclusive acceptance of the primacy of grace offered in the Word of salvation – was the common property of all Protestants, albeit with different practical consequences; and most certainly differently interpreted in its range of meanings as specific situations suggested. There was absolutely nothing devious about this. In the case of Puritans the interpretation was inextricably bound up with releasing the most effective meaning from a commitment to Calvin's doctrine of double predestination: of the elect to salvation from the beginning, and of the non-elect to damnation from the beginning. Such double predestination manifested itself most frequently in a desire to build a

---

18 Patrick Collinson, *The Religion of Protestants. Ford Lectures 1975*. London 1982, p. 1.
19 Alan Ford (as note 8), pp. 54-55.

godly community of true believers and, by implication, to exclude those who, as reprobates, fell short of the required standards. Applied to the contemporary situation in Ireland, such a vision could provide fervent Puritans with a ready-made model to explain the manifest failure of the religious policy – allegedly grounded in the laws of 1560 – to persuade most of the Irish to be 'saved' by it.[20] No assessment of likely reasons for such a failure was undertaken. It did not need to be undertaken. It was clearly not a question of policy failure at all, since there was a predestined scheme that had made some Irish 'irredeemable from the beginning'. I am not, however, suggesting that such arguments were employed as a general Puritan excuse for doing nothing; many preachers did try – as they put it – to satisfy the Irish and to 'bring the gospel to them'. But when the success was not forthcoming, the explanation was readily to hand, to some at least.

In practice, Puritanism took shape – that is, as dictated by the conditions that existed in reality – along the lines of the secular authority's willingness or ability to enforce conformity to the letter of the law. Such a project, too, permitted a multiplicity of interpretations. From the start, the Anglican Church in Ireland, although allegedly independent, adopted the same principles of conformity as the Anglican Church in England. However, the Church of Ireland could not rely on the same potentially accommodating social conditions or instruments that one might have been able to use in England to enforce conformity. The Irish situation could be used to the advantage of 'dissenters' from England who were willing to work in Ireland when matters became too uncomfortable for them in England. From the time of the arrival of Adam Loftus in Dublin in May 1560, there were within the Church of Ireland far greater opportunities than in the Church of England to accommodate and even incorporate Puritan features, and these opportunities grew as the century progressed. Adam Loftus was at the centre of this accommodation of and with Puritanism.[21]

What then is to be made of the accusation by modern critics that Loftus discarded the Puritan convictions and attitudes in the late 1580s and early 1590s in order to placate the English queen and her privy council and thus to ensure his survival in Ireland? The available evidence, closely examined, is capable of a somewhat different construction.

Loftus's original commitment to further reformation is clearly enunciated in a letter which he wrote to his patron, William Cecil, in July 1565. To mark the final stage of the vestments controversy, the English government had removed from office those clerics who refused to wear the traditional surplice when celebrating communion. Loftus fervently urged the reinstate-

---

20 Terence P. McCaughey, *Memory and Redemption: church, policies and prophetic theology in Ireland.* Dublin 1993.
21 Alan Ford (as note 8), pp. 52-68 offers a somewhat different reading.

ment of the 'many learned preachers' whom he characterised as having been expelled from their benefices merely on account of their 'detestation of these popish rags'. Loftus used strong language in his letter to Cecil; he adopted the stance of an Old Testament prophet; he threatened Cecil with the destruction of his person and his whole household, if he failed to follow the whisperings of his evangelical conscience. He ended his letter, revealing his deep commitment to Puritanism, with the following phrase:

> But I know your zeal and godly mind, and how careful you are to restore again the true and sincere ministry of the Church of Christ, which in mine opinion you shall never do, unless you remove and take away all the monuments, tokens and leavings of papistry; for as long as any of them remain, there remains also occasion for relapses into the abolished superstition of Antichrist.[22]

The passage contains all the key Puritan concepts: zeal, godly mind, sincere ministry, tokens and leavings of papistry and the pope as Antichrist. Twelve years later, in March 1577, Loftus wrote to Walsingham:

> Some little inkling hath been given me (whether truly or no, God knows) that her Majesty hath been informed that I am a puritan, and a favourer of Mr Cartwright and his doctrine. Truly Sir, I am utterly ignorant of what the term and accusation meaneth.[23]

What is one to make of this? Does this not demonstrate that Loftus was only too ready to abandon principle and old friends just to save his skin? Thomas Cartwright and Christopher Goodman had been 'like-minded' friends of Loftus in Dublin in the 1560s; they had even been proposed as suitable archbishops of Armagh and Dublin respectively at the time, because, it was stressed, they were such excellent preachers of the gospel. However, by 1577 things had changed fundamentally. Presbyterianism had offered itself as a means of enshrining Puritanism in a different and distinctive form of

---

[22] Dated 16 July 1565 see Shirley (as note 11), No. LXXI = S.P. 63/14/26. This adopts the same tone of severe admonition which is also present in a letter by Peter Martyr to John Jewel, Bishop of Salisbury, 24 July 1562 in H. Robinson (ed.), *Epistolae Tugurinae* (Parker Society). Cambridge 1845, App. Letter I, pp. 339-341. The controversy triggered by the 'Second Reformation' within the Holy Roman Empire revolved around the same issues, especially in Brandenburg-Prussia, which was in the process of consolidating its territory into a state; see Rudolf von Thadden, 'Die Fortsetzung des "Reformationswerks" in Brandenburg-Preußen' in Heinz Schilling (as note 9), pp. 233-250; there is also an instructive summary of these problems and their impact in R. Po-chia Hsia (ed.), *Social Discipline in the Reformation. Central Europe 1550-1750*. London 1989, pp. 28-32.

[23] Loftus to Walsingham, 16 March 1577 S.P. 63/57/36.

church government, challenging the basic principles of the Anglican settlement. The word Puritan only then gained wider currency and, more importantly, it designated a specific religious party which explicitly rejected accommodation within the Anglican episcopal system. Loftus as archbishop of Dublin found the Presbyterian position utterly detestable, as it engendered schism within the one Anglican Church that needed to muster all its Puritan strength to withstand the assault of the abolished, but still active, 'superstition of the Antichrist'. Loftus's utterances in the late 1580s certainly suggest that he considered the established Anglican Church perfectly capable of beneficially serving the purpose of further reformation in the Puritan manner which he knew from the 1560s. He had not changed since then; his former friends had changed prompted by different circumstances.

When the Presbyterian Movement in England was finally dismantled by royal command and intervention in 1586-1857, Adam Loftus enthusiastically agreed with those who separated Puritan convictions and fervour from exclusive advocacy of Presbyterian church discipline; the Puritan sentiments must be retained and put to good use within the Anglican Church, the Presbyterian church discipline must be consigned to the rubbish tip of history.

Adam Loftus in Dublin read the dismantling of the Presbyterian Movement in England as a God-given sign indicating the appropriate time to found a university in Ireland. Such an Irish university had always been understood as a means to inculcate civility and a deep appreciation of established law and order. There were now 'unemployed' men in England, Cambridgemen, dedicated teachers and preachers who were willing and able to fill these ideals with vigorous life.[24] These men had to be rescued from England and absorbed into the Church of Ireland which was better suited to accommodating Puritan sentiments. A few of the best of them could educate the next generation of leading Protestants in Ireland, while combining teaching with preaching and being materially provided for out of the benefices of St Patrick's. This was the moment, Loftus argued, for which St Patrick's Cathedral had been preserved. The whole scheme would, of course, only work out, if the godly learned men truly abandoned the loathsome Presbyterian discipline.

What I have just argued is largely surmise. Now I wish to test out my assertions by a close reading of the government correspondence and the Loftus speeches relevant to the foundation of Trinity College, Dublin. To state my previous assertions again: I have been assuming that Loftus never lost sight of the university issue, that he was convinced that it could not be realised at the expense of the commensurate remuneration of the preaching

---

24 Patrick Collinson (as note 15), pp. 385ff., 432ff.; also my doctoral dissertation (as note 3), pp. 224ff.

clergy, but that he was aware that nothing in the matter of the reformation could ultimately be achieved without a local university; and that this university had to be academically of the highest calibre in the tradition of Christian humanism.

While suitably qualified staff, combining teaching with preaching in the desired fashion, was theoretically plentiful, there still remained the problem of the site for the appropriate location of the university. Loftus had preserved the integrity of St Patrick's Cathedral for the 'preaching clergy'. Even if one considers this a spurious argument, there remains the indisputable fact that Loftus's defence had nevertheless been accepted by the court, the queen herself included, who had originally given quite contrary instructions. One thing is clear: Loftus wished for a fully-fledged university which offered 'good letters' to all who were willing and able to be taught there. Although he had argued against transforming St Patrick's Cathedral into a university, he had never advanced any arguments against establishing a university in Ireland, as his Marian and early Elizabethan predecessor, Archbishop Hugh Curwen, had done. (Curwen was continued as archbishop of Dublin after Elizabeth's accession, since he had accepted the Reformation changes made by the Irish Parliament of 1560.) Curwen had pointed out in a letter of June 1564 that St Patrick's should not be converted into a university, since this would give 'the Irish enemy' an opportunity to spy on the government by sending its offspring there allegedly to study but in reality to wreak havoc. However, quite apart from this he deemed it very misguided to educate clergy to preach the Reformation in an academic manner. Such training would only raise the expectations of such clergy, and they would insist on higher remuneration in line with their academic training.[25] Loftus never argued against the need for academic training of the preaching clergy.

The 'appropriate site' was eventually donated by the Dublin corporation; and Loftus undoubtedly helped. In later years he certainly kept reminded the college community that it owed its existence to the generosity of Dubliners, enjoining the members of the college never to forget that the structure had been raised 'out of the bowels of the city's bounty'.[26] However, in addressing the corporation, Loftus could not count on 'like-mindedness' in the matter of Puritan convictions. He appealed instead to the civic pride and to the commercial interests of the members of the corporation. There was nothing unprincipled in such an appeal. No university founded in the early modern period could ignore the commercial interests of the urban centre in which it was placed. Every single one of the towns which agreed to the establishment of a university, insisted that the educational institution thus promoted must benefit the corporation directly and serve it in the long run by demonstrat-

25 Shirley (as note 11), No. LVIII.
26 Colm Lennon has chosen this as the title of his article in *Long Room* 37, 1992, pp. 10-16.

ing the college's practical, material usefulness. Incidentally, that was not reassuring enough for Brussels in the 1580s. The burgesses of Brussels refused to permit the founding of a university in their midst for fear of student unruliness and the menace which the presence of an excessive number of young men presented to the daughters of good families.[27]

In the case of the Dublin corporation, it is evident that the patricians were ultimately motivated by the conviction that founding a university provided them with an opportunity to make a last-ditch effort to give their loyalty to the English crown an anchor that would hold. The issue, as it presented itself in the early 1590s, was to provide for the education of the future civic elite at home. The consensus between the leading members of the Dublin corporation and the Loftus circle was established on the notion of and commitment to civility. In the early 1590s this meant support for the established law and order in the face of plots and threats inspired by Jesuit missionaries trained and directed from abroad. While most members of the Dublin corporation might not have cared much for Puritanism (had they known what it might lead to), they were at that time still largely indifferent to the finer nuances of religious beliefs. Only a small band of the Dublin patriciate – all connected in extended kinship groups with Adam Loftus – were actively committed to a decidedly more Puritan orientation for the new university as the indispensable condition of bringing civility to the country.[28]

It is interesting to note that when the College was first established there were no religious tests at matriculation; but that was not a sign of religious toleration: rather it was a case of translating principle into pragmatic practice. There was clearly no point in introducing religious tests, when the correct appreciation of religious truth had yet to be instilled. Mere outward conformity was no longer satisfactory: conviction had to be nurtured. And Adam Loftus, as the first provost of the College, did take an interest in giving the university not only a religious but also the appropriate academic profile; there is no doubt that he championed the adoption of the working norms of certain of the most 'advanced' Cambridge colleges.[29]

One can indeed catch illuminating glimpses of Loftus's vision of the university in his Latin resignation speech.[30] He shows himself supremely committed to sound foundational studies, useful to officials in state and church.

---

27   John W. Stubbs (ed.), *Archbishop Adam Loftus and the Foundation of Trinity College, Dublin: Speeches delivered by him on various occasions* ... Dublin 1892, pp. 1-3; there were indeed no universities in the largest cities at the time: London, Madrid, Amsterdam, Marseille, see Willem Frijhoff, 'Grundlagen' in Walter Rüegg (ed.), *Geschichte der Universität in Europa*. Munich 1996, pp. 53-102, here especially p. 80.
28   Colm Lennon, *The Lords of Dublin in the Age of Reformation*. Dublin 1989, pp. 128ff.
29   His resignation speech makes much of this, see Stubbs (as note 27), pp. 8-13, here especially p. 11 & p. 13.
30   Stubbs (as note 27), pp. 8-13.

Young men must be trained in the approved manner of letter-writing, and in organizing their thoughts for effective public speaking. Loftus especially mentions Poliziano and Erasmus as the reliable instructors in the ground-rules of what would be called 'effective communication' in late twentieth century parlance. He represents their method as the sure way to overcome 'the barbaric Roman style'. The Florentine humanist professor Angelo Ambrogini Poliziano (1454-1494) had influenced the development of a new philology throughout Europe. He had provided the instruments for the analysis of texts and had thus helped to teach the appreciation of a 'purer', 'non-barbaric' style. He had refined his own 'word-for-word' approach to texts by cutting out the tedium of the irrelevant; in his books written by and for the scholar he had evolved the new style that dealt 'selectively with difficult and interesting problems'. He had also been the first to treat textual criticim as a historical study; this had been his most sweeping innovation in philological method. While it is demonstrable that his principles did not triumph at once and it is unknown through what channels they were eventually passed on, Loftus's reference to him reveals an unreserved commitment to the new philology which had by then come into its own. In the epistolary endeavours the lead of Erasmian text-based humanism should be followed. Furthermore, Loftus recommends the careful study of texts and scholarly exercises in the humanist mode, also as the basis for theological training. He argues that since people are no longer instructed by Christ directly, they have to be persuaded to rely on the purest texts of his teaching. This was an argument prevalent among the most distinguished educators of the Reformation era who adhered to classical Christian humanism, which Philip Melanchthon had so clearly set out as his aim. During Melanchthon's lifetime the 'pure text' argument had been directed against the spiritualists's endeavour to retrieve Christ's authentic voice through preparing oneself by suffering to receive Christ's message in the whisperings of the Spirit. This had resulted in their discarding any formal learning. When Loftus refers to becoming like Christ's disciples who were simple fishermen, he was not rejecting learning for the elite; rather he was anxious to promote the kind of uncluttered message that Erasmus and Melanchthon and many others had in mind for those lower down the social ladder.[31]

In the Holy Roman Empire of the German Nation the tension between learning and simplicity (as rejection of learning) had gone through its critical refiner's fire much earlier than the Tudor monarchy had had to face up to such a problem. There, in central Europe, some of the leading scholars,

---

31 Stubbs (as note 27), p. 13; on Poliziano see especially Anthony Grafton, 'The Scholarship of Poliziano and its Context' in Anthony Grafton, *Defenders of the Text. The Traditions of Scholarship in an Age of Science, 1450-1800*. Cambridge, Mass. 1991, pp. 47-75; here pp. 50, 55, 64, 73 and 75.

expecting the imminent end of the world, had discarded their learning. The radical abandonment of academic training by the spiritualists, for instance at the time of the Münster Anabaptist Kingdom, had led to the overthrow of all existing social and political norms. Such a development had to be avoided in future. One became even more anxious to stress continuity of law and order which also called for humanist training of an elite (those who were able and willing to become officials in state and church), so that those who entered the church could instruct in simple terms those whose predetermined situation in life did not require learning. Such a scheme was also considered to suit the situation in Ireland very well.[32] The aim of studying in this manner was the simple communication of God's truth, adopting indeed the simplicity of the first apostles who were fishermen. All these instructions and guidelines contain Erasmian insights and sentiments echoing, in this instance, Cambridge influences.

Enforcement of moral discipline among scholars – as indicated in their dress and haircut – is perceived and represented for the sake of social discipline and harmony within the university. The religion to be practised in the institution is described as 'reformed Catholico-Anglicanism or the original British Christian religion'.[33] This is a very unusual formulation; it suggests a wish to return to a pure Christian religion in the Celtic tradition, going back to before the year 597; that is, before St Augustine was sent to England by Pope Gregory I to win the people of Kent and beyond to the form of Catholicism directed by the pope in Rome. Such a construction as that advanced by Loftus denotes a search for stability, since the exercise of true religion is shown merely to involve a rekindling of the purer ways that allegedly existed in the early days of Christianity, which had in the course of the Middle Ages been overlaid by man-made inventions and accretions, largely through the intervention of the pope in Rome. While all magisterial reformers everywhere in Europe naturally adopted such a stance of maintaining continuity, they did not necessarily present their arguments in this way. However, one thing is clear: all changes, even radical breaks with the past, were introduced, in line with contemporary thought and expression, as reform, as a reshaping of something that had been ideal before, but had lost its original shape in the intervening time. Innovation was a total anathema, it was considered the work of the devil. Here, in Adam Loftus's formulation, there is even the distinct echo of a recognition of Celtic Christianity as an original line of orientation, included perhaps because it sounded good.

Loftus, far from discarding his principles here, showed himself a totally committed reformer. He never abandoned his Puritan stance, his aspirations

---

32 G.H. Williams, *The Radical Reformation. Third Edition* (=Sixteenth Century Essays and Studies, vol. XV). Kirksville, Missouri 1992, pp. 553 ff.
33 Stubbs (as note 27), p. 12.

to a further reformation or what might have been seen as the 'Second Reformation' on the continent of Europe. Rather, it was precisely in the interest of Puritanism, as the further reformation, that he stressed the need for stability. Stability was the outward condition to ensure the progress of the pure gospel as a matter of conviction. It may be possible to demonstrate that his Puritan views expressed themselves more and more in endeavours to inculcate conviction in others, especially in the young, through 'sound' education. Loftus most certainly became less and less convinced that coercion in matters of religion could achieve anything good or sustainable.

Loftus's Puritan convictions which informed his vision of the university are most evidently revealed in that seemingly bizarre speech he made in 1594 when Walter Travers had been elected provost of Trinity College, Dublin as his successor.[34] The speech appears to be one long stern admonition. Such admonition, however, far from being perceived as tactless or generally tedious – as it surely would be, were it to be made nowadays – was recognised in Puritan circles at the time as the well-established practice of early Christians when the occasion demanded it. However, the speech is also one of the best testimonies to the type of university Loftus was holding out for. The case of Walter Travers certainly called for admonition in that biblically enjoined and sanctioned sense. However, here was also an opportunity to show oneself conversant with early Christian practice.

Walter Travers, a Cambridgeman, had been one of the foremost leaders of the recently dismantled Presbyterian Movement. In 1586 Travers had been charged before the Ecclesiastical High Commission in London with being 'author or at least the finisher' of the Presbyterian *Book of Discipline*. However, nothing could be proved. Yet Travers had without doubt been one of the principal *ideologues* of the English Presbyterian Movement. Twelve years earlier he had composed the most authoritative account (in Latin) of the Calvinist scheme of church order, the *Ecclesiasticae Disciplinae ... explicatio*, translated into English by Thomas Cartwright, the other *ideologue*, as *A full and plaine declaration*.[35] (This is sometimes confused with the *Book of Discipline* of the 1580s.) One the other hand, Travers was also renowned as an exquisitely learned and authoritative teacher and preacher. He had been acclaimed, as Loftus put it, for the 'laborious search he ... made in the depth of such learning as may make him *useful* to our society'. (Society was the customary contemporary reference to the university.) The separation of his deep-seated Presbyteriansm from his useful Puritan learning was obviously not going to be easy; it was certainly more difficult than in the case of a mere

34 Stubbs (as note 27), pp. 14-21.
35 R. Bauckham, 'Hooker, Travers and the Church of Rome in the 1580s' in *Journal of Ecclesiastical History* XXIX, 1978, pp. 37-50; see also S.J. Knox, *Walter Travers: Paragon of Elizabethan Puritanism*. London 1962.

fellow-traveller. However, Adam Loftus the Puritan, was prepared to attempt such a beneficial separation in the name of the pure gospel by admonition in the manner of the early Christians. He was all the more convinced of the acceptability of such an attempt since he had also received encouragement from England, from those who wished to rescue Puritanism from the damnable Presbyterian discipline which was so dangerously out of step with the hierarchically structured monarchy. The compatibility of state and church had to be retained, particularly in a country like Ireland where so much else was uncertain and contested. In his speech before the fellows of the college Loftus stressed the need for the provost to set the leading example. Addressing Travers directly he insisted: 'You shall now have the greatest influence on the regulation of the behaviour [of those] whom you are to governe both in doctrine, discipline and moralle course of life for your actions are the transcript of your doctrine.'[36]

As far as moral discipline was concerned, he warned Travers not to admit 'those who in their blooming youth have been precontracted to vicious habits'. Strict moral discipline must be practised, Loftus repeated, since 'one ill member in the college is like a perished tooth, which is apt to corrupt its fellows'. This observation in fact expressed a deep conviction on which all well-regulated communities were organised, from Calvinist Geneva to Jesuit Salamanca.

Furthermore, Loftus enjoined upon Travers the promotion of 'good letters', so as to rekindle and recapture 'ancient learning and piety'. To achieve the aim of engendering this thirst for knowledge and understanding, Travers was instructed to begin with basics: younger students were to be catechised. The older ones were to be taught from a catalogue of approved books to be read as foundational learning both human and divine, 'either to their own good or to the salvation of others'. Loftus reminded Travers sternly that the university was not a place for controversy of any kind. On the contrary, the university's activities must be embedded in peace, which is represented as the only promoter of true religion based on learning and sound understanding.[37] Controversy, on the other hand, was deemed to lead to discord and

---

36 Stubbs (as note 27), p.16.
37 These were indeed standard instructions to professors and preachers in territories where there was diversity of religion. For an interesting parallel see the document in which Elector John Sigismund of Brandenburg deprecates fanaticism, 1614 in C.A. Macartney (ed.), *The Habsburg and Hohenzollern Dynasties in the Seventeenth and Eighteenth Centuries. Selected Documents*. London 1970, pp. 223-227: '... you are to cease, eschew, and avoid all berating and abuse of other Churches, which are not in your charge, even if they have not yet overcome certain generally recognizable errors, nor are you to brand them with the name of sectaries. For We cannot in conscience any longer watch this, nor hold Our peace on the subject; ... if We learn that one or more of you ... continues to disregard this, Our strict command, which accords with the word of God (and it will not remain hidden from

rash action, such as the premature, forcible removal of idols from the uncomprehending idol-worshippers. It was the common conviction of all magisterial Protestant reformers that such injudicious expressions of religious zeal did not further the love of the pure faith; rather, as one could witness in the religious civil wars of France and the Netherlands, it led to the most detestable and loathsome rites of violence. The university must promote learning and understanding. Trinity-trained preachers had better refrain from becoming iconoclasts. So far Walter Travers had only ever been in a subordinate or even 'subversive' position, but now he was called upon to take on the highest responsibility in an academic institution which afforded him no previous local model that he might have been able to follow. This was a baptism of fire indeed.

Despite all the difficulties he encountered and failed to master, according to his own judgement, Travers, nevertheless, presided over a fairly well-functioning academic institution. This is evident from an early account drawn up in connection with the studies of James Ussher, one of the first and subsequently the most famous graduate of the university: scholarly disputations *more Socratico* seem to have worked for him, namely to use debate to elicit the best reading (to get at the truth), not to engage in intellectual internecine war.[38]

What conclusion can one draw from the arguments and activities of the first provost of Trinity College, Dublin and his role in shaping its foundation and early scholarly orientation? Like most universities anywhere in the early seventeenth century, Trinity College, Dublin was constantly hovering on the edge of collapse. Where the contemporary sources paint a bleak picture this merely shows that Trinity College, Dublin was no exception to the rule. Like many other early modern foundations the college showed a most amazing resilience despite the bleak prospects. The shortcomings were undoubtedly very great, at times even overwhelming, but that is hardly worth dwelling upon. Mahaffy let the sources speak for themselves; in fact, they spoke only to his early twentieth century prejudices; and he discovered much that he found utterly distasteful. A late twentieth century inspection of the evidence might easily fall into the same trap, not from ignoring the distinctly different problems, thoughtworld and language of the end of the sixteenth century, but from a desire to make the sixteenth-century foundation of Trinity College fit in better with our society's need for tolerance; in an attempt to approximate the spirit of the early university to the possibly more 'ecumenically-minded Irish society' of today. That is indeed the error of con-

---

Us), such persons may be well assured that they will be summoned to Court and there be suitably admonished by Us ... for the maintenance of peace and unity ...'

38 TCD MSS C.5.15 contains James Ussher's notes of lectures and sermons attended at Trinity College, Dublin.

ciliatory blandness which has not always been avoided in celebratory statements. There is no concealing the fact that Adam Loftus and Walter Travers and all the early seventeenth century provosts that followed, presided over a decidedly 'Puritan', elitist institution. Trinity College, was indeed the ideological counterpart of the Irish colleges abroad, especially the Irish college in Salamanca, founded by Jesuits in the same year, 1592. Universities in the confessionally devided Europe of the early modern period were established as rival fortresses in the wars of religion which were to rage for another century. They served their respective societies in the only manner they could. However, religious conflict forms only one part of the history of the foundation of the university. The academic requirements which Adam Loftus set down for the teaching in the College, drew upon a common and shared European humanist cultural heritage which survived the wars of religion. This legacy of the common European culture is still present in the College's Library (the Long Room) and its impressive early collections.

Who went to Trinity?
The early students of Dublin University

Alan Ford

Each university has its list of alumni, familiar to historians, biographers, genealogists alike. Oxford has its Foster, Cambridge the Venns, and Dublin University Burtchaell and Sadleir.[1] Though no sane person sits down and reads these volumes from beginning to end, they are nevertheless of fundamental importance to all scholars. Individually the entries enable the careers of particular students to be traced; aggregated, they can be used as the basis of elaborate analyses of the composition of the student body, the role of the universities, and the nature of educational and social change.[2]

The historian's dream is to have a register of all the students that attended university which also provides full details of their background, degrees and subsequent careers, that can in turn be used as the basis of sophisticated, often computerised, analysis to produce reliable evidence about the size and composition of the student population, including their social and geographical origins, and their subsequent careers. The reality, unfortunately, is rarely so simple, particularly in the case of mediaeval and early modern universities. At every stage from compilation to analysis, difficulties about sources, their availability and their interpretation, repeatedly intrude. Putting together a register of students seems initially to be a straightforward task. Foster described his work on Oxford simply as the matriculation records of the university 'alphabetically arranged, revised and annotated'.[3] But this uncomplicated aim gives a misleading impression of the practical difficulties. There are times when no matriculation records were kept. For other periods

---

1 J. Foster (ed.), *Alumni Oxonienses: The members of the University of Oxford, 1500-1714*, 4 vols. Oxford 1891-1892; J. Venn and J.A. Venn (eds.), *Alumni Cantabrigienses ... Part I from the earliest times to 1751*, 4 vols. Cambridge 1922-1927; G.D. Burtchaell and T.U. Sadleir (eds.), *Alumni Dublinenses*. Dublin 1935.
2 For some examples see: T.H. Aston, 'Oxford's mediaeval alumni' in *Past & Present* 74, 1977; T.H. Aston, G.O. Duncan and T.A.R. Evans, 'The mediaeval alumni of the University of Cambridge' in *Past & Present* 86, 1980; Joan Simon, 'The social origins of Cambridge students, 1603-1640' in *Past & Present* 26, 1963; Lawrence Stone, 'The size and social composition of the Oxford student body, 1580-1910', in Lawrence Stone (ed.), *The university in society*. Princeton 1974, vol. 1.
3 *Alumni Oxonienses* (as note 1), vol. 1, title page.

the matriculation books have failed to survive. Even where they do, their comprehensiveness varies, and contemporary compilers (and, indeed, later editors) fall prey to inevitable mistakes in transcription. Close comparison with college records can show that not all students were actually recorded in the matriculation lists.[4] And finally, more thorough exploitation of records of both the university and the world outside can expand still further the number of students known to have attended university.[5] The task of compiling registers of alumni seems, as a result, sisyphean. Foster has been criticised by the Venns, and has in turn been greatly improved on by Emden's remarkable work on the mediaeval students of Oxford and Cambridge.[6] Each generation of researchers thus adds to the lists of students by enlarging the breadth and thoroughness of the search.

Though the tracing of sources and compilation of registers consists largely of minute attention to often-tedious detail, the results produced by analysing this data have wide ranging significance. In England, Lawrence Stone has dubbed the expansion of higher education between 1560 and 1640 an 'educational revolution', giving a detailed quantitative analysis based upon matriculation registers and college records, which suggests that admissions to Oxford and Cambridge began to expand in the 1560s reaching a peak $c.1583$, then after a lull growing again from 1604 until the years leading up to the Civil War, when the number attending university reached a level not surpassed until the 1860s.[7] Having added in those who went to the Inns of Court or were educated abroad or privately, Stone arrived at a total of 1,230 students entering higher education each year during the peak decade of the 1630s, a minimum participation rate which he estimates to be about 2.5 per cent of the male cohort reaching the age of 17 each year.[8] Studies of the social composition of higher education, have concluded that nobility, landed gentry and middle and professional classes all took increasing advantage of these opportunities.[9] Though fascinating, the degree of certainty that can be attached to such conclusions is open to question, given the recalcitrance of many of the primary sources. It has been argued, for instance, that the dramatic expansion in student numbers in England may be a product of faulty sources, a mere opti-

---

4 *Alumni Cantabrigienses* (as note 1), p. v.
5 A.B. Emden, *A biographical register of the University of Oxford A.D. 1501 to 1540*. Oxford 1974, p. xvii.
6 A.B. Emden, *A biographical register of the University of Oxford to A.D. 1500*. 3 vols., Oxford 1957-1959; A.B. Emden, *A biographical register of the University of Cambridge to 1500*. Cambridge 1963.
7 Lawrence Stone, 'The Educational Revolution in England' in *Past & Present* 28, 1964, pp. 47-51.
8 Lawrence Stone, 'The Educational Revolution' (as note 7), pp. 54-57.
9 Lawrence Stone, 'The Educational Revolution' (as note 7), pp. 57-68; Joan Simon, 'Social origins' (as note 2), pp. 58-63.

cal illusion, and that the social composition of the student body did not change as dramatically as has been claimed.[10] Considerable problems also arise in using the information given in matriculation registers about the social class or profession of the student's father, with terms such as gentleman, esquire or plebeian proving so flexible and indeterminate as to undermine attempts at statistical investigation of the social composition of universities.[11]

But at least in the case of the English universities the task of compiling and analysing, postulating and arguing about sources is well under way. In the case of higher education in Ireland, the study of the social role of the universities remains largely uncharted territory, not merely with regard to analysis, but also in relation to the essential sources. Part of the problem lies in that familiar complaint of early modern Irish historians – the paucity of those sources and the consequent shortage of primary information upon which to base analysis. In the sixteenth century in particular, essential facts about Irish population and educational provision are hard to come by, resulting in startlingly contrary evaluations of the condition of Irish education.[12] A further impediment is the fragmented nature of Irish higher education. Trinity College Dublin, founded in 1592, catered primarily for the new Protestant community in Ireland. The Catholic majority of the Irish population could hardly resort to a college which referred in its statutes to 'papal and other heretical religions', nor to the English universities which in the later sixteenth century became firmly Protestant – instead they had to turn increasingly to the continent, to the counter-reformation centres of learning on mainland Europe, both to existing universities, and to Irish colleges founded specifically for training Irish missionary priests.[13] The laborious task of gathering from the matriculation and graduation lists of the various continental institutions the names of these Irish students was begun in the later nineteenth century, and has produced significant results which indicate the links between particular colleges and universities and specific regions of Ireland.[14] Much remains to be done, however, at the level of both sources

10   Elizabeth Russell, 'The influx of commoners into the University of Oxford before 1581: an optical illusion?' in *English Historical Review* 92, 1977; Rosemary O'Day, *Education and society 1500-1800. The social foundations of education in early modern Britain*. London 1982, p. 81.
11   Joan Simon, 'Social origins' (as note 2), pp. 60-64; Lawrence Stone, 'The Educational Revolution' (as note 7), pp. 57-68.
12   R.D. Edwards, *Church and state in Tudor Ireland. A history of the penal laws against Irish Catholics 1534-1603*. Dublin 1935, p. 71; Brendan Bradshaw, *The dissolution of the religious orders in Ireland under Henry VIII*. Cambridge 1974, pp. 224f.
13   T.J. Walsh, *The Irish continental college movement. The colleges at Bordeaux, Toulouse, and Lille*. Cork 1973; H. Hammerstein, 'Aspects of the continental education of Irish students in the reign of Queen Elizabeth' in *Historical Studies* 8, 1971.
14   M.J. O'Doherty, 'Students of the Irish College Salamanca' in *Archivium Hibernicum* 2-4, 1913-1915; Timothy Corcoran (ed.), *Facultates Lovanenses, 1426-1797, praecipue quae*

and analysis. Even the most recent and by far the most thorough and impressive attempt to list and analyse Irish students at French universities already needs supplementing.[15]

At first sight, historians of Trinity College appear better off. They have at least a basic register, Burtchaell and Sadleir's *Alumni Dublinenses*, which brings together in one volume the students and graduates of Trinity from the foundation to 1846 – a total of over 35,000 students during a period of more than 250 years.[16] So far, however, little has been done to analyse this mass of data in a systematic manner.[17] Part of the purpose of this article is to begin this process by looking at a small but important group of students – those who matriculated during the first half-century of the college's existence. By identifying the size and some of the key characteristics of the student body it is hoped to replace the previously rather speculative and often contradictory conclusions that have been drawn about the early students with more accurate facts and analysis.[18]

I THE SOURCES

Before engaging in any detailed analysis of the students in *Alumni Dublinenses*, it is essential to check the accuracy and reliability of the data, since, as will be seen, compiling a list of the early *alumni* presents unusual difficulties both for the compilers and, indeed, for subsequent historians.

nomen Hibernicum spectant. Dublin 1939; Brendan Jennings, 'Irish students at the University of Louvain', in Sylvester O'Brien (ed.), *Measgra i gcuimhne Mhichíl Uí Chléirigh. Miscellany of historical and linguistic studies in honour of Brother Michael Ó Cleirigh, O.F.M. chief of the four masters 1643-1943.* Dublin 1944.

15 L.W.B. Brockliss and P. Ferté, 'Irish clerics in France in the seventeenth and eighteenth centuries: a statistical study' in *Proceedings of the Royal Irish Academy* 87 C, 1987, reviewed in *I.H.S.* 27, no. 107, 1991, pp. 279f.
16 *Alumni Dublinenses* (as note 1), p. xi.
17 R.B. McDowell and D.A. Webb, *Trinity College Dublin 1592-1952.* Cambridge 1982, pp. 499-501, have computed the total matriculations for the period 1668-1950.
18 Amongst the many and varied claims: 'the sons of the protestant burghers of Dublin and Drogheda' provided Trinity with the 'mass of its [early] students', whilst the college soon began 'to attract the sons of the high born in influential', with the result that by the early seventeenth-century it had between two and three hundred students: Eda Sagarra, 'From the pistol to the petticoat? The changing student body 1592-1992', in C.H. Holland (ed.), *Trinity College Dublin and the idea of a university.* Dublin 1991, p. 111; 'there were hardly any native Irish in the college – the early students were predominantly Anglo-Irish and English, but hardly any of the paying students in the early seventeenth century were 'people of quality': J.P. Mahaffy, *An epoch in Irish history. Trinity College, Dublin: its foundation and early fortunes, 1591-1660.* London 1903, pp. 97, 184; 'there were about 90 members of the College in 1620, 42 of whom were 'natives by birth', according to J.W. Stubbs, *The history of the university of Dublin, from its foundation to the end of the eighteenth century.* Dublin 1889, p. 42.

Alumni Dublinenses is based, like almost all such works, upon the college's matriculation registers. The early modern students are culled from the first matriculation volume which covers the seventeenth and early eighteenth centuries. This usually (but not always) gives details of when the student matriculated, whether he was a fellow commoner, scholar commoner, pensioner or sizar, the name and social standing or profession of his father, age, place of birth, school and teacher, and college tutor, all of vital interest to the social historian. In addition the editors recorded students' degrees, mostly taken from the College Register,[19] and information about subsequent careers and date of death from family, official and ecclesiastical records. Not all the students, however, were recorded in the matriculation lists. There are two minor gaps in the seventeenth century, in 1688 and from the end of 1644 to the middle of 1652, and one major one, from the foundation to January 1638.[20] Though the two later gaps are almost certainly a product of the internal difficulties of the college which virtually closed down in a time of national crisis, and do not represent any significant fall in the total number of recorded students, the lack of matriculation details for the formative years of the college is a serious defect, which Burtchaell and Sadleir tried to make good by turning to alternative sources, and using these to trace as many of the early students as possible.

The pre-1638 data was compiled from two kinds of sources. First, and by far the most important, are the college records, most especially the *Particular Book*.[21] The latter is a bound volume containing entries from the foundation to the 1640s, but heavily weighted towards the period 1592-1630. Careful reading of its financial accounts, exeats, degrees awarded, punishments, and appointments to College posts can provide the names of a large number of students. The *Particular Book* can be supplemented by the first College Register, which lists both degrees and scholarships, and deals with punishments of students from 1627, and is the main source on students who attended Trinity in the 1630s, and also by the many papers contained in the college muniments.[22] Second, there are the state papers and official ecclesiastical records. The major source here was the grants of wardship, contained in royal letters patent, which in many instances specify that the ward should be educated in Trinity College. H.F. Berry listed 110 such cases as 'probable early students of Trinity College', all of which were included in *Alumni*

19 J.H. Todd (ed.), *A catalogue of graduates who have proceeded to degrees in the University of Dublin, from the earliest recorded commencements to July, 1866: with supplement to December 16, 1868*. Dublin 1869 is utterly unreliable: see *Alumni Dublinenses* (as note 1), intro., p. xi.
20 *Alumni Dublinenses* (as note 1), intro., p. vii.
21 J.P. Mahaffy (ed.), *The Particular Book of Trinity College, Dublin*. London 1904.
22 TCD Muniments V/5/1.

Dublinenses.²³ Other records used included ecclesiastical visitations, calendars of state papers, chancery and exchequer inquisitions and funeral entries.²⁴

Though the range of these sources is impressive, reflecting a lifetime of genealogical and historical research by the editors, the reliability and comprehensiveness of the entries are affected by sins both of commission and omission. The former fall into three categories: errors of transcription, errors of identification, and mistaken inclusions. The first two are almost inevitable in any such project, and certainly occur in *Alumni Dublinenses*,²⁵ though it is difficult to check all entries thoroughly since the editors, though giving a summary list of records consulted, frustratingly fail to identify sources for individual entries.²⁶ Considerably more serious are the errors of inclusion, not so much the individual examples of 'students' who never attended Trinity,²⁷ but the collective inclusion of a whole class of alumni whose presence seriously distorts any attempts to investigate the social, political and racial composition of the student body – the wards of court.

---

23 H.F. Berry, 'Probable early students of Trinity College, Dublin (being wards of the crown), 1599-1616' in *Hermathena* 16, 1911.
24 *Alumni Dublinenses* (as note 1), intro., p. vii.
25 Errors of transcription: John Blease is given as 'Sch 27 October 1626', but the entry in the *Particular Book*, 199a, is for the same date in 1621: since he received his BA in 1623, this is clearly the correct date: John Brodest is mistakenly credited with the scholarship awarded to John Broder in 1633: Registry, p. 42; 'Richard Linsdon' is in fact 'Richard Purdon'; 'John Debrishire' = 'John Derbishire'; S.P. 63/216/201.

Errors of identification: the entry for Lancelot Lowther conflates two different persons of the same name: H. Owen, *The Lowther Family*. Chichester 1990, pp. 111f., 125; Nicholas Meyler the ward and Nicolas Meyler the graduate of Trinity are not necessarily the same person, as *Alumni Dublinenses* (as note 1) assumes: the ward forfeited his lands after the 1641 rebellion as a Roman Catholic: O'Hart, *Irish landed gentry*, pp. 220, 267; the Trinity graduate can be confidently identified with the Ossory churchman who was aged 60 in 1642 and cannot therefore have been young enough to be a ward in 1604: James B. Leslie, *Ossory clergy and parishes; being an account of the clergy of the Church of Ireland in the Diocese of Ossory, from the earliest period, with historical notices of the several parishes, churches, etc.* Enniskillen 1933, pp. 85, 268. The award of an MA to Edward King in 1596 is a mistake, the result of confusing the fellow, Edward King, who arrived in Trinity in 1601, with Mr John King, a benefactor of the College listed in the accounts 1596 and subsequent years: Alan Ford, 'The Protestant reformation in Ireland, *c*.1590-1641', Cambridge University Ph.D. Thesis, 1982, p. 174. The simple entry in *Alumni Dublinenses* of 'Garr' as being a student in 1606 needs supplementing if his identity is to be established: he is almost certainly the same as Owen McGiarre [= Eugene or Hugh Maguire], a poor scholar beneficed in Clogher and supported at Trinity by the state and Sir Hugh Montgomery, who became a vicar in the Church of Ireland before becoming a Roman Catholic priest: H.F. Berry, 'Probable early students' (as note 23), p. 26; 'O'Kane papers', *Analecta Hibernica* 12, 1943, p. 105; Historical Manuscripts Commission, *The manuscripts of Earl Cowper*. 3 vols., 1888-1889, pp. ii, 357.
26 *Alumni Dublinenses* (as note 1), intro.
27 Though these do occur: the entries for 'Allin' and S. Allen seem to refer to the same student; there is no evidence that the 'Atkin' presented to a Trinity living in 1615 had been

A typical example of a grant of wardship is that of Fergal O'Gara, granted to Sir Theobald Dillon on 12 January 1617 with the standard provision that from the ages of 12 to 18 years he be maintained in Trinity 'in the English religion and habits'.[28] Berry compiled his list on the not unnatural assumption that this requirement was usually met. However, in this, as in so many other cases in early modern government, one has to be wary of mistaking enactment for enforcement. Remarkably few – probably less than half a dozen – of these 110 wards feature in the college's own records.[29] Whether through the desire to save on the expense of education, or because of the reluctance of Catholic grantees to send their wards to a Protestant institution, the provision was rarely put into effect.[30] The 1622 commissioners, sent over to Ireland to investigate the efficiency and effectiveness of the Dublin administration, reported that no ward was then studying in the College.[31] As late as 1661 the earl of Orrery concluded that the court of wards had been a failure: 'we cannot find six instances in the memory of men of any converted to the Protestant religion by the education of the Court of Wards'.[32]

This significantly alters both the social and religious composition of the student body of Trinity in the early seventeenth century. The College was not a means of proselytizing the sons of the deceased Catholic gentry: those wards who are definitely known to have attended Trinity come from

at Trinity; similarly Samuel Busshop is simply given in the regal visitation of 1615 as a student, without any indication of which university he is attending: BL Add MS 19,836, fol. 71rh; Thomas Morton was invented out of a misreading of Jho [= John] Morton in the *Particular Book* – see Mun P/1/124 and 127 both of which contain only one Morton; there is nothing to associate either Richard Purdon or John Derbishire with Trinity: S.P. 63/216/201.

28 M.C. Griffith (ed.), *Irish Patent Rolls of James I: facsimile of the Irish Record Commissioners' Calendar prepared prior to 1830*. Dublin 1966, p. 311.

29 Valentine Browne (*Particular Book*, 184a), Henry Colley: presented goblet, 1609 (*Particular Book*, 199b), Thomas Comerford (TCD Muniments P/1/127), Thomas Cromwell: presented a standing piece, 1608 (*Particular Book*, 199b; T.C.D., Muniments P/1/136), Edward Nugent: 1605 (*Particular Book*, 29b), Thomas Thornton (Fellow Commoner 1606: *Particular Book*, 29a; presented pot: *Particular Book*, 29b); possible: Nicholas Stafford (*Particular Book*, 199a), Richard Talbot (*Particular Book*, 29b); Thomas Aylmer (a Mr Elmer appears as a Fellow Commoner in TCD Muniments P/1/54₅); Walter Dougan (a W. Dougan appears in TCD c.1602-1603 – TCD Muniments P/1/54₅, but this is more probably William than Walter, since Walter was married by 1600 and became a 'Catholic lord of the pale': see T.P. Dungan, 'John Dougan of Dublin, an Elizabethan gentleman' in *Journal of the Royal Society of Antiquaries of Ireland*, 118, 1988.

30 S.P. 63/234/17 (C.W. Russell and J.P. Prendergast (eds.) *Calendar of State Papers relating to Ireland, of the reign of James I*. 5 vols., London 1872-1880, vol. 1615-1625, p. 203

31 National Library of Ireland, MS 8014/iv/9; British Library, Add. MS 4756, fol. 69r; see also the case of Nicholas Darcy, where the English Privy Council in 1612 tried in vain to ascertain whether in fact he was being educated at Trinity: Public Records Office, London, Phildaelphia Papers 31/8/200/103, vol. 1611-14, pp. 266f.

32 S.P. 63/307/200.

Protestant families.³³ The oft-quoted and frankly unbelievable example of Trinity's inclusiveness – its education of O'Gara, who in his later life and political career was quite clearly identified as a Catholic, and, moreover, was the patron of that decidedly unprotestant venture, O'Cleirigh's *Annála Ríoghachta Éireann* – is, therefore, simply untrue.³⁴

In addition to including those who did not attend Trinity, *Alumni Dublinenses* also left out those who did. How many did Burtchaell and Sadleir miss? M.C. Griffith, in compiling her definitive catalogue of the early Trinity muniments, came across 156 names not included in *Alumni Dublinenses*.³⁵ Though more omissions have been and will continue to be discovered,³⁶ it will never be possible to identify all the students for these vital early years. Nevertheless, it is practicable to perform one useful task: to establish rough guides to the degree of inclusiveness of *Alumni Dublinenses*. This can be done by taking key documents which provide comprehensive snapshots of college membership at three stages of its development, and which were not used by the editors. From c.1605 there is a buttery list of the names of 75 students taking commons.³⁷ Of these, a total of thirty-three are not found in *Alumni Dublinenses*.³⁸ In 1619 Provost Temple compiled a list of the 99 students then in college. Of these only nine are not included.³⁹ In 1640 the college sent a gift of poetry to one of its noble students, Lord Deputy Wentworth's son, William: it was signed by 102 students. Even though all those who matriculated after December 1637 are recorded in the matriculation book, and there-

---

33 The Colleys were Protestant: John McCavitt, 'The Lord Deputyship of Sir Arthur Chichester in Ireland, 1605-16', Queen's University Belfast, Ph.D. thesis, 1988, p. 368; the Brownes were a well known Protestant settler family, as were the Cromwells.

34 Amongst those that assume O'Gara studied at Trinity: Mícheal MacCraith, 'Ireland and the Renaissance', in Glanmor Williams and R.O. Jones (eds.), *The Celts and the Renaissance: tradition and innovation*. Cardiff 1990, p. 81; Alexander Boyle, 'Fearghal O'Gadhra and the Four Masters' in *Irish Ecclesiastical Record* 1963, pp. 103f.; Brendan Jennings, *Michael O Cleirigh, chief of the four masters, and his associates*. Dublin 1936, p. 143; Fearghus Báiréad, 'Muintir Ghadhra', in Sylvester O'Brien (ed.), *Measgra i gcuimhne Mhichíl Uí Chléirigh* (as note 14), p. 53, on the other hand, is rightly puzzled by O'Gara's presence at Trinity.

35 'An addendum to *Alumni Dublinenses*', typescript in TCD Manuscripts Room.

36 A list of 32 further students not noted either in *Alumni Dublinenses* or by Griffith is given in the addendum below.

37 TCD Muniments P/1/54₅.

38 TCD Muniments P/1/54₅: Arthur Ussher, Hector, Dillon, St Laurence, [Richard] Evans, Winston, White, Oshallie, Lynch, Kyrwane, Barker, [John] Piggott, Bowen, Ben Steare, Rider sen., Rider jun., Ledwich, Owin, Cooke sen., Cooke jun., Skereth, Ferdinando, Kennon, Fleminge, John Weston, Dicke, Linch, Younge, Edward Smith, Connor, Page, Warren sen., Warren jun.. Two further students might possibly be identified as wards who attended Trinity: Elmer (=Aylmer) and Dougan (see above, note 29).

39 TCD Muniments P/1/124: Fulke Dobbe, Brien Neale, John Tomson, Robert Ford, Archibald Hamilton, Richard Hamilton, Ferdinando Poole, William Somner, John Whitton.

fore in *Alumni Dublinenses*, at least 31 of the remainder are not included.⁴⁰ These snapshots would suggest that there was a high rate of omission – 44 per cent – for the early years of the century; a low rate – less than 10 per cent – for the late 1610s, and a higher rate again – 30 per cent or more – for the end of the 1630s. The explanation for this pattern lies in the editors' reliance upon the *Particular Book*, whose comprehensiveness varies considerably depending upon who was keeping the records. Temple during his provostship (1609-1627) maintained a meticulous account of scholarships and degrees: it is significant that seven of the nine students in the 1619 list who were omitted from *Alumni Dublinenses* were either fellow commoners or pensioners, the kind of students who were the least likely to become scholars or take a degree. His successors and predecessors were much less careful, however: prior to Temple the *Particular Book* mostly contains accounts rather than degree and scholarship lists; in the 1630s, it contains hardly any details of students.

How confident, therefore can the historian be in using *Alumni Dublinenses* as a record of pre-1638 students? Given the omissions, false inclusions, mistranscriptions and other errors, it is clearly not possible to treat the list as a full or accurate record of all those students who attended the college. It is certainly a starting place; indeed, it contains the fullest published list. But it is far from complete, and must be used with caution.⁴¹

II THE COMPOSITION OF THE STUDENT BODY IN THE FIRST HALF OF THE SEVENTEENTH CENTURY

When these corrections are taken into account, what is the picture that emerges of the composition of the student body during the first half-century of the college's existence? Given the lack of comprehensiveness in the surviving sources and, above all, the sheer randomness, variability and incompatibility of the information they contain, it is impossible to resort to that panacea of unimaginative historians, the computer, and compile a database from which the nature of and changes in the student body can be calculated. Rather, an alternative method has to be tried. The three key sources that have been used to produce the snapshots of the student body above can be analysed together with the matriculations 1638-1641 to give an

40 T.U. Sadleir and H.M. Watson, 'A record of 17th century alumni' in *Hermathena*, 89, 1957, list 33 students in italics as not being recorded in *Alumni Dublinenses*: in fact two of these students can be identified with entries in *Alumni Dublinenses*: William Baxter with 'Baxter ... Sch. 1639', and Edward Browne with 'Browne ... Sch. 1639'.
41 I have compiled a card index of students who entered before the matriculation book begins in January 1638, upon which much of the above is based.

indication of the changes in the nature of the student body over the first fifty years.

The buttery accounts often provide a very welcome listing of the early students of Trinity just at the time when the College was expanding rapidly after the privations of the Nine Years War. Though precise dating is difficult, internal evidence suggests that they come from the middle years of the first decade of the seventeenth century.[42] They consist of loosely bound papers containing the names of fellows and students, with indications of how often each dined during the academic year. They are, as a result a reliable indication of the resident members of the College. The fullest list, which may date from 1605, contains 75 students and 8 fellows. The composition of the student body is difficult to judge precisely, for want of detailed information about many of the names. It can however be suggested on the imprecise but not wholly inaccurate evidence of the surnames of the students, aided by the details that are available in some cases, that the racial composition of the College was roughly as follows:

10 Anglo-Irish
16 Native Irish
49 New English/English.[43]

This suggests two surprising conclusions. First that a significant number of indigenous students attended Trinity College in its early years – almost 35 per cent. And second that amongst the fellow commoners – those students of higher social class – it was not, as might have been expected, the new English who predominated: on the contrary, eight of the total of thirteen were from either an Anglo-Irish or a native Irish background. Overall, of course, more than 65 per cent of the students seem to be of English origin, thus confirming the predominantly anglicised nature of the new university. But a third of the student population was a not inconsiderable proportion in itself, and in terms of potential it was even more significant. For it raises fundamental questions about the aims of Trinity and the nature of its social, cultural and political impact on Ireland.

One of the original hopes of Elizabeth in founding Trinity had been that it would act as a 'civilising' force in Ireland, an objective strongly endorsed by her successor, James I, who hoped that, over time, Trinity would produce 'good numbers of natives' who could go out and teach the 'rude Irish' 'civility, learning and religion'.[44] It is generally, and, as shall be seen below, right-

---

42 See the discussion of their possible dating by M.C. Griffith in 'An addendum to *Alumni Dublinenses*'.
43 See Chart 1.
44 M.C. Griffith (ed.), *Irish patent rolls* (as note 28), p. 471.

ly, assumed that ambitious plans for Trinity to assume a sweeping role in establishing English norms throughout Ireland fell victim to the coincidence between the college's founding and the growth of a much sharper religious divide in Irish society. Trinity was from the beginning firmly identified with Protestantism, the vast majority of the Irish population, Anglo-Irish and native Irish, opted for Catholicism: *ergo* Trinity failed to attract indigenous students and fulfil the role which Elizabeth and James had envisaged. The figures from c.1605 and, as shall be seen, from 1619, suggest, however, that, initially at least, Trinity attracted some students from the Anglo-Irish and native Irish communities. Clearly, this phenomenon, since it cuts across the conventional wisdom about confessional exclusiveness, needs closer investigation.

There are two sides to the investigation: the efforts made to attract such students to Trinity, and the response of the two communities to those efforts. With regard to the former there is considerable evidence that, in the aftermath of the Nine Years War, as the attention of the English King and the Dublin government turned away from the short term necessities of military conflict to the longer term process of establishing peace in Ireland, the role of education assumed much greater importance in official thinking. James always stressed the need for persuasion and teaching if the next generation of Catholics – what he called the 'future tense of Papistry' – was to be turned into Protestants.[45] His Privy Council in England repeatedly stressed to its Irish counterpart the need for a policy of 'diligent instruction' in Ireland.[46] The Lord Deputy, Sir Arthur Chichester, was equally convinced of the importance of education and rapidly acted to put the instructions from England into effect. Acknowledging in 1606 the older generation as obstinate papists, he argued that 'our better hopes must be in the next age, by the good and careful education of the children'.[47] He identified Trinity as having a major role to play in this process, urging the king to pay for native students to be educated there.[48] Indeed Chichester had already put his proposal into action. A series of Irish students from the province of Ulster, were in 1605-1606 funded by the Dublin government and the income from ecclesiastical benefices to attend Trinity 'forasmuch as they being of the country birth and having the language, may prove profitable members hereafter, either in the church or commonwealth'.[49]

---

45 J.J. LaRocca, '"Who can't pray with me, can't love me": toleration and the early Jacobean recusancy policy' in *Journal of British Studies* 23, 1984, p. 31.
46 P.R.O., London, Philadelphia Papers, 31/8/199/75; see also P.R.O., London, Philadelphia Papers, 31/8/199/36, 39; S.P. 63/218/21; Historical Manuscripts Commission (ed.), *Salisbury MSS*, 16, pp. 419f.; SP 63/218/23 ; S.P. 63/221/42.
47 S.P. 63/218/65.
48 S.P. 63/218/65.
49 H.F. Berry (ed.), 'Early students of Trinity' (as note 23), p. 25; 'O'Kane papers', pp. 102, 105; S.P. 63/217/63.

The provision of scholarships for poor Irish students was but a part of the process of turning Trinity into an indigenous university. The other essential element was attracting richer students from the landed and mercantile classes, thus ensuring that Trinity was also in a position to shape the education of the influential upper reaches of Irish society. The recitation of the surnames of the fellow commoners from the *c.*1605 and other buttery accounts – Ussher, Carroll, Dillon, Elmer (=Aylmer), Walsh, St Laurence, Nelius (=O'Neill), two Neals (=?O'Neill), Connor, Cahan, Moore, Kavanagh[50] – is tantalising, because it contains a number of surnames of prominent Gaelic and Anglo-Irish families, without giving sufficient information to identify precisely the parentage of the students.

This brings us to the question of the response of the Anglo-Irish and Gaelic communities to these efforts to attract their offspring to Trinity. As can be seen from the study of the effectiveness of the prescriptive educational requirement in grants of wardship there was strong resistance to Trinity from Catholics who were granted wardships. How, then, do we explain the presence of names such as Carroll, St Laurence, O'Connor and O'Cahan amongst the fellow commoners? If none of them were coerced there through wardship: was it then parental choice? In some cases this was almost certainly so, though the parents were not necessarily Catholic. Some of the students were sons of parents who were amongst the small minority of Anglo-Irish or native Irish who opted for Protestantism. Thus, the Ussher family had in the late sixteenth century split into Catholic and Protestant lines, with the latter providing a steady succession of students for Trinity; the student Roger Carroll was the son of the conformist Dublin alderman, Sir James Carroll; and the presence of a St Laurence could similarly be explained by the fact that Lord Howth was a Protestant.[51] Other students, however, may have been the offspring of Catholic parents who had been persuaded to send their children to Trinity. The received wisdom is that such efforts had little success. Henry Fitzsimon, the chief Jesuit missionary in Leinster, dismissed Trinity in 1611 as a foundation of 'Satan and other heretics' which was

> by none of account approached, by no number of reckoning frequented, notwithstanding all fraud and force that might be to the contrary, [and] came to little effect according to the prediction of our saviour: 'All planting which my heavenly father hath not planted shall be rooted up'.[52]

50 TCD Mun P/1/54₁₋₅.
51 W.B. Wright, *The Ussher memoirs; or, genealogical memoirs of the Ussher families in Ireland*. Dublin 1889; Brendan Fitzpatrick, 'The municipal corporation of Dublin 1603-40', Dublin University, Ph.D. thesis, 1984, pp. 225, 250; Lambeth Palace Library, MS 629, fol. 28r (*Calendar of Carew Manuscripts, 1603-1623*, p. 170).
52 Henry Fitzsimon, *Words of comfort ... letters from a cell ... and a diary on the Bohemian War of 1620*. Edited by E. Hogan. Dublin 1881, p. 68f.

But at the start of the seventeenth century, when the English were extending their power to Ulster, prior to the alienating impact of mass plantation, there were certainly some native Irish willing both to conform to the established church and to attend its chief seminary.[53] And indeed in 1603 Fitzsimon had acknowledged that there was a problem about Catholics attending Trinity:

> A certain illustrious baron, whose lady is my principal benefactress, sent his son to Trinity College. Notwithstanding my obligations to them for affording me support, I with the utmost freedom, earnestness, and severity, informed and taught them that it was a most impious thing, and a detestable scandal, to expose their child to such education. The boy was taken away at once, and so were others, after that good example. The college authorities are greatly enraged at this, as they had never before attracted any pupil of respectability, and do not now hope to get any for the future.[54]

Was Fitzsimon right that he, exploiting the ever-increasing sense of religious exclusiveness, succeeded in preventing other Catholic parents from making the same mistake? Analysis of the next complete record of Trinity students, from 1619, tends at first sight to contradict the Jesuit's claim. In a list prepared by Provost Temple of all the fellows and students in the college in 1619, he claimed that 78 of the 97 students in the college were Irish, an improvement which appears startling until, that is, one begins to examine his figures and his definitions more carefully.[55] To begin with he included 15 fellows amongst the students; and of the 82 students remaining he included as Irish all those new English who had been born in Ireland. Using categories more familiar to historians, the breakdown is as follows, again a rough estimate based largely upon surnames:

54 New English/English/Welsh
9 Anglo-Irish
19 Native Irish[56]

---

53 Between the establishment of English power in Ulster, immediately after 1603, and the coming of the English and Scots settlers in the second decade of the century there was a brief attempt to build up an indigenous church in Ulster staffed by native clergy, often converted priests. During this period there is evidence of limited conformity on the part of some of the native clergy. See Alan Ford, *The protestant reformation in Ireland, 1590-1641*. 2. ed. Dublin 1997, pp. 127 ff.; Alan Ford, 'The reformation in Kilmore to 1641' in Raymond Gillespie (ed.), *Cavan: an Irish county history*. Dublin 1995, pp. 73-98.
54 Henry Fitzsimon, *Words of comfort* ... (as note 52), p. 56.
55 TCD Mun P/1/127.
56 See Chart 2.

In short, the proportion of truly indigenous students is about 34 per cent, an almost identical figure to 1605, and still surprisingly high for an anglicising institution. In one respect, however, the native student population had changed: of the eighteen fellow commoners listed, four were probably of Gaelic origin, none obviously from the Anglo-Irish community. Fitzsimon's patrons amongst the Pale gentry had clearly listened to his admonitions. There were Anglo-Irish amongst the students, but now predominantly from families that had already an established Protestant branch, such as the Usshers, Cusacks and Eustaces: Trinity was a means of confirming such families in their existing religious faith rather than of converting Catholics to Protestantism.[57]

By the late 1630s, Trinity was a markedly different institution. Under the watchful eye of its new chancellor, Archbishop William Laud and his protégé as provost, William Chappell, it had been purged of its pronounced Calvinist outlook, and stripped of refractory fellows. To replace malcontents, Chappell imported fellows and students from his old Cambridge college, Christ's. Under his guidance Trinity also increased substantially the number of fee paying students, especially fellow commoners. The results of these changes are apparent in the composition of student population in 1640:

87 New English/English
10 Anglo Irish
5 Native Irish[58]

There has been a dramatic fall in the number of Anglo-Irish and native Irish students since 1619, from 34 per cent to just under 15 per cent. Amongst the now 30 fellow commoners, the most notable change was the influx of new English names, led by the sons of the recently ennobled members of the new English community such as Viscount Lecale and the earl of Cork, and of leading English officials in Dublin, such as Wentworth himself and his closest adviser Sir Christopher Wandesford. The predominance of the English and new English in the Laudian Trinity is confirmed by the more reliable figures of the matriculation books from 1638 to 1641, which produce the following break-down of student origins:

136 New English/English
12 Anglo-Irish
12 Native Irish

---

57 W.B. Wright, *The Ussher memoirs* (as note 52); Hubert Gallwey, 'The Cusack family of counties Meath and Dublin' in *The Irish Genealogist* 5, 1974-1979, pp. 298-313, 464-470, 591-600, 673-684; E.F. Tickell, 'The Eustace family and their lands in County Kildare' in *Journal of the County Kildare Archaeological Society* 13, 1955, pp. 270-287, 364-413.
58 See Chart 3.
59 See Chart 4.

At merely 15 per cent, the percentage of indigenous students is the same as in 1640.

III TRINITY AND THE INDIGENOUS STUDENTS

Given the difficulties with the sources that have already been outlined, the above figures indeed cannot be anything but approximate. But even allowing for inaccuracies the general trend in the composition of the Trinity studentbody is abundantly clear. For its first three decades at least, the university, despite its predominantly English provosts and anglicising ethos, succeeded in attracting a significant proportion of indigenous students. And not just the sons of new English settlers, born in Ireland and therefore technically 'natives' in Temple's terms, but the offspring of Anglo-Irish and native Irish families. Some of these, it is true, were the products of parents who had already opted for Protestantism, but others may have been sent to Trinity by Catholic parents. Given the size of the Trinity student body which, far from the two to three hundred which has been claimed, in fact grew during this period from c.70 to c.100, the fact that 34 per cent of the student population were indigenous was hardly earth-shaking: it could not hope to match the emigration of Catholic Irish students to Catholic centres of learning on the continent. Nevertheless, it does force a re-evaluation of the traditional portrait of the College as solely the preserve of the sons of the burghers of Dublin and Drogheda. The composition of the student body in the first few decades of the seventeenth century was both more interesting and more complex than such stereotypical analyses would suggest. By the end of the 1630s, however, the university had changed significantly as the indigenous element declined and the new English dominance became more marked.

The pattern may well have been linked to the hardening of the religious divisions in Irish society. After much debate amongst historians about the timing and the causation of confessionalisation in Ireland, the period 1590-1620 has emerged as a decisive period when, on the one hand, the Protestant Church of Ireland for the first time filled every bishopric in Ireland and created a committed ministry with a firmly Calvinist confession of faith, catering for a mainly settler population. On the other hand, it was during this same period that the Catholic church established a rival episcopate in control of a separate parochial system which successfully challenged the established church for the allegiance of the mass of the native Irish and Anglo-Irish people.[60] Counter-reformation trained priests such as Fitzsimon repeatedly

---

60 Brendan Bradshaw, 'Sword, word and strategy in the reformation in Ireland' in *Historical Journal* 21, 1978, pp. 475-502; Brendan Bradshaw, 'The reformation in the cities: Cork, Limerick and Galway, 1534-1603', in John Bradley (ed.), *Settlement and society in medieval*

stressed the need to refrain from contact with the heretical religion of Protestantism. The presence of a significant number of indigenous students in Trinity was thus a remnant of an earlier period, before the lines of religious demarcation had become clear, when it was possible to bridge the divide and treat institutions such as Trinity as a national university rather than a Protestant seminary. By the 1630s such ambiguity was no longer possible and the true nature of the Trinity student body had begun to emerge. Where there is evidence of native conformity it is in those few families, native Irish and Anglo-Irish, who opted for Protestantism.

Certainty is not easy to come by in relation to the early students of Trinity. As with all such prosopographical enterprises, what seems at first encounter to be a simple and straightforward exercise – to enumerate all the students of Trinity – becomes on further investigation much more complex. The primary printed source for Trinity students, the *Alumni Dublinenses*, is, for the pre-1638 period, seriously flawed, leading to significant misjudgements about the kind of students who went to Trinity. In trying to correct it, however, and in suggesting alternative figures for the size and the composition of the student body, the best that can be done is to improve upon what went before: it is not and, given the nature of the sources, will never be possible, to claim precision or complete accuracy. As a shrewd reviewer has warned:

> The quantification of student populations is a very approximate art; the best practitioners are those who stress this constantly.[61]

Ireland: studies presented to Francis Xavier Martin, O.S.A. Kilkenny 1988, pp. 445-476; N.P. Canny, 'Why the reformation failed in Ireland: *Une question mal posée*' in *Journal of Ecclesiastical History* 30, 1979, pp. 423-450; K.S. Bottigheimer, 'The failure of the reformation in Ireland: *une question bien posée*' in *Journal of Ecclesiastical History* 36, 1985, pp. 196-207.

61 Review in *History of Universities* 8, 1989.

Who went to Trinity? The early students of Dublin University

NOTE ON CHARTS

It must be stressed that these figures are approximate, for a number of reasons. To begin with the distinction between new English, Anglo-Irish and native Irish is far from rigid, with many families having Gaelic and Anglo-Irish branches, whilst others subtly metamorphosed from Anglo-Irish in the mediaeval period into native Irish by the sixteenth century. To categorise rigidly is often to be insensitive to the nuances and complexities of the situation on the ground in early modern Ireland. Equally, as the seventeenth century progresses the difference between the Anglo-Irish who opted for Protestantism and the new English who had made their home in Ireland for several generations becomes increasingly irrelevant. Secondly, where there is no detailed information about a student and his family they have been assigned to one or the other group on the basis of their surname. This is a useful approximation but it can be no more than that, because of a number of difficulties:

- some names could be of English as well as Irish origin: e.g. Jordan, Reynolds, White. These have generally been assumed to be English unless there is evidence to the contrary.

- some families had both Gaelic and Anglo-Irish branches: e.g. Lynch (these have been allocated to both groups).

- anglicization of surnames – e.g. MacGowan into Smith – can swell the number of apparently new English names.

1605 (Chart 1)
Anglo-Irish: Ussher(4), Dillon, St Laurence, Elmer, Walsh, Ball, Lynch.

Native Irish: Carroll, Connor, Nelius, Lynch, Donnellan (2), Kirwan, Mooney, Dougan, Nellie, Owin, Skereth, Kennon, Lallie, Lennon, Oshallie.

1619 (Chart 2)
Anglo-Irish: Lynch, Eustace, Bourke, Fitzgerald, Ussher(2), Pierce, Comerford, Jordan.

Native Irish: Donnellan(3), Cuffe, Hogan, Lysaght(2), Conrey, Lynch, Neale, Power, Higgins, Savage, Grady, Kelly, Brady, Hussy, Buckley, Barry.

1640 (Chart 3)
Anglo-Irish: Bourgh, Cusack(2), Ussher, Dowdall, Fitzsimons, Ball, Butler(2), Bodkin.

Native Irish: Reardon, Raylie, Coghlan, Coffey, Neyland.

1638-1641 (Chart 4)
Anglo-Irish: Bourgh, Dowdall(2), Fitzgerald, Fitzmorrice, Sinnod, Ussher, Prendergrasse, Briscoe, Power, Blaney, Esmond.

Native Irish: Brady, Donnellan(2), Hurgan, Malloy, Lynch, Lysaght, Neilan, McGillicuddy, O'Sullivan, Ryan, Fyeagh.

ADDENDUM

Students not listed in *Alumni Dublinenses*, nor in M.C. Griffith's addendum.

Adair, Archibald: given as Trinity alumnus in 1633 visitation of Achonry: TCD MS 1067, 153, 159ff.
Aessop, Constantius: given as BA TCD in subscription book of Salisbury: Barrie Williams (ed.), *The subscription books of bishops Townson and Davenant 1620-40*. Wiltshire Record Society, 27, for the year 1976 Devizes 1976, p. 48.
Alcock, John: *Particular Book* 29a; Prebendary of Tombe (Ferns): Leslie, Ferns, 95.
Anderson, William: to perform exercises for doctor's degree 1635: Mun P/1/242.
Birne, Gearald: granted commons till next scholars election: Registry p. 27.
Birkett, John: in TCD 1635: *Particular Book*, 157b.
Boyle, Lewis: 3rd s of Rich. E. of Cork: sent to Trinity 5 May 1630 aged 11: K.M. Lynch, *Roger Boyle*. Knoxville 1965, p. 7.
Bridgeman, Thomas: studied in TCD: 1634 visitation of Killaloe: TCD MS 1067, p. 273.
Brock, John: MA 1616 according to W.M. Brady, *Clerical and parochial records of Cork, Cloyne and Ross*. 3 vols., Dublin 1863-1864, vol. 1, p. 20.
Cahan [Chahan=O'Cahan]: in TCD *c.*1603: Mun P/1/544.
Cambell: in TCD 31 Dec 1597: TCD MS 2640, p. 12.
Carny, John: restored to schol., Sept 1630: Register, p. 30.
Conwaye, Mr: Fellow Commoner c. 1603: Mun P/1/544.
Cooke, William: to perform exercises for doctor's degree 1635: Mun P/1/242.
Cosgreffe, Thomas: punished 1630: Register, p. 38.
Dodsworth: student 1595: TCD MS 2640, p. 8.
Dumvill, William: BA by 1637: Mun P/1/259: see Brady, *Records of Cork, Cloyne and Ross*, i; Foster, *Alumn. Oxon.* and A.G. Matthews (ed.), *Walker revised* (Oxford, 1988), 90.
Elliott, Francis: punished 1630: Register, pp, 26, 28.
Fitzsimons, Philemon: BA 1638 MA 1640: see Brady, *Records of Cork, Cloyne and Ross*, i, 67.
Garrett, John: native schol. 1617: PB 170b.
Gefrey: commons a/c 27 Aug 1596: TCD 2640, p. 12.
Hall, John: *Particular Book*, 197b.
Hector, Mr: Fellow Commoner *c.*1604: Mun P/1/543-545.
[O']Heirke, Philip: Student in College in Dublin: Cashel regal visitation 1615: BL Add MS 19836, fol. 51v.

Hench: In TCD 1595: TCD MS 2640, p. 7.
Kean, Adam: Punished 1630: Registry, p. 27.
O'Donnell, Neachtain: At TCD in 1608, supported by the state; 'the wickedest boy I ever dealt with' according to Lord Deputy Chichester: Paul Walsh, 'O'Donnell genealogies', *Analecta Hibernica*, viii (1938), p. 391.
O'Farran, Denis: in TCD c.1609: 'O'Kane papers', Analecta Hibernica 12,1943, p. 102.
O'Flaherty, Roger: Schol. 1612: PB, 77b, 81b.
O'Sherin, Cornelius: Student in TCD: regal visitation of Killaloe 1634: TCD MS 1067, p. 275.
Piggott, Robert: Punished 1630: Registry, p. 28.
Poole, Ferdinando: Pensioner in 1619: Mun P/1/124: became Puritan minister in England: R.A. Marchant, *The puritans and the church courts in the diocese of York 1560-1642*. London 1960, p. 310; A.G. Matthews (ed.), *Calamy revised*. Oxford 1988, p. 394.

Who went to Trinity? The early students of Dublin University   73

Chart 1: Trinity Students: 1605
From Mun P/1/545

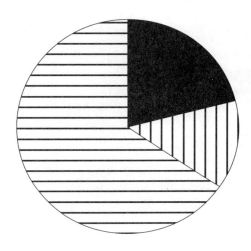

■ Native Irish 16 (21.3%)
▥ Anglo Irish 10 (13.3%)
▤ New English/English 49 (65.3%)

Chart 2: Trinity Students: 1619
From Mun P/1/127

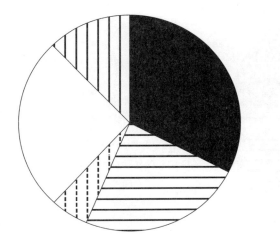

■ New English 24 (29.3%)
▤ English 26 (31.7%)
▥ Welsh 4 (4.9%)
☐ Native Irish 19 (23.2%)
▥ Anglo Irish 9 (11.0%)

Chart 3: Trinity Students: 1640
From New Year's gift to William Wentworth

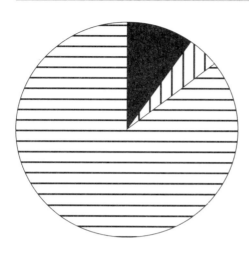

■ Anglo Irish 10 (9.8%)
▥ Native Irish 5 (4.9%)
☰ New English/English 87 (85.3%)

Chart 4: Trinity Students: 1638-1641
From Mun P/23/1

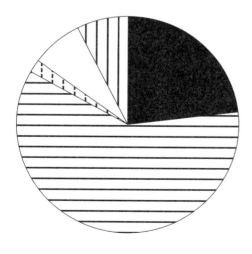

■ English 37 (23.1%)
☰ New English 96 (60.0%)
▥ Welsh 3 (1.9%)
☐ Native Irish 12 (7.5%)
▥ Anglo Irish 12 (7.5%)

The libraries of Luke Challoner and James Ussher, 1595-1608

Elizabethanne Boran

John Dury's declaration in 1650 that the chief purpose of any university was 'for the advancement of Pietie and Learning' summarises the guiding principles behind the construction of the library collections of Trinity College, Dublin in the early seventeenth century.[1] Dury's views on the pre-eminent role of the library as an institution within any university likewise mirror the views of early members of TCD, so evident in their decision to commit a large sum of money to the development of a college library, at a time when the college was going through a serious financial crisis. Evidently the library was regarded as the most important element of the university to develop. As such it served to define the new college-university.[2] But the college library did not stand alone – it was ably supplemented by a number of private libraries of members of TCD and of these libraries the most important were undoubtedly the collections of James Ussher and Luke Challoner. These collections are of interest in a number of ways, not least because these men were the principal book buyers of the college library and, as Richard Parr declares, were given the arduous task of procuring 'such books as they should judge most necessary for the library, and most useful for the advancement of learning, which they accordingly undertook.'[3] Any attempt to reconstruct the chief intellectual interests of members of College in the early period must take into account not only what little information may be gleaned from the statutes, student notebooks, and the college library, but also from the subsidiary library collections of these two men.

The first of the pair, James Ussher, needs little introduction, given his high standing in the intellectual life, both within and without the college, at this time. What concerns us here is not his meteoric rise within the ecclesiastical establishment, as evidenced by his accession to the bishopric of Meath in 1621 and his appointment as archbishop of Armagh and Primate of Ireland

---

1 John Durie, *The Reformed Library Keeper*. London 1650, p. 15.
2 See Elizabethanne Boran, 'Libraries and Learning: The Early History of Trinity College, Dublin from 1592 to 1641.' TCD unpublished Ph.D., 1995.
3 Richard Parr, *The Life of the most Reverend Father in God, James Ussher, late lord archbishop of Armagh. Primate and Metropolitan of all Ireland*. London 1686, p. 9.

in 1626.[4] Rather, I intend to focus on his intellectual interests as refracted through his library collection from the period 1592 to c.1610.

The fame of his father-in-law, Luke Challoner, has inevitably been somewhat overshadowed by Ussher's. Though Challoner (1550-1613) never served as provost of Trinity College, he played a crucial role in its early history. Newport White presents Challoner as an ardent supporter of early plans for a university in Dublin, and suggests that he may have accompanied Henry Ussher on his mission to London to secure royal approval for the new college, a view reflected in sources such as the Ulster Funeral Entries where he is described as 'the first mover and the earnest Solicitour for the buildinge and foundinge of Trinitie Colledge by Dublin'.[5] His name appears among the first fellows of the college in the Elizabethan Charter, and Constantia Maxwell goes so far as to describe him as the 'real founder'.[6] Nevertheless, relatively little is known about his early life, save that his family was comparatively wealthy and well connected – indeed his connection with the Ussher family may account for the zeal with which he undertook the setting up of Trinity College Dublin, as that family played a major role in both organizing and sustaining the foundation.[7]

Certainly, Challoner was active in the subsequent fundraising campaign as Richard Parr, a biographer of James Ussher, indicates: 'He received and disbursed the monies, had the oversight of the fabrick, which he faithfully procured to be finished'.[8] Material in the college archives likewise attests to the keen interest Challoner took in the administrative affairs of the college – not only in the recording of leases and benefactions but also in the missions to Elizabeth's court to obtain more financial assistance for the college/university.[9] His central role in the administration of the college is undisputed, particularly during the frequent absences of Provosts Alvey and Temple when Challoner (as either Vice-Provost or Vice-Chancellor) presided over official functions. Among these were the first commencements in 1601, at which he himself took the degree of Doctor of Divinity, having received his initial qualifications from Trinity College Cambridge in the 1580s.[10]

---

4 Richard Parr (as note 3); see also Nicholas Bernard, *The Life and Death of the Most Reverend Father of our Church, Dr James Ussher*. London 1656, and C.R. Elrington (ed.), *The Life and Works of the Most Reverend James Ussher*. London 1864, as well as Robert Buick Knox's more recent biography of Ussher, *James Ussher, archbishop of Armagh*. Cardiff 1967.
5 N.J.D. White, *Four Good Men: Luke Challoner, Jeremy Taylor, Narcissus Marsh, Elias Bouhereau*. Dublin 1927, p. 11; W. Ball Wright, *Genealogical Memoirs. The Ussher Families in Ireland*. Dublin 1889, p. 108.
6 Constantia Maxwell, *A History of Trinity College Dublin, 1591-1892*. Dublin 1946, p. 8.
7 N.J.D. White (as note 5), p. 8.
8 Richard Parr (as note 3), p. 14.
9 J.P. Mahaffy (ed.), *The Particular Book of Trinity College, Dublin*. London 1904.
10 H.L. Murphy, *A History of Trinity College Dublin, from its foundation to 1702*. Dublin 1951, p. 8.

It is, however, misleading to relegate Challoner's influence exclusively to the administrative sphere. Challoner had been named as one of the three fellows in the 1592 Charter and it seems likely that he held the post of professor of divinity at TCD from 1601 to 1607.[11] The origins of this professorship are shrouded in mystery and it has sometimes been assumed that James Ussher was the first appointee, given his high standing in the college's intellectual life.[12] Unfortunately, there appears to be no conclusive evidence that he was the first incumbent of this post, a vitally important one in Dublin. It seems odd for a college so theologically inclined to wait until 1607 to inaugurate a professorship of divinity, particularly when the university had received a grant for such a purpose as early as 1595.[13] Instead, acceptance of 1601 as the foundation date of this professorship seems to make better sense, and on at least three grounds. Firstly, the college was then able to recover money after the troublesome preceding years; secondly, even as early as 1601, students were being conferred as Masters of Arts and might therefore be expected to proceed to the higher faculty of theology; thirdly, Challoner himself took the degree of Doctor of Divinity, thus qualifying himself for the post. Finally, and of substantial interest here, there is the internal evidence of his library catalogues which seems to suggest a major reorganization of his collection on theological grounds, a reorganization that appears to have been started at least as early as 1601. For all these reasons, then, it seems appropriate to assume that Challoner was the earliest professor of divinity in TCD.

Both Challoner and Ussher played a major role in the development of the college in their capacity as the principal book buyers for the college library, helping to construct the repository of knowledge which was necessary if Trinity was to operate as a centre of learning. We know that Challoner accompanied James Ussher to England on at least three occassions to procure books for the college library – 1603, 1606 and 1609 respectively.[14] It seems likely that they used these opportunities to develop their own libraries.

Two complete and one partial catalogue of Challoner's library exist in the TCD archives.[15] The partial catalogue, which contains books purchased up to November 1595, numbers 473 titles. The second catalogue, entitled 'Catalogus Librorum Lucae Challeneri. Decembris 14 1596', contains 853, while the third, dated 1608, has 885. It is likely that some sections are missing from

---

11 Constantia Maxwell (as note 6), p. 120.
12 J.W. Stubbs, *The History of the University of Dublin from its foundation to the end of the eighteenth century*. London 1889, p. 46.
13 J.W. Stubbs (as note 12), p. 48.
14 Constantia Maxwell (as note 6), p. 53 and C.R. Elrington (ed.), *The Whole Works of the most reverend James Ussher D.D.* Dublin 1864. vol. 1, pp. 23-27.
15 Trinity College Dublin (TCD) MS. 357 fols 1r-15v.

the first list as it contains no reference to any bibles or biblical commentaries, subject areas which are well developed in the following catalogues and which were considered essential to the library of any fellow of the period. The fact that the first two lists are costed enables us to substantiate this conclusion since there is a discrepancy between the cost figure given at the end of the first list and the total cost calculated from the titles itemized.

There are minor differences between the 1595 and 1596 lists – for example, some books in the 1595 list are not to be found in that of 1596; subject headings undergo some slight changes, while many prices in the second catalogue are lower than in 1595. The reason for this latter development remains obscure but the figures might possibly be the result of a valuation of the collection which would naturally decrease somewhat with the increased age of the works, as in the case of secondhand books. In the main, however, the 1596 list bears a strong resemblance to what is left of the 1595 catalogue. This is most apparent when one examines the individual subject collections themselves. Such an enquiry also throws valuable light on Challoner's intellectual interests.

While the identification of Challoner's catalogues presents no problems, the significance of Ussher's has been overlooked, partly due to uncertainty concerning its ownership. This catalogue, begun in 1608, may be found in one of James Ussher's notebooks, TCD MS 793.[16] As such, it is catalogued by Colker very cautiously as a 'list of books and manuscripts dated May.3.1608.'[17] Colker mentions that one work in the catalogue was once owned by Ussher, but hesitates to draw conclusions from this. Nevertheless, close examination of the manuscript reveals that this catalogue is undoubtedly the earliest catalogue of Ussher's collection.

A number of elements identify it firmly as an Ussher library. Firstly, the fact that it is one of his notebooks in his own hand, while certainly not conclusive, is suggestive. Secondly, an intensive examination of the catalogue, relating it to other catalogues of Ussher's, appears to confirm this suggestion. A comparison with a much later Ussher catalogue, dated *c*.1666, composed to mark the acquisition of the Ussher collection by Trinity College, reveals that almost one third of the works in MS 793 are direct matches with those in the later list, with at least 33 other possibilities.[18] Obviously, this begs the question of the fate of the other two thirds. Perhaps there may have been some reorganization in Ussher's collection, or indeed possibly works may have been lost in the various transfers of books, from Drogheda to England and back again, which his collection underwent.

Luckily, other material may be brought to bear on the question in order

16 TCD MS 793 fol 170r-186v.
17 M.L. Colker, TCD. *Late Latin Manuscripts* c.*1980 unfinished*.
18 TCD MS 6.

to solve the problem. Hugh Jackson Lawlor has identified four lists of books, found in the Ussher collection in the Bodleian Library as being lists of works missing from Ussher's collection.[19] He states that these lists cover the period $c.1625$–$c.1641$.[20] The first and fourth lists merely give the call numbers of the missing books, but luckily the second and third lists afford us slightly more information. A comparison of the 1608 catalogue with both lists must inevitably take into account the fact that both these lists contain material printed after 1608 and also, that even those works in the lists dated prior to 1608, the year of our catalogue, may be later acquisitions. Hence, though there are only 12 direct and one other possible match out of a 'possible' 75 from the second list, one cannot totally discount a relationship. A more enlightening feature is that all 12 works in the 1608 catalogue and this list have exactly the same title, date and place of publication. The figures from the third list again seem disappointing – 23 out of 75 – yet, again one finds that the positive identification are actually direct matches as in the case of the second list.

More conclusive proof may be found in the evidence of Ussher's own notebooks, in particular two lists in MS 790.[21] The first such list is the first list we possess of Ussher's library. It is by no means a complete catalogue – rather it represents a price list of books bought by Ussher in England in 1606. Almost half the works cited here may be found in the 1608 catalogue. The other list in MS 790 is a borrowing list, which we shall examine later, in conjunction with others of Challoner and Ussher. Many of the works cited in these lists, particularly in the lists of book loans from Ussher's own collection may be found in the 1608 catalogue. It seems fair to deduce then, that with the catalogue dated 3 May 1608 in MS 793, we are in fact dealing with the earliest catalogue we possess of Ussher's library, and, like Challoner's, it affords us insights into the intellectual interests, not only of James Ussher himself, but also of the college as a whole.

Subject classification in library catalogues is an issue fraught with difficulties, not least because certain authors may belong to more than one subject category and therefore one has to rely on information about the work itself. The scarcity of bibliographical information that Luke Challoner and James Ussher offer in their catalogues makes the task more difficult as, at times, the author's name is given with only a shortened title or indeed no title at all. That both catalogues are *classis* catalogues, that is, catalogues divided into various subject headings does, however, render the endeavour somewhat more profitable and in the following section I propose to examine

19   Hugh Jackson Lawlor, 'Primate Ussher's Library before 1641' *Proceedings of the Royal Irish Academy* 22, 1900, pp. 216-264.
20   Hugh Jackson Lawlor (as note 19), p. 263.
21   TCD MS 790 fol. 67r-v and fol. 49 r-v.

the main subject groupings, firstly in Challoner's three catalogues, and then in that of Ussher.

Taking Challoner's 1595 'philosophy' section first, we find that it actually corresponds with the 1596 natural philosophy section – the emphasis being on cosmological and mathematical works, and indeed, the collection here should be studied in tandem with the mathematics section. The most obvious branches of natural philosophy, as perceived by contemporary intellectuals, are codified by Thomas Blundeville in his *Exercises* (1594), a work in the 1595 philosophy section. Blundeville arranges the relationship of some of the disciplines. He describes cosmography as 'the description of the whole world, that is to say, of heaven and earth and all that is contained therein'. Cosmography is further divided into four 'speciall kindes of knowledge – Astronomie, Astrology, Geographie and Chorographie.' Astronomy is described as 'a science which considereth and describeth the magnitudes and motions of the celestiall or superior bodies' while astrology ranks as 'a science which by considering the motions, aspects and influences of the starres, doth foresee and prognosticate things to come'. Geography is rendered as 'a knowledge teaching to describe the whole earth, and all the places contained theirin, whereby universall Maps and Cardes of the earth and sea are made' and, finally, chorography is defined as 'the description of some particular place, as Region, ile, Citie, or such like proportion of the earth severed by itselfe from the rest.'[22]

Challoner's astronomical collection contains many of the most popular works. Ptolemy's occupy pride of place. While no title survives, in the context of this particular catalogue we are probably dealing with his *Almagest*, his chief work in astronomy which covered the whole of mathematical astronomy known to the ancients. In its 13 books it deals with such topics as solar and lunar theory, generally in an Aristotelian framework. Its tables of astronomical computations ensured its popularity until the early years of the seventeenth century.[23] Another great authority, also well known in the middle ages – the *De Sphaera* of Johannes de Sacrobosco – is present in the philosophy section. Based on Ptolemy, it proved very popular in the sixteenth century, and even in the seventeenth century it was recommended by Thomas Sixsmith to his pupils in the 1620s.[24]

In 1595 Challoner added to these two heavyweights one of the more popular contemporary textbooks, Peter Apian's *Cosmographicus liber*, first printed at Landshut in 1524 but subsequently augmented by Gemma Frisius, an

---

22 S.K. Henninger, Jr, 'Tudor Literature of the Physical Sciences' in *The Huntington Library Quarterly* 32 no. 2., 1968, pp. 118-119.
23 Mordechai Feingold, *The Mathematicians apprenticeship. Science, universities and society in England 1560-1640*. Cambridge 1984, p. 142.
24 Mordechai Feingold (as note 23), p. 67.

author whose work appears in the 1608 list. Other continental authors include Scaliger and Cardano; evidently Challoner was interested in sixteenth century controversy.[25] By 1608 Challoner had also acquired a copy of Robert Recorde's *Castle of knowledge*, a contemporary English study of the Sacrobosco text which attempted to modernise it. The essentially Ptolemaic structure of his collection, and the absence of Copernicus's *De revolutionibus*, while it suggests an outdated view of the cosmos, should be assessed in the context of contemporary absence of knowledge of the heliocentric theory. In fact, as Mordechai Feingold has demonstrated, the heliocentric theory only became widely known in the second decade of the seventeenth century.[26] Certainly, the name of Copernicus is markedly absent from the probate inventories of libraries owned by students and fellows in Cambridge in the period 1575-1610.[27] Challoner seems to have developed a blend of continental writers on astronomy with English authors, the latter primarily interested in the practical side of cosmographical enquiry – for example, Thomas Hood's *Use of Both the Globes, Celestiall, and Terestiall* (1592), and Blundeville's aforementioned *Exercises* which was used for navigational purposes.[28]

Ussher's astronomical collection likewise includes a commentary on Ptolemaic mathematical astronomy by one of the foremost mathematical astronomers of the sixteenth century – Erasmus Reinhold (1511-1553). A copy of Reinhold's famous *Prutenic Tables* may also be the subject of a stray reference in one of the borrowing lists in College.[29] The presence of Reinhold's commentary is significant in Ussher's catalogue as Reinhold, as a member of the Melanchthonian circle, became acquainted with Copernican cosmology through a fellow mathematics lecturer at Wittenberg, Georg Joachim Rheticus. Reinhold's works may be seen as a bridge to those of Copernicus. He himself had a high opinion of them as his reference to Copernicus as 'a modern scientist who is exceptionally skillfull' indicates.[30] His *Prutenic Tables* enhanced Copernicus's reputation by its incorporation of much of his material. It is therefore interesting to see that Ussher, unlike Challoner, whose collection was certainly begun earlier than James Ussher's, had purchased a copy of the *de Revolutionibus*, edited by Georg Joachim Rheticus. Again, our interpretation of this must be edged with caution, for mere possession of the work does not necessarily imply acceptance of the key

---

25 Henry Morley, *The Life of Girolamo Cardano, of Milan, Physician*. London 1854, pp. 175-179.
26 Mordechai Feingold (as note 23), p. 7.
27 Elizabeth Leedham-Green (ed.), *Books in Cambridge Inventories. Book lists from Vice-Chancellor's court probate inventories in the Tudor and Stuart Periods*, 2 vols. Cambridge 1986.
28 S.K. Henninger, Jr (as note 22), p. 127.
29 TCD MS 790, fol 49 v.
30 C.C. Gillespie (ed.), *Dictionary of Scientific Biography*, vol. 11. New York 1975, p. 366.

heliocentric theory; indeed, Reinhold himself, while fully accepting all else, baulked at this suggestion. Nevertheless, the presence of these works does indicate that, at least by 1608, Ussher was looking forward to the 'new' astronomy.

This trend is also continued in Ussher's collection with Michael Maestlin's *Epitome Astronomiae* (Heidelberg, 1582). Maestlin's chief claim to fame was in his role as a transmitter of Copernican theories, particularly to his pupil, Johannes Kepler.[31] Taught by Apian, whose work was in Challoner's 1595 collection, Maestlin was recognised as an influential teacher in sixteenth century astronomical circles, indeed Tycho Brahe incorporated some of his work into his own treatises. Maestlin's most famous work is present here. Designed primarily for laymen it proved popular, running to seven editions. It stands between the ancient Aristotelian outlook and that of Copernicus and, as Feingold relates, was one of the comprehensive works of astronomical theory which, at the start of the seventeenth century was beginning to supersede elementary textbooks such as those by Robert Recorde and Gemma Frisius, works found in Challoner's library.[32]

Ussher's other works dealing with astronomical theory occur in compilatory volumes such as Liebler's *Epitome Philosophiae naturalis* and the *Isagoge Sphaericae* of Scribonius. Ussher also owned another work by the latter author, his *Physica*. In the area of physics Ussher and Challoner shared one common interest: the controversy between Scaliger and Cardanus. Both own copies of Scaliger's *Exercitationes contra Cardanus*. An attack on Hieronymus Cardanus's *De subtilitate*, Jensen has described it as 'standard reading for the intellectually more aventurous students of physics in England at the end of the sixteenth century'.[33] No doubt its chief appeal for both Ussher and Challoner lay in its connection with metaphysical enquiry and its use by some writers as a counterbalance to works by Ramus, an author whose works proved popular in both collections.

Unlike many of his scholarly contemporaries, Challoner seems to have had little time for the astrological component of cosmography. In this he differs slightly from Ussher, whose collection includes a small number of astrological works. One of these, Schoenfelt's '*Astrologicall prognostication for ye year 1564*', occurs in his 'Libri Mathematici, Physici et Medici' section. Its presence here should cause no surprise given that one might well expect to find astrological works alongside those of astronomical or indeed a mathematical bent, as John Dee's definition of astrology suggests:

---

31 David Abbott (ed.), *The Biographical Dictionary of Scientists: Astronomers*. London 1984, p. 107.
32 Mordechai Feingold (as note 23), p. 215.
33 Kristian Jensen, *Rhetorical Philosophy and Philosophical Grammar. Julius Caesar Scaliger's Theory of Language*. Paderborn 1990, p. 46.

> Astrologie is an Arte Mathematicall, which reasonably demonstrateth the operations and effects, of the naturall beames of light, and secrete influence: of the Starres and Planets: in every element and elementall body: at all times.[34]

Of considerably more interest, however, is Ussher's inclusion of Johannes Lichtenberger's notorious *Prognosticatio* among his 'Scripta Theologorum, qui ab anno 1000 ad 1500 claruerunt'. A combination of astrological and visionary prophecy, its inclusion here appears idiosyncratic. Most likely Ussher felt that it tied in with his preoccupations concerning apocalyptic thought. Certainly, as a treatise which included well nigh every millenarian prophecy, its possible application was wide![35]

Challoner, on the other hand, spent more money on geographical works. These likewise are classified with his mathematical and philosophical works, primarily because of geography's dependence on the science of astronomy, though actual maps are held together in a separate grouping. The standard medieval texts, the *De situ orbis* of Pomponius Mela and Pliny's *Historia Naturalis*, are present, but the emphasis is on sixteenth century treatises. Of these the most important include works by Mercator and Ortelius. The popularity of Gerard Mercator's *Geographia* is evidenced by its presence in such libraries as John Rainold's, Andrew Perne's and Lancelot Andrewes's.[36] Mercator's remarkably accurate maps of western and southern Europe continued to be used in the seventeenth century as the purchases of the Newdigate Brothers in Oxford in *c.*1618 demonstrate.[37] In 1608 Challoner added this famous Atlas to the collection. Also present in the 1595 Philosophy section is the *Theatrum orbis terram* of Abraham Ortelius, a friend of Mercator's and the principal cartographer of the sixteenth century. Published in 1570 as a comprehensive atlas of the world, it proved immediately successful and ran to numerous editions. Ortelius's *Synonymia geographia*, a work on ancient geography, later revised as the *Thesaurus geographicus*, may also be found in the 1595 mathematics section. It is interesting to note that one William Bedwell, M.A. 1588 TCC and therefore a contemporary of Challoner's at Cambridge, actually translated the *Theatrum* into English in 1606, and, indeed this work was added to Challoner's collection by 1608.

---

34 S.H. Henninger, Jr (as note 22), p. 119.
35 For a discussion of Lichtenberger's prophecies see Elizabethanne Boran, 'Johannes Lichtenberger' Prophecy and Propaganda in the Later Middle Ages.' TCD, 1989, M.Phil. thesis, unpublished.
36 Mordechai Feingold (as note 23), p.58. For Andrew Perne's library see Elizabeth Leedham-Green (as note 27), p. 463; a copy of Lancelot Andrewes' library may be found in D.D.C. Chambers, 'A Catalogue of the Library of Bishop Lancelot Andrewes (1555-1626)' in *Transactions of the Cambridge Bibliographical Society* 5, no. 2, 1970, p. 114.
37 Mordechai Feingold (as note 23), p. 107.

Also bought by 1608 was another great sixteenth-century author's work, Sebastian Münster's edition of Ptolemy's *Geographia*, while Richard Hakluyt's *Navigations* (1589) augmented the corpus of English authors. Chorography, or historical geography as opposed to descriptive geography, is likewise represented by works such as Camden's *Britannia* and Stow's *Cronicle*.[38] Though Challoner prefers to classify them as 'History Books Civil', they undoubtedly fit Vadian's description of a geographer as one who 'in addition to listing places, concerns himself generally with their histories and with inquiries about the origins of cities, races, nations and peoples.'[39]

Perhaps in line with this interpretation, Ussher prefers to categorise his geographical works alongside his historical works. Ussher's geographical collection is far inferior to that of Challoner. In fact his only major geographical work is yet another edition of Ptolemy's *Geographia*, this time by Willibald Pirckheimer, with a commentary by Moletius (Venice, 1562). Descriptive geography is represented by Camden's ever popular work, but in general the emphasis here is on historical works other than those of chiefly geographical interest.

Closely linked to cosmography was the related discipline of mathematics. As Joseph S. Freedman in his study of the curriculum in central European universities during the Reformation has pointed out, mathematics was consistently classified under the broad subject heading of philosophy.[40] Challoner's library includes the principal works in this field. The primary text was Euclid's *Elements*, and an edition of this by Christopher Clavius was added by 1596. Peter Ramus's *Geometria* appears to have been an equally popular work, though, again, Challoner seems to have favoured the more practical side of geometry by including works by Robert Tanner, and Leonard Digges's *A Boke named Tectonicon*. Arithmetical texts were of less interest: the aforementioned *Castle of Knowledge* and books seven to nine of the *Elements* were two of the few works on this subject. Indeed, it is interesting to note that in this demonstration of partiality towards geometry rather than arithmetic, Challoner continues a general trend to be found in libraries of clerical students, which continued into the seventeenth century as the book purchases of Joseph Mede's pupils demonstrate.[41]

Ussher likewise possessed a copy of Ramus's *Scholae mathematicae* (Basel 1569). The popularity of this work is attested to by the frequency with which

---

38 S.K. Henninger, Jr (as note 22), pp. 130-1.
39 Gerald Strauss, 'Topographical-Historical Method in sixteenth-century Scholarship' in *Studies in the Renaissance* 5, 1956, p. 99.
40 Joseph S. Freedman, 'Philosophical Instruction within the Institutional framework of central European schools and universities during the Reformation era' in *History of Universities* 6, 1985, pp. 117-166.
41 J. Looney, 'Undergraduate education at early Stuart Cambridge' in *History of Education*, 10 no. 1, 1981, p. 14.

it occurs in the inventory lists of Oxbridge dons and students.[42] Savile's lectures from 1570 to 1575 used Ramist mathematics as did those of Henry Briggs, a lecturer in St John's College, Cambridge in the year 1587 to 1588.[43] Inventories at Cambridge in the late sixteenth century reveal Ramist geometry appearing in the library of William Ball, a fellow of TCC who died in 1601, and in the library of John Rainolds.[44] Indeed, as early as 1545 we find a reference to it in the list of Nicholas Pilgrim's library.[45] The appeal of Ramist works continued into the seventeenth century: Brian Twynne, a Fellow of Corpus Christi from 1605 to 1623 used his works, as did Henry Dunst at Harvard in 1642.[46]

This, however, is the only mathematical work Ussher and Challoner have in common. No reference to Euclid or Recorde may be found in Ussher's list. Instead his purchases include Schenbelius's *Algebra*, Münster's edition on Geometry, Curtes' *Arte of Navigation* and Digges' *Pantometria*. The last work, begun by Leonard Digges but finished by his son Thomas reminds us that both collections, though combining different authors, in the main evince an interest in practical mathematics linked to geometry, a tendency also demonstrated by Challoner's inclusion of John Shute's *Chief Grounds of Architecture* in this section. It is interesting to note that, just as Ussher catalogues all three trivium subjects together, so also does he attempt to combine the quadrivial subjects in this section by his inclusion of Faber's *Musica* of 1551.

Cumulatively insignificant in terms of the total catalogue, both Ussher's and Challoner's scientific collections should come as no surprise given the attitude of Puritan divines in general to science. William Fulke, a favourite theological author of Challoner's called astronomy 'of all the humayn sciences ... the most divine', while Melanchthon's preface to Sacrobosco suggests a link between the study of astronomy and evangelization.[47] Robert Recorde likewise argued that mathematical studies were closely connected to the overall search for the truth.[48]

The other element in the philosophical corpus in Challoner's catalogue is logic, specifically dialectic. Dialectical works are classified alongside rhetorical texts in a section denominated as 'Scole books'. Though misleading, this subject heading should not be taken as an indication that the books contained therein are actual grammar school texts, rather the 'Scole Books' of the title refers to the various schools, or what might now be called departments, in

---

42 Elizabeth Leedham-Green (as note 27), vol. 2, p. 654.
43 Mordechai Feingold (as note 23), pp. 47 and 50.
44 Elizabeth Leedham-Green (as note 27), vol. 1, p. 544.
45 Elizabeth Leedham-Green (as note 27), vol. 1, p. 61.
46 Mordechai Feingold (as note 23), pp. 73 and 94.
47 P.H. Kocher, 'The Old Cosmos: A Study in Elizabethan Science and Religion' in *The Huntingdon Library Quarterly* 15 no. 2, 1952, p. 108.
48 P.H. Kocher (as note 47), p. 100.

contemporary universities. For example, while Challoner himself was studying in Cambridge the B.A. course was primarily based on the trivium – grammar, rhetoric and logic – books which on the whole seem to be classified in this group. Logic appears also to have played an important role in the early curriculum of TCD judging by student notebooks which discuss many titles still in use in the first decade of the seventeenth century.[49] The textbooks most widely used in Cambridge in the second half of the sixteenth century are present: Seton's *Dialectica*, Melanchthon's *Dialectices* and Ramus's *Dialecticae institutiones*.[50] The first of these, Seton's *Dialectica* was based on lectures of the 1540s and was considered an elementary textbook until the end of the century. Seton's aim was to explain Aristotle's Organon in the light of earlier treatises of Melanchthon and Rudolph Agricola which had sought to reinterpret the logical works of Aristotle. Ramus's own dialectical textbook had been even more popular in Cambridge during Challoner's stay, judging by inventories of booksellers and stationers.[51] Indeed, from the spread of Ramist works throughout his catalogues, one may surmise that Challoner was deeply influenced by this author.

While Ramus had not specifically rejected all of Aristotle's works and indeed, in part, owed much to him, he had freely criticised the scholastic approaches to the *Organon*. Applying humanist methods of emphasising the original sources rather than later accretions he radically overhauled Aristotelian logic by abandoning the predictables, reorganising the categories, and reducing the importance of the syllogism.[52] His fundamental break with Aristotle came, however, in his declaration that there was only one system of logic rather than Aristotle's two and in his specific rejection of metaphysics.[53] Such a simplification of logic may account for the popularity of this text, while the biblicism of English Ramists such as Perkins, Fenner, and Downham – all present in Challoner's library – may have rendered the novelty of the approach more palatable to divines. Though Challoner has continental Ramist writers in his collection, notably Beurhaus and Scribonius, he seems to have concentrated on the English Ramists.

Dudley Fenner's work, *The Artes of Logicke and Rethorike* contains much unacknowledged translation of the *Dialecticae Libri Duo*.[54] It proved a popu-

---

49 TCD MS. 790, MS. 782, MS. 788.
50 Lisa Jardine, 'The Place of Dialectic Teaching in sixteenth century Cambridge' in *Studies in the Renaissance* 31, 1974, p. 51.
51 Elizabeth Leedham-Green (as note 27), vol. 2, pp. 652-654; see also Lisa Jardine (as note 50), p. 57.
52 The two main authorities of Ramist philosophy are Walter Ong, *Ramus, Method and the Decay of Dialogue*. Cambridge Mass. 1958 and W.S. Howell, *Logic and Rhetoric in England, 1500-1700*. New York 1961.
53 Hugh Kearney, *Scholars and Gentlemen: universities and society in pre-industrial Britain, 1500-1700*. London 1970, p. 49.
54 W.S. Howell (as note 52), p. 216.

lar book primarily because of its juxtaposition of Ramist works on dialectic and rhetoric, a combinaton which was highly favoured by preachers who accepted logic and rhetoric as essential elements in evangelization. Ramist rhetoric was dominated by the work of Omer Talon, whose preface to his rhetoric neatly summarizes the Ramist revolution in this subject;

> Peter Ramus cleaned up the theory of invention, arrangement, and memory and returned these subjects to logic, where they properly belong. Then, assisted by his lectures and opinions, I recalled rhetoric to style and delivery (since these are the only parts proper to it).[55]

At the same time, however, Challoner does not neglect key authors such as Cicero, Virgil and Erasmus.

Ussher prefers to categorise the three subjects of the trivium together under the section 'Libri Grammatici, Rhetorici, Dialectici, Lexica'. This section is dominated by rhetorical and grammatical works, with very few treatises of a logical nature present. Ussher has only three works directly connected with logic: Johannes Sturm's *Partitione Dialecticae*, his uncle Richard Stanyhurst's *Dialecticae in Porphyrianos* and the *Quaestiones Logicae et Ethicae* of Freige. The last work, by a noted continental Ramist, continues the trend seen in Challoner's dialectical section. The absence of Ramus's own Dialectica is surprising, given the high regard in which the work was held, a factor obvious from the student notebooks of TCD. A possible reference to it may be the 'P.Rami. Basileae. 1571', but this seems to bear little relation to works by Ramus codifed by Walter Ong.[56]

In regard to rhetoric, no such doubts exist as regards a Ramist ascendancy. Ussher's catalogue includes Rudolph Snel's commentary on Talaeus' *Rhetorica* (1596) as well as a 1577 edition by Ramus and Talaeus, and indeed a first edition of the *Rhetorica*. While Ussher has no copy of Fenner's *Rhetorike* he does not entirely ignore English Ramist rhetoricians as his inclusion of Charles Butler's *Rameae Rhetoricae Libri Duo* (1597) shows.

Closely linked to the rhetoric section was the third element in the trivium, grammar. Challoner's works are divided between the 'Scole books', 'Books for Toungs' and a mixed section at the end of Challoner's 1595 catalogue – books seemingly bought between August and November 1595. Ancient moralists such as Cicero, Quintilian, Isocrates, Livy, Seneca, Horace, Ovid and Plutarch predominate in this section with very few actual grammatical works present.

During the Renaissance humanist grammarians had divided grammar into four parts, dealing with orthography, prosody, etymology and syntax respec-

---

55   W.S. Howell (as note 52), p. 148.
56   Walter J. Ong, *Ramus and Talon Inventory*. Cambridge Mass. 1958.

tively. However, though Latin grammarians such as Guarino Veronese might stress that 'Partes grammaticae sunt quatuor, videlicet littera, syllaba, dicto et oratio', this format was not always followed by textbooks.[57] The true emphasis was always on the relationship of grammar to rhetoric. Moving away from the medieval attempt at speculative grammar, humanists asserted definitions of ancient grammarians such as Quintilian, who had emphasised the important role of literature. One sixteenth century definition of grammar illustrates this trend: "Grammatica est iter nobis ad studium litterarum et omnium liberalium artium"[58] – a sentiment which is echoed in an English context by Elyot in his *Book called the Governour*.[59]

This trend may be seen in one of the most famous fifteenth-century treatises on Latin grammar, Lorenzo Valla's *Elegantiae linguae*, a copy of which is present in Ussher's library. In this work Valla uses quotations from ancient authors to explain his points. The *Elegantiae* was divided into six books and 475 chapters: a major work.[60] In the preface to the first book Valla outlines the importance of grammar as a basis of all knowledge and he proposes the replacement of logic by rhetoric. While his main aim was to improve the quality of written Latin, he also asserted the importance of Latin philological skills in the understanding of Scripture and theology, and perhaps for this reason the work proved very popular, with 34 editions printed in France, Germany and Italy from 1501 to 1544.[61]

One drawback of the Elegantiae was its very structure, however. For instead of being a textbook it was a series of essays on the nature of language, and as such proved difficult to use. It comes as no surprise, therefore, that Ussher felt the need to purchase a more readily accessible textbook. His choice fell on two of the most popular grammatical works of the early modern period: treatises by Donatus and Despauterius. Donatus's two treatises had been extremely influential in the formulations of early humanists and his influence continued well into the early sixteenth century.[62] His *Ars Minor* had become the standard Latin textbook used in grammar schools and its companion volume, the *Ars Maior*, proved equally popular, judging by the number of editions in the late fifteenth and sixteenth centuries.

57 W.K. Percival, 'Grammar and Rhetoric in the Renaissance' in J.J. Murphy (ed.), *Renaissance Eloquence. Studies in the Theory and Practice of Renaissance Rhetoric*. London 1983, p. 304.
58 W.K. Percival (as note 57), p. 306.
59 James Wortham, 'Sir Thomas Elyot and the Translation of Prose' in *Huntingdon Library Quarterly* 11, no. 3, 1948, p. 227.
60 David Marsh, 'Grammar, Method and Polemic in Lorenzo Valla's Elegantiae' in *Rinascimento* 19, 1979, p. 91.
61 G.A. Padley, *Grammatical theory in Western Europe*. Cambridge, vol. 1, 1976, p. 18.
62 G.A. Padley (as note 61), p. 15.

Despauterius, otherwise known as Johannes van Pauteren, was a very popular sixteenth century grammarian. His *Rudimenta* had first been published in 1514, but in 1537 the celebrated Robert Estienne published his whole corpus of works in the *Commentarii grammatica*, a work which dominated Latin teaching in Flanders and France well into the seventeenth century, and in the latter country into eighteenth century.[63] Ussher has a 1537 edition of the *Rudimenta* while Challoner's 1596 collection includes presumably the same work; the '*Despauterius gram*' might refer to the *Rudimenta* or to the compilatory volume. If it is the latter, then Despauterius's other works would be included: his treatise on accidents (1521); syntax (1513); accents (1511); poetic genres (1511) – to name but four.[64]

Challoner's 1596 collection is extremely interesting as it contains some of the key works of the later sixteenth century grammarians. Though Ussher has a copy of Freige's grammar, the emphasis in his catalogue on Donatus, Valla and Despauterius seems to echo the concerns of early humanists, while Challoner's, with the inclusion of books by Ramus, Lily and Scaliger, mirrors the later developments of sixteenth-century grammatical study.

Both Scaliger and Ramus were interested in metagrammatical issues rather than specific problems. Scaliger in particular seems in some cases to reformulate the arguments of the medieval *grammatica speculativa* of the primary role of *ratio*.[65] His most famous work, the *De causis linguae Latinae*, by its very title heralds its debt to Aristotelian philosophical concepts, ideas which Scaliger attempts to apply to grammar. Moving away from the humanist emphasis on the role of literature in the understanding of grammar, Scaliger underlined the orality of the language. For Scaliger the true end of grammar was *recte loqui*.

Ramus's work on Latin grammar, the *Grammatica*, had been published in 1559 and translated into English by 1585.[66] Like so many of his works, it proved to be very popular in Puritan circles. Indeed works by Ramus were the only Latin grammatical works in Challoner's first list – the other work was Ramus's *Scholae in liberales artes*, purchased in November 1595.[67] Like Scaliger, Ramus emphasised the importance of Aristotelian rules in grammar – seen in his division of word classes. His similarity with the Scaligerian approach may be seen in his insistence that logical criteria must be applied to grammar.[68] In the *Scholae* he wrote that a grammarian must know logic and that grammatical categories must adhere to a logical framework. He

---

63 G.A. Padley (as note 61), p. 20.
64 W.K. Percival (as note 57), p. 321.
65 See K.Jensen (as note 33) for an indepth study.
66 G.A. Padley (as note 61), pp. 77-78.
67 TCD MS 357, fol. 3r.
68 G.A. Padley (as note 61), p. 85.

seems to have agreed with Scaliger's definition of grammar as an *ars bene loquendi* though it is clear that he saw it more as a handmaiden to logic than rhetoric.[69] Nevertheless his insistence on usage led him to emphasise that 'good' Latin might be found in Cicero and Varro, though not in the poets, so beloved by rhetorical humanists.[70]

The inclusion of Ramus's grammatical works doubtless should be viewed in the light of the dominance of Ramist thought as evidenced in these catalogues and the surviving College notebooks of the time. The inclusion of Lily's grammar should equally cause no surprise. Its place as the standard school textbook of Tudor England had been aided by the monopoly of printing grammars held by the king's printers, which had encouraged uniformity. Lily's grammar, like Valla's, followed that of Donatus, yet unlike the earlier work concentrated on the pupil rather than on the teacher.[71] Finally, the absence of Ramus's Latin grammar from Ussher's collection is exceedingly surprising, given his emphasis on it in his notebooks, where it is characterised as a key grammatical work.

The opposite is true in the Greek grammar section of Ussher's collection where there exists a 1581 octavo edition of his *Grammatica Graeca*. Both Challoner and Ussher devote more attention to this grammatical section than that concerned with Latin grammars. Challoner's complement of Greek grammars includes some of those most in demand in Cambridge at this time, judging from the inventory lists. In particular the grammars of Cleonardus and Ceporinus were exceedingly popular.[72] The grammar of Cleonardus, or Cleynaerts (1495-1542) was widely used and its popularity is attested to by its many reprints. In an English context one finds it prescribed for use in the grammar school of Shrewsbury in 1551.[73] Challoner's Greek dictionary is another favourite. The author, Calepinus, or Ambrogio da Calepio (*c*.1440-1511) had first published his dictionary at Reggio in 1502.[74] Since that date it had continued to be used throughout Europe; indeed, in Italy it was still in use in the eighteenth century. Challoner also had a copy of Constantine Lascaris's Greek grammar which had been the first book printed in Greek (1476).[75]

Both collectors had a copy of Friedrich Sylburgius' grammar. Sylburgius (1536-1596) was a prodigious editor of Greek works as his activities in Frankfurt and Heidelberg demonstrate.[76] This grammar is, however, the only

---

69 G.A. Padley (as note 61), p. 84.
70 G.A. Padley (as note 61), p. 84.
71 G.A. Padley (as note 61), p. 26.
72 Elizabeth Leedham-Green (as note 27), vol. 2, pp. 226-227; pp. 196-197.
73 J.E. Sandys, *A History of Classical Scolarship*. London 1967, vol. 2, p. 239.
74 J.E. Sandys (as note 73), p. 373.
75 J.E. Sandys (as note 73), p. 77.
76 J.E. Sandys (as note 73), p. 270.

Greek grammar which occurs in both collections. Ussher complements Sylburgius by adding such works as Thomas Smith's *De recta lingua Graeca* and Bernard Salignaci's *Rudimenta Graeca*. Smith (1514-1577) is perhaps best known as the regius professor of civil law at Cambridge and as an introducer of the Erasmian reform of Greek pronunciation which by Elizabeth's reign was in general use.[77] Indeed, his work seems to have had some influence on a treatise, in Challoner's 1596 collection, by Beza, on the pronunciation of Greek. Smith had been aided in this reform by the regius professor of Greek, John Cheke, and in Ussher's catalogue we find a work concerned with the Cheke-Gardiner controversy over the new pronunciation. Again the trend in Ussher's collection appears to be of a slightly more modern flavour than in that of Challoner's. Like Challoner's section, Ussher's would also have found useful works among ancient writers. While Challoner preferred to categorise them alongside his grammatical works, Ussher isolated them in a separate section, entitled *Authores Classici qui claruerunt ad annum Dom. 600*. The core works are here: Ovid, Seneca, Lucian Virgil, Pliny and Cicero.

The third biblical language is likewise represented in both collections. Challoner's 1596 collection is the same as that of 1595. By 1608 he had, however, added more works, probably due to a reorganization which took place at this time. His early collection contains two works by a very popular author, Santes Pagninus (1470-1536), described as 'one of the most learned Hebraists of his day'.[78] In 1528 he had published his version of a translation of the Bible from Hebrew and Greek – *Veteris et novi Testamenti nova translatio* – to enthusiastic reviews from both Christians and Jews. As a literal translation it proved very popular and indeed it was included in the Royal Polyglot Bible of 1572. As an aid to this work he had also published a grammar and a dictionary. These show the influence of Jewish grammarians, in particular the works of David Kimchi, whose *Michlol* is the basis for Pagninus's *Institutiones Hebraicae*, while his *Book of Roots* also provides much of the content of the *Thesaurus linguae Sanctae seu lexicon hebraicum*.[79]

John Brindsley, headmaster of the grammar school at Ashby de la Zouch, mentions Pagninus in his *Ludus literarius* of 1612.[80] He specifically mentions the work found in Challoner's catalogue: the *Epitome* of Pagninus' *Thesaurus*, edited by Raphaelengius and published in 1570. Ussher likewise has a 1577 folio edition of the *Thesaurus*, edited by Joannes Mercerus, Antonus Cevallerius and Bartholomaeus Cornelius Bertramo. The frequency with which it occurs in Cambridge inventories demonstrates its popularity.[81]

77 J.E. Sandys (as note 73), p. 232.
78 G. Lloyd Jones, *The discovery of Hebrew in Tudor England: a third language*. Manchester 1983, p. 40.
79 G. Lloyd Jones (as note 78), p. 41.
80 G. Lloyd Jones (as note 78), p. 260.
81 Elizabeth Leedham-Green (as note 27), vol. 2.

Another equally popular author found in Chaloner's first two catalogues, and that of Ussher, is Petrus Martinius. Martinius, a professor of Hebrew at the Protestant seminary in La Rochelle, had published his *Grammaticae Hebraicae Libri duo* in 1567 and 1591. Brindsley once again commends him for his method and brevity, which perhaps account for the popularity of the work.[82] In fact, it was to serve as the basis for the only English grammar of Hebrew, Udall's *The Key to the Holy Temple*.[83] Ussher owns a 1591 Rupellae edition. Evidently he considered this an important Hebrew grammar: he singled it out as such in one of his notebooks.[84] Challoner's unfortunately undated copy is accompanied by a copy of Martinius's Hebrew-Chaldaic grammar.

Works by Drusius may also be found in both catalogues. John Drusius had studied at the trilingual college at Louvain. He had spent some time teaching at Cambridge and Oxford before returning to the continent to become Hebrew professor at Leiden.[85] Challoner has three works by him, his *Observationes, Miscellanea* and *Quaestiones*, while Ussher has his *Alphabetum Hebraicum vetus et veterum Sapientum Hebraeorum* (1587). Franciscus Iunius's *Grammatica hebraea* (1590) also makes an appearance in both collections. Most famous for his collaboration with his father-in-law Immanuel Tremellius in his translation of the Old Testament, he formed part of a distinguished circle of continental Christian hebraists whose works dominate both collections.

The only other author whose name is duplicated in the collections is Genebrard, a French Hebraist often quoted by Whitaker in his diatribes against Bellarmine. Probably most famed for his 1577 Latin translation of the *Seder 'Olam Zuta*, the work by him here is *Isagoge Rabbinici Tabulae Rabbinica ejusd. R. Davidis Jehajae poetica* (1587). Ussher and Challoner have other hebraist authors in their catalogues. Challoner includes works by Gronbeck and Avenarius, the latter's book also receiving praise from Brindlsey.[86] Ussher's collection contains three works by the celebrated Sebastian Münster, and one each by Bertram, Reuchlin and Levita.

Münster (1489-1552) was a contemporary of Pagninus, who had become a Protestant *c*.1526. A prolific author and translator (his published works number 75), many of his commentaries may be found throughout Ussher's and Chaloner's lists. Lloyd Jones describes him as the chief conduit by which the Targum and works by rabbis were introduced to the biblical scholars of Tudor England.[87] His works here include the *Institutiones Grammaticae in*

---

82 G. Lloyd Jones (as note 78), p. 257.
83 G. Lloyd Jones (as note 78), p. 257.
84 TCD MS 790, fol. 36r.
85 G. Lloyd Jones (as note 78), p. 203.
86 G. Lloyd Jones (as note 78), p. 260.
87 G. Lloyd Jones (as note 78), p. 48.

hebraeam linguam (1524), the *Elementorum Hebraicae linguae* (1525) and an edition of Levita's *Capitula Cantici* of 1527.

Levita, otherwise known as Elijah Bachur (1469-1549) had acted primarily as a mediator between rabbinical works and Christian interpreters. As such he was well liked in Christian humanist circles and proved a popular author. Ussher's edition of his *Methurgeman* was edited by Paul Fagius, who, like Münster and Bertramo, had acknowledged his debt to Levita, and who, like Drusius, had taught in Cambridge.

Finally, Reuchlin's 1518 edition of the *De accentibus et orthographia linguae hebraicae*, a work which examined pronunciation and the use of accents, is present in Ussher's section. In this he continued his endeavour to establish philology as an independent discipline. Reuchlin is, however, best known for his defence of Jewish books in 1510, and for his cabbalistic writings, none of which appear here. Indeed both collections tend to concentrate on basic grammatical aids, particularly by continental Christian hebraists such as Münster, Pagninus, Drusius, Iunius and others rather than on post-biblical Jewish writings. When contact is made with rabbinical works it is invariably through these contemporary sixteenth century hebraicists, rather than direct access to the works of David Kimchi, Ibn Ezra, Isaac Abravanel and Gersonides. Perhaps one reason why these works are not bought at this time is the fact that all these authors are represented in the college library.

Other Hebrew instruction might also be found in Hebrew bibles available in the collections. Ussher has a copy of the Complutensian Bible, which incorporated Pagninus's very literal translation. He also has a Hebrew edition of the Psalms, catalogued in the Biblia section. This, of course, reminds us of the chief use of Hebrew to theology scholars. As Reuchlin himself stated:

> I assure you that not one of the Latins can explain the Old Testament unless he first becomes proficient in the language in which it was written. For the mediator between God and man was language, as we read in the Pentateuch; but not any language, only Hebrew, through which God wished his secrets to be made known to man.[88]

The Reformers, Luther, Zwingli and Calvin, had all recognised the importance of Hebrew. Old Testament commentary produced on the continent helped to stimulate English interest in the language, and though the growth in esteem was gradual, one may infer from isolated instances that Hebrew learning were slowly spreading. This interest was not restricted to philology as such but in its theological application, particularly in conjunc-

---

88 G. Lloyd Jones (as note 78), p. 24.

tion with polemics. There were first of all the various translations of the Bible which claimed attention, but then there were also the controversies such as the Fulke-Martin debate and Whitaker's works directed at Bellarmine.[89] Indeed the issue of the use of Hebrew affected the whole debate on the authority of the Bible: Roman Catholics desperately defending the Vulgate against an onslaught of Protestant attacks, which were inspired by the humanist injunction to return *ad fontes*.

Hebrew versions of the Bible in conjunction with rabbinical texts were used in doctrinal controversies to strengthen the Puritan position; an example of this is the Rainolds-Hart debate concerning papal authority. Yet another use of Hebraic material might be found in the growing interest in apocalyptic thought, especially in the works of Hugh Broughton and Thomas Brightman. Broughton's *Consent of Scripture*, of which Ussher has a copy, stresses the value of Hebrew in unravelling the prophecies of the Old Testament. Indeed Broughton appears to have been one of Ussher's favourite authors, judging by the volume of works written by him which are present in Ussher's theological section.

Perhaps Ussher's interest in chronology and apocalyptic thought may explain his larger Hebrew collection. Another possible explanation lies in his friendship with Edward Lively (1545-1605), who was a professor of Hebrew at Cambridge.[90] Like Ussher he was interested in chronology, as his *Chronologie of the Persian Monarchy* demonstrates. As a student he had been taught by Drusius and, like Ussher, he owned a copy of Drusius' work. In May 1575 he had been elected to the regius professorship of Hebrew, which post he held until his death in 1605, while he had been appointed to take part in the construction of the authorised version in 1604. His library contained works by Pagninus, Martinius, Levita, Reuchlin, Münster and Drusius, in short, much the same as Ussher' collection.[91] Indeed among his other works he had written a commentary on Martinius's Hebrew grammar. On his death both Ussher and Eyre eulogised him and Ussher's correspondence reveals that Lively was a mutual friend of both. In fact, Samuel Ward's letter to Ussher, dated 1626, indicates that Ussher had been trying to get Lively's chronological work published.[92]

Challoner shows considerably more interest in history than in grammar, or indeed in politics. True, works of an ecclesiastical nature predominate but the 1595 catalogue does contain a section of 'History Books Civil'. The English works of Camden and Stow have been mentioned in connection with historical geography and many other works might also be added to this cat-

89 William McKane, *Selected Christian Hebraists*. Cambridge 1989, pp. 76ff.
90 See entry in the *DNB*.
91 Elizabeth Leedham-Green (as note 27), vol. 1, p. 548.
92 R. Parr (as note 3), p. 369.

egory, for example Caius's *De Cantabrigia*. As one might expect, ancient authors like Herodotus, Diodorus Siculus, Sallust, Iustinus and Plutarch are also represented. Some care has, however, been taken to construct an adequate 'local history' section, not only by buying medieval texts such as the *Flores Historicum*, a chronicle from the creation to the year 1326, but also more contemporary works by Polydore Vergil, Leland's histories and the *Historia Hiberniae* ostensibly written by Richard Stanihurst but greatly influenced by Edward Campion.[93]

The other two history sections are dominated by what one might call the Protestant interpretative histories. The most influential of these was *The Centuries*, written by Matthias Flacius Illyricus whose theological-polemical approach to history emphasised the role of God rather than man in history. Divided into thirteen volumes, the work devoted itself to church history up to the thirteenth century. Protestants accused of breaking with tradition desperately needed to demonstrate that they were in fact only following earlier traditions which the Roman Catholic Church had abandoned. As a condemnation of papal historical claims to authority, while at the same time serving as a source of legitimation for Protestant reformers, it produced a popular genre. Other works in this genre are also present in Challoner's catalogue – Melanchthon's revision of Johannes Carion's *Chronicle* and the *History* of David Chytraeus.[94] The English polemicists Fox and Bale are likewise present, though slightly more impartial works, such as, Sleidan's *Commentariorum de statu religionis et reipublicae Carolo V caesare libri XXVI*, can also be found alongside earlier texts such as Eusebius's *Ecclesiastical Histories* and Platina's *Lives of the Popes*.

Ussher's history section dominates his catalogue alongside his collection of works on Protestant controversy. Entitled '*Libri Chronologici, Historici, Geographici, de re Antiquaria*', it numbers some 84 works. Treatises by Funceus, Bunting, Alfragani and Preyer, to name but four, illustrate Ussher's well known interest in matters chronological. His interest in local history seems even more acute than Challoner's – not only do we find Hector Boethius's *Historici Scotorum* (1575), Buchanan's *Rerum Scoticarum* (1584), John Major's *History of Britain* and John Harding's *Chronicle of England*, but also some Irish material: Ralph Birchinsawes's *Discourse of ye victory at Kinsale* (Dublin 1602) and William Farmer's *Almanack, Ireland for ye year 1587*.

Roman histories by Livy also appear and some news reports from the continent, for example, An explanation of ye T*itle of Don Antonio to ye kingdome of Portingall: wth a briefe historye of all that passed concerning that matter, usque ad annum 1583* and *The Declaration of ye French King, and ye king of Navarre,*

93   Levi Fox, *Tudor Historical Writing*. Huntingdon 1967, p. 185.
94   J.W. Thompson, (1942), *A History of Historical Writing*. New York 1942, pp. 527-528.

concerning ye truce agreed upon between them and ye passage of ye River of Loire. 1589.

Ussher's ecclesiastical history must, however, be found elsewhere: alongside his works on the Bible, Fathers and Councils. Like Challoner, he also possessed the key work for Protestant historians interested in history's polemical uses: the *Centuries* of Flacius Illyricus. Ussher's historical works are more difficult to trace as he spreads them out over more than one section – for example he places Flacius Illyricus's *de Translatione Imperii* in the *Libri Prot. de Controversiis* section. In general, however, his collection is sparse, compared to that of Challoner. Apart from the *Centuries*, the historical works he has are different from those of his father-in-law.

Both Ussher's and Challoner's history sections might be viewed as a subsection of the primary subject division in all their catalogues: Theology. In Challoner's 1595 selection theology is subdivided into sections such as 'Papist Books and Scripture', 'Confuta. of Papists', 'Books against Lutherans', 'Books against and for Discipline' and the 'Fathers'. It seems likely that theology sections in the 1596 list, such as, 'Theologia- Biblia et Commentarii', and possibly some of the 'Loci Communes' and 'Tractatus theologici' sections, may simply be missing from the earlier catalogue.

In any theological endeavour the Bible was the lodestone. Luther's insistence on *sola scriptura* had emphasised the importance of the Word of God. Subsequent Protestant formulations of this principle led to an increase in intellectual examination of the text itself and a veritable outpouring of commentaries. A key issue was the search for correct editions, a quest which was made possible by the increased interest in linguistic skills in the biblical languages of Greek and Hebrew and Aramaic. The increased publication of works, such as those described above in the section dealing with the respective grammar collections of Challoner and Ussher, enabled a deeper investigation of the true meaning of passages in the Bible from which all preaching and, indeed, all conception of the community would spring.

In England this principle had been enunciated in the 39 Articles where it was stated that 'Holy Scripture containeth all things necessary to salvation'.[95] Puritans such as Cartwright and his followers placed added emphasis on the text, a fact acknowledged by Whitgift in his reply to the 'Admonition to the Parliament' (1572):

> As though they should say nothing is to be tolerated in the church of Christ, touching either doctrine, order, ceremonies, discipline, or government, except it be expressed in the word of God.[96]

95 S.L. Greenslade, *The Cambridge History of the Bible. The West from the Reformation to the present day*. Cambridge 1963, p. 6.
96 J.S. Coolidge, *The Pauline Renaissance in England. Puritanism and the Bible*. Oxford 1970, p. 1.

Coolidge quite rightly points out that the chief stumbling block between Puritan and Anglican lay in this appeal to scriptural authority, as evinced by the following statement of Cartwright's concerning Christian liberty and edification:

> So that you see that those things which you reckon up of the hour, and time, and day of prayer, etc. albeit they be not specified in the scripture, yet they are not left to any to order at their pleasure, so that they be not against the word of God, but even by and according to the word of God they must be established, and those alone to be taken which do agree best and nearest with these rules before recited.[97]

Challoner's 1596 catalogue contains two English Bibles, two Hebrew Bibles, a Bezan text, the Vatablus Bible and an edition by Tremellius-Iunius, while his 1608 collection has only one English Bible, one Hebrew, one French, one Syriac, the Vatablus, the Bezan and two of Tremellius. Unfortunately, the scarcity of bibliographical information present in Challoner's catalogues renders the task of identifying the different editions well nigh impossible in some cases. For example, his English Bibles, 'Bible *Anglice* 8o and 4o' respectively, could be editions by Tyndale, Coverdale, Rogers or the Genevan Bible. Equally, they might be the 1568 Bishops Bible or, indeed, that of Douai-Rheims. His inscription 'Biblia Heb 4o.et 8o' poses similar problems of identification, and could refer to any of the well known Hebrew versions available: Daniel Bomberg's Bible, first published in 1516-1517, or that of Sebastian Münster (1535), or the edition of the printers – Robert Estienne's 1539-1544 and Christoper Plantin's famous Polyglot of Antwerp – though equally, we could be dealing with the Complutensian Polyglot of Alcala of 1514-1517.

The Challoner 1608 references to an octavo Syriac Testament and a French Bible prove equally tantalising. A Syriac version of the New Testament had first appeared *c.*1555 and had been of polemical use to Protestants in their endeavour to discredit the use of the vulgate. A version was incorporated into the Royal Polyglot, while Tremelius worked on his own edition of 1569. Whichever edition one is dealing with, the only conclusion one may reach is that it must have been based on the core text of Widmanstadt's full Syriac version of the New Testament.[98] The 'French Bible' likewise creates difficulties as it could refer to any of the sixteenth-century French Bibles – Olivetan's, Castellio's or the Genevan revision by Beza and Bertramo, a more unlikely contender being the Catholic Louvain version of 1578.

97 J.S. Coolidge (as note 96), p. 5.
98 S.L. Greenslade (as note 95), p. 74.

With the 'Biblia Vatabli' we are on firmer ground. François Vatable (d.1547) was a Hebrew scholar at the Collège de France during Calvin's sojourn in Paris. Both Calvin and Whitaker had used his commentaries. Between 1539 and 1546 he had co-operated with Robert Estienne in the printing of two editions of the Hebrew Old Testament and this is probably the work in question here, though Challoner lists it as a trilingual work.

Immanuel Tremellius's work was probably the most popular edition of the Bible in the sixteenth century. Tremellius himself had taught at Cambridge in 1549 at Cranmer's invitation and he was also a close friend of another archbishop of Canterbury, Matthew Parker. Responsible for the Latin translation of rabbinical sources such as the Targum Jonathan and an Aramaic/Syriac grammar, Tremellius's chief claim to fame lay in his Latin translation of the Old Testament in which each book was accompanied by an introductory preface. This work, in which he had been aided by his son-in-law, Franciscus Iunius, was dated 1575-1579, and was the last Latin translation to appear. One reason for the extent of its popularity was its close identification with the Protestant cause, demonstrated in the various dedications in its prefaces to Lutheran leaders such as the Elector Frederick of Saxony, Johann Casimir and William of Hesse respectively.[99] Challoner has this edition and, in his 1608 list, he had acquired a later edition, which included a Latin version of the Greek New Testament by Beza.

Both the 1596 and 1608 catalogues of Challoner have two editions of other Bezan New Testaments. Beza had used Tremellius' work on the New Testament, along with Henri Estienne's notes, in this important Greek edition published in 1565. In all, Beza published no less than nine editions between 1565 and 1604. His editions popularized the *textus receptus* which had been largely based on Erasmian translation and, in an English context, his 1588-1589 and 1598 editions proved very influential in the compiling of the 1611 authorised version. Unfortunately, Challoner gives us no information as to the exact edition, but one appears to have contained English notes.

Ussher's Bible collection contained far fewer complete Bibles than that of his father-in-law: two Latin and one English Bible. Luckily in the latter case, he identifies his English edition as that of the 'Genevan translation 1601. Lond. 8o.' The Geneva Bible, first printed in 1560, was the most popular English edition of the Bible in Protestant, and, more particularly, in Puritan circles. Based on Hebrew and Greek originals, it was undertaken by Protestant exiles from the England of Queen Mary – particularly William Whittingham and Anthony Gilby. It broke new ground in a number of areas, being the first English quarto Bible and the first in Roman type. A compar-

---

99 J.A. Van Dorsten, 'Sidney and Franciscus Junius the Elder' in *Huntingdon Library Quarterly* 42, 1978, p. 8.

ison of publication figures between 1560 and 1611 of other English Bibles demonstrates the wide appeal of this version:

Tyndale's New Testament: reprinted 5 times.
Great Bible: reprinted 7 times.
Bishops' Bible: reprinted 22 times.
Geneva Bible: reprinted more than 120 times.[100]

Even after 1611 more than 60 editions appeared, showing that even the authorized version could not displace it. Frequent citations by sixteenth century writers likewise attest to its wide appeal, though some discussion remains as to the reasons for its popularity. Greenslade says that one reason for its persistent popularity in Puritan circles was the attendant notes which he describes as 'somewhat distinctly Calvinist'.[101] Partridge counters this by emphasising its use by Whitgift and Hooker.[102] Levi, however, manages to explain the apparent contradiction by suggesting that the earlier editions contained no offensive material to Calvinists such as Parker and Whitgift, but that editions of the 1590s, published under the aegis of Walsingham, adopted a more controversial tone, including notes by Beza and Camerarius.[103] Certainly though Laud himself cited from it in his sermons, he found these editions problematic, and, in 1616, forbade its printing in England. This is why editions after 1616 are invariably printed in Amsterdam. In this context it is interesting to note that Ussher's edition was printed in 1601.

Ussher's other two complete Bibles are Latin editions. One is an edition of the controversial Vulgate, which Protestant writers had been trying to supplant and which the Roman Catholic Church at Trent had authorised as the true version of the Bible. Obviously its presence here should be analysed as a purchase to aid polemical research, rather than an indication of devotion to this particular edition! The other Latin edition is referred to as *Romanae Correctionis in Latinis Bibliis jussu Sixti V. recognitus, loca insi juiora, observata a Franc. Lucam brugensi. Antwerp. 1603. 160.* The Sixtine edition of Rome 1590 had created certain problems in the Catholic camp. Though supported by its own bull declaring it to be the new Roman Catholic authorised version, it had been attacked by Cardinal Bellarmine. A result of this was a re-edition, now directed by Bellarmine under the aegis of Clement VII, which declared itself to be a new Sixtine edition of 1592. Brugensis' is obviously one of these later editions, and again its purchase should be viewed in the same light as Ussher's purchase of the Vulgate.

100 Peter Levi, *The English Bible. 1534-1859.* London 1974, p. 27.
101 S.L. Greenslade (as note 95), p. 158.
102 A.C. Partridge, *English Biblical Translation.* London 1973, p. 77.
103 Peter Levi (as note 100), p. 29.

Ussher's remaining biblical editions are evenly divided between testaments and psalters. One of the Old Testaments was also linked to Sixtus V, this edition being by Cardinal Carafa in 1587, while the other was a Greek version of the Pentateuch edited by Zephyrus. The two New Testaments are both Greek, the former being edited by Robert Estienne and the latter a part of the famous Complutensian Bible. Estienne had published four editions of the Greek New Testament. The third, first printed in 1550, had popularised the Erasmian versions, and, as Metzger states, became 'the received or standard text of the Greek Testament' in England.[104] In his earlier editions Estienne had also utilised the Complutensian Greek New Testament and it is this that was the basis for Ussher's second New Testament in Greek, published in 1591. Part of the celebrated Complutensian Polyglot of Cardinal Ximenes de Cisnero, it included the other languages: Hebrew, Aramaic and Latin.

Finally, Ussher seems to have made rather a collection of translations of the psalms: comprising Greek, Latin, English, French and Polyglot versions. His English version is a manuscript Old English translation rather than one of the 85 printed English editions then available by such luminaries as Thomas Rogers, Anthony Gilby, or indeed, his own uncle, Richard Stanyhurst. His purchase of a French edition by Clement Marot, combined with Genevan forms by Beza, is unexceptionable, given the extent of the popularity of this edition in Calvinist circles. As Pidoux emphasises: 'en 1562, le Psautier a joui d'une veritable canonicite les textes de Marot et de Beza, de même les melodies genevoises, ont ete reproduits de varietur comme une nouvelle Vulgate'.[105]

The presence of these editions, along with his Greek, Latin and quadrilingual versions shows the popularity of the Psalms in Calvinist circles for devotional use. The increase in publication in the sixteenth century of devotional works – as many as 80 collections from 1558-1603 – was undoubtedly linked to the increased responsibility placed on the individual by the religious controverisal debates.[106] The principle of the priesthood of all believers laid a greater emphasis on an individual's private spiritual life. The moderate Puritans, as authors of the majority of devotional works, recognised this need. The Biblical model inherent in the Psalms proved a strong attraction. As Rivkah suggests, the 'psalm model's peculiar importance derived from its representation of an individual's self revelation in direct and artful colloquy with God'.[107] This intense focus on self-revelation, allied as it was to assur-

---

104   B.M. Metzger, *The text of the New Testament. Its transmission, corruption and restoration.* Oxford 1968, p. 104.
105   Pierre Pidoux, *Le Psautier Huguenot.* Basel 1962, vol. 2, p.v.
106   Horton Davies, *Worship and Theology in England from Cranmer to Hooker. 1534-1603.* Princeton 1970, p. 407.
107   Zim Rivkah, *English metrical Psalms. Poetry as Praise and Prayer 1535-1601.* Cambridge 1987, p. 204.

ance of salvation, was intrinsically connected to interpretations of predestination which, as a central concept in late sixteenth century debate, is likewise present in both collections.

More precisely the Psalters should be included in the sections on Biblical commentary and indeed both authors include their collections of Bibles in their sections of commentary. An examination of Challoner's library in 1596 reveals that the number of commentaries on Old Testament books are almost double that of New Testament works, and, with some minor changes, his 1608 list tells the same story. In the New Testament sections the emphasis is on the Pauline books – Romans and the epistles especially – though the Book of Revelations also had five different commentaries in each catalogue. The vast majority of the commentaries are by contemporary writers, some Lutheran, but mostly Calvinist. Continental authors predominate, the English exceptions being Fulke and Pilkington.

During the sixteenth century the growing interest in Hebraic studies had, as we have seen, led to a number of Hebrew translations of the Bible by such Christian hebraists as Sebastian Münster. These, in turn, had acted as an impetus to publication of Old Testament commentaries which had thrived from the eleventh century to the fourteenth but which had since then, been somewhat in decline due to the rise of Lombard's *Sentences*.[108] However, from 1530 onwards a whole range of commentaries was published, taking advantage of the linguistic skills now more readily available, but also, and perhaps more importantly, answering a need in the continuous religious controversy. The Protestant emphasis on *sola scriptura* inevitably led to more contemporary discussions of scripture and these, in turn, forced Roman Catholic apologists to turn their minds to counteract them. Calvin's output in particular, in this regard, was phenomenal.[109] Producing commentaries on Isaiah, Genesis, psalms, Hosea, lamentations and prophets such as Daniel, Jeremiah and Ezekiel, he also incorporated discussion from sermons and lectures given at Geneva; this is a timely reminder for us that other material would have been utilised in exegesis rather than works solely classified as biblical commentary.

Indeed, Ussher includes sermons in his biblical commentary sections entitled 'Recentiorum Theologorum Commentarii in S. Scripturani et Conciones'. His collection differs markedly in terms of authors from Challoner's. Ussher's emphasis is placed on sermons by English authors, particularly those of a Puritan slant, ranging from Dering to Udall. As regards the balance of New and Old Testament commentaries, Ussher likewise does not mirror Challoner's library; his New Testament section almost rivals that of his Old Testament in number. Both collections do, however, favour mul-

---

108 T.H.L. Parker, *Calvin's Old Testament Commentaries*. Edinburgh 1986.
109 T.H.L. Parker (as note 108), p. 9.

tiple copies of the same Old Testament books – Genesis, psalms and individual prophets, with Revelation also proving popular in Ussher's New Testament collection, though interestingly Ussher seems to have had a personal preference for sermons on Matthew. This avoidance of duplicating material by the same authors suggests a concerted plan of action on the part of the two collectors to expand the pool of knowledge available.

Editions of the *Harmonia Evangeliorum* were also popular with both collectors. Connected to scriptural exegesis was the study of earlier interpretation by both the Church Fathers and later medieval commentators. Challoner's 1595 catalogue lists 22 authors in this section entitled 'Fathers', while his collections in the following year had risen to 31 and, by 1608, stood at 37. Ussher's collection of 1608 incorporated his patristic material with that of his collections of ecclesiastical history and Church Councils, a tendency to which Challoner also succumbed.

Both collections had assembled the key works outlined in the 1559 Westminster Conference: Justin, Irenaeus, Tertullian, Cyprian, Basil, Chrysostom, Hierome, Ambrose and Augustine, though Greenslade points out that other later commentators might also be included, John of Damascus, for example, in Challoner's 1608 list.[110] The trend seems to have favoured Greek commentators such as Gregory of Nazianz, John Chrysostom, Cyrillus of Alexandria, some of these works had been edited by Oecolampadius.

The key issue, of course, as regards the Church Fathers was that of their use. Viewed as a necessary supplement to any theological collection, there was yet an ambivalence in Protestant circles as to their possible use and authority that found its way into the writings of men like Bishop John Jewel and others.[111] Yet despite this, it was soon clear that the literature of the Fathers provided valuable ammunition in the polemical stakes between Catholic and Protestant. Even beyond this negative use, they could act as a guide to the meaning of scripture. As one sixteenth century source states, 'they have *auctoritas*, weight, they are to be esteemed'.[112]

Richard Parr, Ussher's biographer, informs us that Ussher himself had a fascination for patristic study, which was initially sparked off by his reading of Stapleton's *Fortress of Faith*.[113] Ussher realised the necessity of studying the original sources and, from c.1601 to c.1639, was to spend much time researching the problem. Parr underlines his polemical interest in the Fathers thus:

> Yet before he was Master of Arts he had read here and there divers Books of the Fathers, and most of our Best Authors, who had writ in

110 S.L. Greenslade. *The English Reformers and the Fathers of the Church*. Oxford 1960, p. 5.
111 S.L. Greenslade (as note 110), p. 9.
112 S.L. Greenslade (as note 110), p. 6.
113 R. Parr (as note 3), p. 4.

confutation of the Errors of the Papists, with many of their writers also; by which he had so well acquainted himself with the state of each controversie, that he was able to dispute with any of the popish Priests, as he often did with the chiefest of them.[114]

Again, of Ussher's labours in 1610, Parr writes:

> For at that time he was deeply engaged in the Fathers, Council, and Church history ... So he was now able to judge, whether the passages quoted by our adversaries were truly cited, or not, or were wrestled to a wrong sense : And this he did, not out of bare Curiousity, but to confute the Arrogance of those men who will still appeal to Antiquity (though with little success), and the Writings of the Fathers.[115]

The polemical value of patristic studies is apparent from the above quote. Theological controversies formed the most important areas in both Challoner's and Ussher's collections. Challoner devoted one section to works by Roman Catholic authors such as Harding, Bellarmine and Acquinas in 1595, while in the following year his collection had been augmented to include more 'Books of Papists'. By 1608 we find 41 works in this section alone, not including other contenders in alternative categories.

Ussher likewise has two sections, entitled *Libri Pontificorum de Fidei, etc Controversii* and *Tractatus Theologici Pontificorum [et aliorum Haereticorum]*. Yet again there appears to be very little overlap between both 1608 collections. Interestingly, Ussher includes another section in his catalogue, entitled *Scripta Theologorum, qui ab anno 1000 ad 1500 claruerunt*, obviously he considered these works as less controversial. In his polemical sections Ussher concentrates on English Roman Catholic apologists such as Parsons, Stapleton and Wright, while Challoner's collections include more mainstream criticism of the reformed religion. The inclusion of these works, of a primarily polemical nature, by Roman Catholic authors was an essential part of the library of any Calvinist divine who was interested in religious controversy, and we find that both Challoner and Ussher saw fit to include a notable section of these works in the library of the college, even though these books might well be considered dangerous, as Ussher's advice to Challoner on their placement in the college library suggests.[116]

The core sections of both catalogues were the sections concerned with answering these papal controversialists, and other Protestant writings. Ussher devotes one of his largest sections to Protestant works of controversy, with

---

114 R. Parr (as note 3), p. 5.
115 R. Parr (as note 3), p. 11.
116 C.R. Elrington (as note 4), vol. 15, p. 81.

an adjacent subsection of Protestant theological tracts; while Challoner prefers to separate his 'Confutatons of Papists' and 'Books against Lutherans' and 'Books against and for Discipline', although there was some reorganization in his 1608 catalogue. Again a correlation of works in both sections reveals that there was little overlap. Challoner's anti-papal sections are dominated by the works of Whitaker and Fulke; works by the latter author number 13 in the 1596 list. Ussher's collection, while including some of Challoner's authors, inevitably concentrates on alternative authors – such as Thomas Morton and Franciscus Iunius. Both include anti-papal works by the more Anglican of their co-religionists: Bilson in Challoner's and Saravia in Ussher's. This shows yet again that both Anglicans and Puritans could easily join forces when attacking the common enemy. However, this said, the dominant trend in Challoner's catalogues is of a Calvinist-Puritan apologetic rather than an Anglican. Ussher's collection is more of a mixture, including works by Andrew Willet. Indeed he pays more attention to early debates, between Jewel and Harding, and Foxian polemic, than he does to the slightly more contemporary debates favoured by Challoner.

Both collectors have the key works concerning the internal debate in the Protestant churches as regards discipline. Treatises by Cartwright and Travers dominate. Challoner, in particular, seems slightly more interested in this area. Ussher includes the key works by Travers and Cartwright but his works for and against discipline are submerged in his general Protestant controversies sections and come a distinct second to those of his papal controversies. Challoner's collection looks to the theological debates of Cambridge in the 1580s and 1590s but Ussher, while inevitably including some of this material, seems far more concerned with more homegrown problems of defeating Roman Catholic apologists. This, of course, ties in with Ussher's interests at this time, as enunciated by Parr:

> ... his Lectures were Polemical, upon chief Controversies in Religion, especially those Points and Doctrines maintained by the Romish Church, confuting their errors, and answering their Arguments by Scripture, Antiquity and sound Reason, which was the method he still used in that Exercise, as also in his Preachings, and Writings, when he had to do with controverises of the Nature, then most proper to be treated on.[117]

Taken as a whole, the prevalent tone of both collections is that of a Calvinist controversialist, particularly interested in refutation of Roman Catholic writers such as Robert Bellarmine, a trend also to be found in the first main catalogue of TCD MS 2. Undoubtedly, Challoner belongs to the

---

117 R. Parr (as note 3), p. 10.

'Puritan' ethos of TCD if his books are any indication of his interests. He not only has works such as Walter Traver's *Ecclesiastical Dicipline*, but also texts by all the great Puritan writers, William Perkins, Thomas Cartwright, William Whitaker, to name but three. Certainly he attempted to keep abreast of contemporary controversy with a steady increase in books from 1595 to 1596 and then a large increase from the 1596 list to the 1608 catalogue.

Undeniably, Challoner was primarily interested in developing his theological section and it is therefore unsurprising to find very few works of the other two higher faculty subjects: medicine and law. In fact there is no section concerned with law in any of the three catalogues and, even in miscellaneous sections, no references can be found. Medicine fares slightly better, with some works incorporated into the 1595 miscellaneous section entitled 'Polyhistores' and its own section 'Phisike' in the 1596 list. Although there appears to have been a steady increase in this section from 1595 to 1596, 22 works to 40 works respectively, Challoner's interest seems to have declined somewhat by 1608 as only one work from either of these two lists may be found in that catalogue: 'The wonders of Nature' by Fenton.

Challoner's 1595/1596 collection is dominated by authors such as Galen and Fernelius, again two of the most popular works of the period, accompanied by a number of works by continental authors on botany. Challoner seems to have relied on Galen's four costly tomes for general medical knowledge and in this he appears to be following a general trend.[118] Certainly Galen's physiological system proved influential until William Harvey's researches in the seventeenth century.[119] It is therefore unfortunate that we have no indication of the actual edition that Challoner procured. The same must also be said of the more contemporary author, Fernelius, for Challoner regrettably neglects to indicate exactly which work is in question. To hazard a guess, the work could be his famous textbook, the *Medicina*, first published in 1554, which treated subjects such as physiology and pathology from a Galenic perspective.[120] In general the remainder of the section deals with botanical works such as Dioscorides's pharmaceutical guide, though the first English work concerning mental illness, Bright's *Treatise of Melancholy* is also included.[121]

Ussher, on the other hand, does not totally neglect law. He seems to be interested in practical works, for example Littleton's *Tenures*, a work which occurs with great frequency in the Cambridge inventory lists. Sir Edward

---

118 Elizabeth Leedham-Green (as note 27), vol. 2, pp. 365-370 (Galen), pp. 339-340 (Fernelius).
119 C.C. Gillespie (ed.), *Dictionary of Scientific Biography*. New York 1972, vol. 5, p. 233.
120 C.C. Gillespie (as note 119), vol. 4, pp. 584-586.
121 C.D. O'Malley, 'Tudor Medicine and Biology', in *The Huntington Library Quarterly* 32, 1968, p. 16.

Coke described the *Tenures* as 'the most perfect and absolute work that was ever written in any humane science.'[122] Ussher's copy is one of the 13 French editions which appeared prior to 1591.

Another possession of Ussher's was an equally famous law text, Rastell's *Statutes*. Its eight reprints no doubt owed much to the scope of the work which was as comprehensive as possible.[123] Ussher also displayed some interest in Irish law, collecting two works on statutes promulgated in Ireland. However, his investigation of legal matters did not limit itself to local law but included the purchasing of works on canon law such as that by Albericus Gentitlis and the *Decreta* of Gratian, as well as one or two works dealing with medieval German law.

Medicine fares little better. Incorporated into the '*Libri Mathematici, Physici et Medici*' section, his collection bears little resemblance to that of Challoner, for he seems to have collected works of secondary interest: a compilation by Brissianus, Macer's treatise on herbs and two works on old age – one of them by Rantzovius. Evidently the higher faculties of law and medicine proved unappealing to Ussher.

Ussher's catalogue contains some categories that may not be found in those of his father-in-law. Works on politics and economics, though they are not many in number, are present, catalogued alongside law in the *Libri Ethici, Oeconomici, Politici and Juridici* section. The most important work was undoubtetly Aristotle's *Politics*, of which Ussher has an edition. He also demonstrates an interest in early seventeenth-century writing: a 1603 edition of the *Politics* of Althusius is found alongside a 1605 edition of the *Mundus alter et idem* of Joseph Hall, a fellow of Emmanuel College.[124] Another contemporary work was the *Microcosmos* by Sir John Davies, whose name occurs in Ussher's borrowing lists.[125]

A category which receives considerably more attention in Ussher's catalogue than in that of Challoner is his bibliographical section. The collection entitled 'Bibliothecae' comprises thirteen titles, of which eleven are printed works. The most famous bibliographer of the sixteenth century, Konrad Gesner, is represented by his *Bibliothecae Epitome a Josia Simlero et Jo. Jacobo Fisio aucta. Tigure. 1583. fol.* The *Bibliothecae Epitome* was in fact a shorter edition of his more famous work the *Bibliothecae Universalis sive Catalogus omnium scriptorum* (Zurich 1545), described as 'a work ... not only necessary for the building of library collections, but most useful for the better ordering of studies for all students of whatever art or science.'[126] In this

---

122 H.S. Bennett, *English Books and their Readers 1558-1603*. Cambridge 1965, p. 162.
123 H.S. Bennett (as note 122), p. 160.
124 See entry in the *DNB*.
125 TCD MS 790, fol 49v.
126 Rudolf Blum, *Bibliographia*. Kent 1980, p. 35.

Gesner had chosen to list Greek, Latin and Hebrew authors in alphabetical sequence with not only bibliographical information but also contemporary opinions of the treatises, and, in some cases, extracts. Taylor has described it as 'a comprehensive international bibliographical dictionary'.[127] Gesner's work, along with his other magnum opus, the *Pandectae sive Partitiones universalis* (Zurich 1548) proved immensely influential in sixteenth century bibliography. Indeed he popularised the very term *bibliothecae*, for lists of authors and their works had previously been designated as *catalogi, elenchi, indexes* or *nomenclator*.[128] This particular edition, edited by Johann Jakob Fries and Josias Simler, spawned further *bibliothecae*, mere extracts of Gesner. Fries, himself a librarian of the canons of the Zurich Grossmunster, was so deeply involved in Gesner's method that he hoped to bring out a new edition of the *Pandectae*, while Simler had already used the *Bibliothecae* in a shorter format.

Another famous bibliographer, Antonius Possevino, is represented by two later works: a folio edition of *Apparatus Sacri, pars 1a cum Appendice*, published in Venice in 1603 and the second and third part of the *Apparatus* along with the *Catalogi librorum MSS. qui in Vaticanam, et aliis celebriorib. Bibliothecis asservantur*. These works continued on the tradition Possevino, an Italian Jesuit, had established in his earlier *Bibliotheca Selecta*, of combining in one work 'a Select Bibliography, in which is presented a Plan of Studies in History, in the Arts and Sciences, and in the Procurement of Salvation for All' – a work primarily conceived as a guide for Catholic students.[129]

These books should perhaps be seen in the light of Ussher's purchase of two indices – undoubtedly in an attempt to understand the bibliographical concerns of the opposite camp: the *Index librorum prohibitorum a Pio IV primum editus, a Sixto V et Clemente VII auctu. Paris 1599. 16o.* and the *Index Expurgatorius: operam Fr. Iunius et Jo. Pappi editus 1599. 16o*. These works might almost be thought of as required reading in the library of someone who was attempting to construct a suitable collection for a newly formed Protestant institution.

While other bibliographical/biographical works are included – for example, Suffridus Petrus' *de Scriptoribus* – the emphasis in the collection is on trade catalogues. Again this proves unsurprising, given Ussher's position as College book buyer. Though they contained less bibliographical information than works such as Gesner's, the Frankfurt *Messe Kataloge* of which Ussher's collection has 15, were essential tools for this task. His *Catalogi Nundinarium Francofurtensium* were divided into two issues per year, spring and autumn. Ussher has both issues for the years 1600-1606, none for 1607, two for 1608

---

127   Archer Taylor, *General Subject Indexes since 1548*. Univ. of Penn. Press. 1960, p. 40.
128   Rudolf Blum (as note 126), p. 16.
129   Rudolf Blum (as note 126), p. 35.

and the spring edition of 1609. These semi-annual catalogues had succeeded previous lists of books for sale at the Frankfurt and Leipzig Book Fairs, but by 1600 had developed into publications which, not only included books for sale, but also all new works in all subject areas: hence their importance for Ussher and Challoner.

Ussher was also careful not to neglect the Frankfurt *Messe Kataloge* prior to 1600 as his ownership of Nicholas Basse's *Collectio omnium librorum qui in nundinis Francofurtensib. ab anno 1564 usq. ad nundinis Autumnales anni 1592 venales extiterunt. Francofurt 1592. 40.* demonstrates. This represented the first culmination of the Frankfurt catalogues up to 1592. Nor did Ussher neglect the seven year gap from this work to the chief *Messe Kataloge*; his collection likewise included a quarto edition of Henning Grosse's *collectio librorum qui ab anno 1593 usq. ad anno1600 prodierunt* published at Leipzig in 1600.

While his collection seems to be dominated by the Frankfurt Catalogues, Ussher also included some French bibliographical aids, generally of individual publishers such as Henri Petri and the Voegelin press. He likewise did not ignore English works, as his possession of Andrew Maunsell's catalogue of English printed books, published at London in 1595 demonstrates. Challoner also had a copy of this trade catalogue. Maunsell actually published two parts but his failure to complete his projected theology catalogue seems to substantiate the view that the Frankfurt *Messe Kataloge* had cornered the market in theological bibliographical aids.

Ussher's catalogue is primarily a static collection for the year 1608-1609. With Challoner one can, however see a progressive development over thirteen years. While the first two catalogues are in the main similar to each other the third catalogue of 1608 exhibits a startling reorganization of Challoner's library. Three hundred and eighty-seven new titles are added, but, at the same time 555 titles from both the 1595 and 1596 lists are absent. The new additions are principally theological works, while the books which have disappeared from his collection are primarily the B.A. subjects of logic, rhetoric, poetry and the M.A. scientific/mathematical sections. It seems probable that this reorganization is related to Challoner's acceptance of the post of professor of divinity at TCD; and this in itself suggests that he himself may have taken the new position more seriously than has previously been perceived. Clearly the vast majority of his new collection was bought to augment his already dominant theological section, especially the subsection of controversy.

The 1608 catalogue sheds valuable light on the question of the relationship of Challoner's library and that of the college. Our sole piece of evidence concerning the composition of the college library prior to the book buying expeditions of 1601 is a list of books, dated February 1601, in the *Particular*

Book.[130] This lists 32 printed books and a number of manuscripts – hardly a stupendous collection. Challoner's library, on the other hand, is remarkably large for a private library, indeed when compared with Cambridge probate inventories from the same period it has few rivals.[131] It seems reasonable to assume, given contemporary borrowing habits, that Challoner's library was not solely used by himself. There is some evidence to support this view. Firstly, Challoner at times owned more than one copy of the same work.[132] Secondly, in one of the student notebooks of the first decade of the seventeenth century a number of works are mentioned which are in Challoner's library but are not to be found in the college library, while in another notebook there is actually a list of 'books borrowed from Challoner'.[133]

The same argument holds true for Ussher's library of 1608. It, too, was a remarkable size for a private library. Added to this, we possess proof that both libraries were not for the sole use of their owners, in the form of lists of books which may be found in the notebooks of Luke Challoner and James Ussher. Those of Challoner are the earliest and are dated September 1601, and May 1610, respectively.[134] It appears that these lists are actually Challoner's records of book borrowing from his library, and, as such, represent invaluable evidence, not only of the early interests of students and fellows, but also of the direct connection between Challoner's own library and that of the college. The 1610 list is no less interesting for a number of reasons. Firstly, it gives us some insight into further acquisitions by Challoner; for example he now has an edition of Keckermann's *Logic*, one of the systematical approaches to Ramist dialectic lamented by Howell in 1961.[135]

The dating of Ussher's two borrowing lists presents more of a problem.[136] Some dates do occur – May 1610 and June 1611 in MS 790 and 1611, 1616 and 1619 in MS 793, thus indicating that they are what one might term 'accessionary' borrowing lists. However, these lists actually begin slightly earlier that the May 1610 date would suggest. The inclusion of Justice Christopher Sibthorp's name as one of Ussher's borrowers indicates that this main list must be later than 1607, the year in which Sibthorp became the third justice of the King's Bench in Ireland.[137] At the same time, part of the list must predate 1609, as a reference to Sr Bourchier is included, Henry

130 J.P. Mahaffy (as note 9), fols. 216v & 217r.
131 Elizabeth Leedham-Green (as note 27).
132 TCD MS.357, fol 11r.
133 TCD MS.790, fol 35v (Nauclerus); fol37r (Wolfius); fol 38r (Wierus); TCD MS 793, fol 169r.
134 TCD MS. fol. 8r & v.
135 W.S. Howell (as note 52), p. 283.
136 TCD MS 790 and MS 793. Another borrowing list of Ussher, which follows the same pattern, may be found in Bodl. Rawl. 1290, fols. 1r-2v.
137 See *DNB*.

Bourchier only became a fellow in 1609.[138] A date of c.1608 seems likely for the main part of the MS 790 list, continuing up to June 1611. Likewise c.1608 covers some of the material in the MS 793 list as Sr Bourchier appears among the borrowers there.

Challoner's two lists are also accessionary lists. Certainly, although the first list may have been begun in 1601, its references to borrowers such as Sir John Tirrel and Mr Lydiat indicate a later date for some of the material. John Tirrel, an alderman of the city of Dublin, was only knighted in his mayoral year, 1602-1603.[139] Lydiat, the renowned mathematician, was a former Fellow of New College, Oxford where he had graduated B.A. 1595 and M.A. in 1598-1599.[140] In 1609 he was appointed chorographer and cosmographer to Henry, prince of Wales, and it was during that year that he became acquainted with James Ussher. Indeed, it was on Ussher's suggestion that he travelled to Ireland. He spent two years in Dublin, became a fellow of Trinity on 7 March, 1610 and gained an M.A. there in the same year. Ussher seems to have fostered his career in Dublin by arranging that he become a reader. By August 1611, Lydiat had decided to return to London, thus ending his relationship with the college, if not with James Ussher – as their subsequent correspondence demonstrates – and, indeed, he appears as a borrower on Ussher's lists.[141]

In the second list, the inclusion of Mr Warren again suggests a possible accessionary character. Edward Warren had been a scholar in TCD in 1603, and had received his B.A. in 1608, and his M.A. in the summer of 1611.[142] He only became a fellow in August 1612. Yet, on Challoner's list, dated May 1610, he is given the title of a fellow.

One area in which Ussher's lists differ slightly from those of Challoner, apart from in the actual book borrowers themselves, is that the second Ussher list contains material relating to books which Ussher himself had borrowed from other people, and, in turn, lent out to others; in short, it is what one might call a double loan list and, as such, gives us valuable information concerning other possible collections available to members of College.[143]

The true importance of all these borrowing lists lies in the information they afford us, not only concerning the friendship networks in College in the early period, but also, and in the context of this article, more importantly, concerning the intellectual interests one may discern from studying the

138 G.D. Burchaell and T.U. Sadleir (eds.), *Alumni Dublinensis*. Dublin 1935, p. 83.
139 Colm Lennon, Colm (1989) *The Lords of Dublin in the Age of Reformation*. Dublin 1989, p. 69.
140 See *DNB*.
141 C.R. Elrington (as note 4) vol. 15.
142 G.D. Burchaell and T.U. Sadleir (as note 138), p. 860.
143 These alternative collections include the contemporary St Patrick's library and libraries of individuals such as 'Mr Bolger'.

choices of the borrowers.¹⁴⁴ A detailed analysis demonstrates that both Ussher's and Challoner's libraries were still being used to augment College resources, which by c.1608 had increased by approximately 4,000 volumes.

Any study of the book borrowers runs into at least one problem, that of the classification of those few borrowers who are unidentified, and therefore may be classed as either clerical or lay borrowers. Keeping this in mind one can, however, discover trends in both sectors of borrowers. An examination of the non-clerical borrower loans reveals that most of the medical, chorographical and political news items were the subjects which found greatest favour in this group. For those in high political positions a sound knowledge of political conditions was of the utmost importance, especially works concerning Ireland. In 1608 the Lord Chief Justice borrowed a copy of Ussher's *Giraldus Cambrensis*, while Sir John Tirrell's (one of Challoner's borrowers) interests ranged even farther afield with his choice of the *Conference of Hampton Court* and a book on *Description of Italy*. Justice Piggoth contented himself with Ussher's *Book of ye works of ye Gentrye of Ireland*, while Sir John Davies continued this trend by opting for Weatworth's *of ye Succession*.

Ussher himself borrowed from Christopher Sibthorp a book by Crompton, unfortunately unidentified. The Crompton in question is the lawyer Richard Crompton, father of the Puritan William Crompton.¹⁴⁵ The book could, therefore, be any one of the following works that were printed prior to 1608-1609: firstly, his edition of Sir A. Fitzherbert's *Office et Aucthoritie de Justices de Peace* (1583), which had run to five editions by 1608; secondly, *A short Declaration of the Ende of Traytors and False Conspirators against the State, and the Duetie of Subjects to their Sovereigne Governour* (1587); thirdly, *L'Authoritie et Jurisdiction des Courts de la Maiestie de la Roygne*. (1594) – his chief work; or, lastly his *Mansion of Magnamitie*.

Another subject which seems to have appealed primarily to non-clerical borrowers was that of medicine. Two of Challoner's borrowers, Mr Maxfield and Mr Medcalfe, display considerable interest. Maxfield includes two general works – an *Enchiridion medicum* and a treatise by Fernelius – while the vast majority of Medcalfe's loans are of medical works; indeed, it seems likely that he himself was a physician. His book loans include Bahun's *de anotomia*, Almarius's *medicina*, Montan's *de urinis* as well as the *Medici antique of Selvini*, though, like the aforementioned public servants, he also seems to have had some interest in geography and politics, judging by his acquisitions in 1610 of Ptolemy's *geographia* and the *Canker of England*.

Mathematics, it would appear, held a limited appeal for both groups of borrowers. Sir John Tirrell borrowed a geometrical treatise by Ramus from

---

144 See Elizabethanne Boran, 'Town and Gown: Trinity College, Dublin and the City of Dublin from 1592-1641' in *History of Universities* 13, 1995, pp. 61-85.
145 See *DNB*.

Challoner, while Mr Brenden likewise borrowed *questiones mathematici* from him. The majority of works were, however, theological, or theologically related items, such as, sermons by Cranchius, or Crashawe, commentaries by Buchanan, Cartwright, Perkins, Beza and Fulke, or, indeed, the Bibles themselves, such as the Geneva Bible and a Greek testament borrowed by Brenden. In short, these lists of lay borrowers demonstrate that, while some subjects such as politics, geography and medicine might find greater favour in this sector, there was yet an abiding interest in works of a theological nature, and indeed in theological controversies, though to a far lesser extent than one finds when one studies loans of clerical borrowers.

As we are concerned primarily with the libraries of two divines who were loaning works to other clerics, it comes as no surprise that theology accounts for most of the books borrowed, followed by related subjects necessary in the curriculum such as the trivium subjects, and some (very few) quadrivial subjects. Greek Testaments and Bibles, particularly English and Hebrew ones, were in high demand; while the chief contemporary reformed commentators were all represented: Calvin, Beza, Drusius, Marlorat, Piscator and Zanchius. The emphasis seems to have been on Calvinist commentators. The main section, in the theological classification, to be borrowed was that of theological controversy. Puritan polemic dominates this section. Cartwright and Fulke are both mentioned sixteen times in the borrowing lists and 99 per cent of those interested in reading them were clerical readers. Three works by Cartwright were particularly popular: his treatise against the *Romish Testament*, his work on the commandments and his catechism, each being borrowed three times. Fulke's treatise against the Censure was borrowed at least twice, while his anti-papalist polemic proved equally successful. Another moderate Puritan writer whose works were almost as popular was William Perkins. His *Cases of Conscience* was borrowed three times, while his sermons on the Mount and Repentance were just as popular – indeed Ussher himself lists Perkins's *of ye end of ye world* as a loan from Mr Edrige. Whitaker, likewise, is referred to primarily on Challoner's first list and is cited eight times – his treatises on the church and scripture being the favourites there.

Apart from these ever popular moderate Puritan writers, the commentators most in demand include Piscator (10), Marlorat (9), Sutlive (9), Zanchius (8), Broughton (6), Abbott (7), and Danaeus (5). Zanchius's *de tribus Elohim*, was borrowed by Ussher from both Challoner and the Lord Primate, and, in turn, was read by other TCD fellows: Welch, Pillin and Cook. Marlorat's works on the psalms proved popular in both sectors, while his commentary on Esaia was almost exclusively commandeered by Richard Ussher and Mr Richardson on four occassions.

Works by Roman Catholic authors also were of interest, particularly in clerical circles, no doubt for their polemical applications. It therefore comes as no surprise to find Bellarmine as one of the foremost authors cited: no less than eight times, his works on the Roman Pontiff being in particularly high demand by Sr Bourchier. Provost Alvey borrowed a copy of Bristowe's *Motives* which had been attacked by Perkins, while English Roman Catholic authors such as Stapleton and Parson are cited on three separate occassions.

Historical works such as the *Centuries* were borrowed alongside chronological treatises by Calvisius and Bunting. Ancient historians like Tacitus, Suetonius and Julius Capitolinus are also mentioned along with more recent authors like Stanyhurst. Of the remaining arts subjects, grammar, rhetoric and dialectic were deemed of limited interest; being favoured more by clerical students than their teachers. Though Matthew Tirrell is recorded as borrowing a Hebrew grammar it would appear that Greek dictionaries were a more attractive proposition; while Seneca, Tully and Virgil represented the oratorical choice: in this respect, it is interesting to notice that it is the Ramist edition of Cicero which is most in demand.

Equally of interest is the fact that Ramus's dialectical works do not appear, though they are often cited in notebooks. Possibly, as in the case of Emmanuel College, lecturers were expected to have their own copies.[146] One Ramist work which is represented on three of the lists is his geometrical treatise; indeed, it seems to have been the most popular geometrical work with the borrowers. In general, however, interest in science subjects is limited to works on cosmography and some geography; the cosmographical works in question being Reinhold's *Prutenic Tables*, treatises by Sacrobosco and Clavius, along with Merula's *Cosmography*; while the geographical texts include works by Mercator and Ortelius, but are dominated by Ptolemy's geography, which is mentioned no less than five times.

While the borrowing lists must be treated with care, certain assumptions may be deduced. Firstly, the majority of borrowers were either theological students or teachers in TCD, with some clerical borrowers based in England who were connected to the college through Ussher. Secondly, among this clerical group the predominant choice was theological works, usually those geared to controversy, both between Protestant groupings and Protestants and Roman Catholics. Thirdly, subsidiary disciplines such as grammar, rhetoric and logic, along with history, received a somewhat more limited attention. Fourthly, students evinced some interest in mathematical subjects such as geometry and physics, especially the works of Scaliger, but, in the main, other faculty subjects like medicine and law found little favour among such borrowers.

Among non-clerical borrowers the proportions are different, a great majority demonstrating interest in subject areas such as politics, history,

---

146 Frank Stubbings (ed.), *The Statutes of Sir Walter Mildmay for Emmanuel College*. Cambridge 1983, p. 101.

geography and medicine, though all reveal some theological interest too. The theological works tended to be sermons or commentaries, rather than controversial works. As regards popular authors, it appears that moderate Puritans like Fulke, Whitaker and Perkins dominate the scene – a factor mirrored in the examination of Challoner's and Ussher's libraries. The Ramist preponderance is also borne out by the inclusion, not only of his own works, but those of Ramists like Talaeus and Fenner in the lists.

The lists likewise demonstrate that both Challoner's and Ussher's libraries were still being used to augment College resources in the years succeeding the major book buying expeditions of these two men. This suggestion is not as startling as it may first sound when one examines the books bought by Challoner in his major reorganization of pre-1608 and Ussher's catalogue of the same year. A close analysis of these works reveals that both men were buying their material with the college acquisitions in mind, indeed, seeking to enhance and supplement rather than to duplicate them.

It seems likely that Challoner was steadily building up his own library in the period 1595 to 1601 for the benefit, not only of himself but also, of his colleagues. On being appointed to the post of professor of divinity, later to be renamed theological controversy, he sought to redirect his collection into a more useful line which continued to be used by some members of College as a supplement to the new college library. Ussher's acquisition of alternative works to those of Challoner and, indeed the college library, seems to mirror this trend. Both men appear to have operated a network of borrowing from 1601 onwards, not only lending books to each other but also to many members of College. The notion that the loan system was a regularised one seems to be given some support by the fact that both collectors take a census of borrowers in May 1610.

Some questions remain to be answered. What happened to the books that are not recorded in Challoner's 1608 list? Were they granted to the college library or were they sold to fund the new purchases? Neither seems to be the case. On the one hand the books were not officially given to College as no mention is made of them in the first main catalogue of TCD which is an accessions catalogue and therefore covers these years.[147] On the other hand, the suggestion that he sold these works to buy new books creates more problems than it solves. Firstly, if this was the case, it raises the urgent question why he was abandoning some of the most popular works in his collection: for example, works by Ramists which were not only of interest to himself, but were also constantly cited in the student notebooks of TCD and, indeed, appear on his borrowing lists.[148] Why should he sell books, in theological sub-

---

147 TCD MS 2.
148 TCD MS 790; MS 782; MS 872; MS 357 fol 8v.

ject areas, such as the 1596 *Tractatus Theologici* section by authors, many of whose works he bought for his 'new' 1608 catalogue? Such an action would appear to be irrational and uncharacteristic.

Challoner's 1610 borrowing list seems to solve some, if not all, of these problems. On close examination it may be seen that some works on this list belong to the missing section of Challoner's library and were evidently in his possession, if not in his catalogue, two years later.[149] What actually happened to these books remains a mystery, but Challoner may have decided to detach them from his library – whether to keep them elsewhere for himself, or, as a form of unofficial undergraduate library, we must unfortunately abandon to conjecture.

To conclude, a study of the libraries of Challoner and Ussher illustrates a number of points concerning their own particular interests, and, by doing so, augments our understanding of the intellectual interests of the early period in Trinity College, Dublin. The emphasis in the collection on works by Calvinist controversialists, coupled with the relatively large subsection of works by Roman Catholic apologists, bears a marked similarity to the 'Puritan' style college library which both Challoner and Ussher were developing for the college. It likewise challenges us on two points. Firstly, it forces us to reassess our image of Challoner. He should no longer be viewed as solely an administrator, rather he should be recognised as a fellow who nurtured the intellectual development of the university, by taking part in various book buying schemes, and, possibly more importantly, allowing his own substantial collection to be utilised by the college. In this sense, he does indeed deserve to be called the 'real founder' of the University of Dublin. Finally, the degree of care with which these collections were amassed demonstrates beyond all doubt the level of importance which Ussher and Challoner attached to collecting a body of knowledge which would serve as the basis for intellectual endeavour within the University of Dublin in the decades to come.

---

149   TCD MS 357, fol. 8v; for example: 'Natalis Comes Mythology', Ortelius's *Geographia*, and Erasmus's *Adages*.

An early friendship network of James Ussher, archbishop of Armagh, 1626-1656

Elizabethanne Boran

James Ussher (1581-1656) was one of the most renowned scholars of the seventeenth century and his correspondence demonstrates his vast friendship circle, a network which spread across Europe and included contemporaries such as Ludovicus de Dieu, Constantin l'Empereur, Frederick Spanheim, and Gerard Vossius. In this article I intend to limit my investigation of his wide circle of friends to one of his early friendship networks, which he developed during his student years and continued on into the 1630s.

Famous for his learning and for his tenure as archbishop of Armagh, it has sometimes been assumed that his later theological utterings reflect his education in Trinity College, Dublin, a view which has little support from the sources. His last biographer, Ronald Buick Knox, placed particular emphasis on Ussher's 'Anglican' pronouncements and was at pains to disassociate Ussher from any Puritan connection.[1] However, the debate about Ussher's Puritan tendencies, begun as soon as his death in 1656, continues, and the present paper intends to re-examine the evidence in order to determine the extent of Ussher's Puritan affiliations, and, at the same time, relate this evidence to our knowledge of the early history of Trinity College, Dublin.

This, of course, leads us into the thorny question of the definition of the term 'Puritan', and one can, I think, feel not a little sympathy for Emmanuel Downing's desire for a precise definition.[2] In modern times attempts to define Puritanism have floundered between two extremes: an attempt to define Puritanism too narrowly, at war with a desire to define it in such a manner as to include many other elements. The first approach has two tendencies: firstly, it regards Puritanism as an essentially Presbyterian movement, thus concentrating on Puritanism as a movement solely concerned with

---

[1] Ronald Buick Knox, *James Ussher archbishop of Armagh*. Cardiff 1967.
[2] Richard Parr, *The Life of the Most Reverend Father in God, James Ussher*. London 1686, p. 16.

ecclesiological reform.³ The second tendency is a desire to render Puritanism as a movement based on soteriological concerns, based on an experimental predestinarian view of salvation.⁴ Certain problems immediately arise with both tendencies, primarily as a result of their exclusivity. A Presbyterian interpretation, while obviously covering one whole aspect of the phenomenon, invariably excludes moderate Puritans such as William Perkins – and indeed other Puritans after 1593 who do not manifest a desire for a Presbyterian polity. The second tendency, the doctrinal definition, denies the basic level of doctrinal consensus which existed in the late sixteenth- and early seventeenth-century church. The revisionist case has much merit – as Collinson has said: 'Calvinism can be regarded as the theological cement of the Jacobean Church ... a common ameliorating bond uniting conformists and moderate Puritans.'⁵ This view has also found some support from the research of Nicholas Tyacke who fervently disagrees with Peter White's attempt to rekindle interest in doctrinal differences.⁶

Ultimately the debate was not perceived by most Puritans to be on the basic doctrinal issues, for those who did perceive the conflict in this manner usually became Separatists. Rather, those issues were defined by both sides as adiaphora (matters indifferent). C.H. George's definition of Puritanism has much to recommend it. He suggests that Puritans 'should be defined as conforming, beneficed ministers who wished to limit the concept of *adiaphora*, to improve the quality and frequency of sermons, and to influence more aggressively the ethics of the laity.'⁷

Nonetheless, by advocating doctrinal consensus, we too easily run the risk of denying that there was any real unrest in the Church of England, a conclusion patently erroneous as the demand for a conference at Hampton Court alone testifies, not to mention the many suspensions for nonconformity by the High Commission. Obviously there was a perceived difference between the Anglican Church and Puritan demands.

Are we then to resort to the opposite extreme of Hugh Kearney, who, rather than involve himself in a quagmire of definition, decides to define so loosely as to incorporate almost every member of the late Elizabethan and early Jacobean Church?:

3 Basil Hall, 'Puritanism: The Problem of Definition' in G.J. Cuming (ed.), *Studies in Church History*, London. vol. 11, 1965, p. 294.
4 See, for example, R.T. Kendall, *Calvin and English Calvinism to 1649*. Oxford 1979.
5 P.G. Lake, 'Calvinism and the English Church 1570-1635' in *Past and Present* 114, 1987, p. 32.
6 Nicholas Tyacke, 'The Rise of Arminianism Reconsidered' in *Past and Present* 115, 1987, pp. 201-216. See also Peter White, *Predestination, Policy and Polemic. Conflict and Consensus in the English Church from the Reformation to the Civil War*. Cambridge 1992.
7 C.H. George, 'Puritanism as History and Historiography' in *Past and Present* 41, 1968, p. 78.

> Puritanism consisted of various cross currents of thought and emotion, generally Calvinist in tone and possessing a certain continuity from the 1560s to the Cromwellian period and beyond ... I would define Puritanism as the growing circle of discontent both within and without the Established Church from the 1560s onwards.[8]

This definition not only avoids the issue but also ignores one of the boundary lines of any possible definition of Puritanism, namely that Puritanism has two constants: (1) a desire to further reform the church, leading to true edification; (2) though this reform is heartfelt and may lead to nonconformity, it nonetheless is totally opposed to the schism of separation from the church. Hence, Puritanism has both positive and negative attributes. It has no one dominant concern, though Irvonwy Morgan comes close in his definition: 'Of all the names used in the sixteenth century to describe the Puritans, names such as 'precisians', 'disciplinarians', 'the brethren', 'the consistorians', the name, which best sums up their character is the Godly Preacher.'[9] The key concern of any Puritan is for the godly spreading of the Word. Factors, and they can only be regarded so, not as definite characteristics, which can help to identify people as Puritans, may be said to be an aversion to unnecessary ceremony; surplices; a desire for a Presbyterian structure; an intense pursuit of personal piety; an interest in experimental predestination; and a marked tendency to concentrate on the papal antichrist. Not all of these factors may be found in every Puritan; indeed, any attempt at definition must take into account the various phases and different interests of Puritans from the vestiarian controversy in the 1560s, the Presbyterian movement of the 1570s and 1580s, the collapse of the movement in the 1590s to the subsequent forced assimilation of the period following the Hampton Court Conference, a period which still focused on liturgy and ceremony, but now gave more time to doctrinal variations of soteriology and issues of practical divinity. Perhaps the nearest possible definition of a Puritan was given to us by one William Bradshaw, in 1605, who defined a Puritan as: 'One of the Rigidest Sort, of those who held the Main opinions in the Realm of England'.[10]

The Puritan element in Ussher's friendship network is best demonstrated by an analysis of his early correspondents and in his choice of ministers whom he considered *suitable* for appointment to key posts in the Dublin College. Ussher had been among the first students to enter Trinity College, Dublin, which had been founded in 1592. His academic ability had been

---

8 H.F. Kearney, 'Puritanism and Science: Problems of Definition' in *Past and Present* 31, 1965, p. 105.
9 Irvonwy Morgan, *The Godly Preachers of the Elizabethan Church*. London 1965, p. 10.
10 M.A. Simpson, *What is Puritanism?* Tweedale 1981, p. 29.

recognised early in his sojourn there and by 1600 he had received his M.A. and had been appointed catechist.[11] A clear indication of his standing in the college was afforded in the following year, when he and his father-in-law, Luke Challoner, were entrusted with the book buying expeditions for the new library, which was regarded as the centerpiece of the aspirations of the new college-university.[12] At various times Ussher was offered the posts of provost and chancellor of TCD, positions which he did not accept. However, it is abundantly clear that though Ussher might not have accepted official leadership of TCD, he was well capable of working behind the scenes, even following his elevation to the bishopric of Meath in 1621 and the archbishopric of Armagh in 1626. Monck Mason alludes to this fact in his life of Bedell, the fifth provost of TCD: 'He [Ussher] was her first born; and, after his full growth he watched over and cherished her, with more of the anxious fostering of a parent, than the kindness and duty of a son; guarding, supporting and strenghtening her, in the trials of perilous times.'[13] This view is corroborated by an examination of Ussher's correspondence with Provost Bedell. The latter, writing to Ussher in April 1628, describes the election of fellows which 'was not such as gave satisfaction to your grace, and hath bred a new broil in the college.'[14] Bedell, a worthy provost, but lacking in self esteem, was all too ready to defer to Ussher's suggestion, and humbly remarked on the aforementioned troubles that 'I conceive your wisdom saw more to lie in it than I could perceive,'[15] while, in the same letter, Bedell reports Ussher's views on the duration of fellowships. The extent of Bedell's reliance on Ussher may best be seen in a letter of August 1628, where he depends on Ussher to choose suitable commencement *quaestiones*:

> Since my last to your Grace I received from Dr Ussher the questions to be disputed at the commencement. I thank you even from my heart for sparing me the pain of bethinking myself what to choose, which would have troubled me as much as the preparation to defend what I had chosen.[16]

Yet Ussher's role was not confined to such routine matters. He also played a major role in the choices of possible provosts, particularly following the demise of William Temple, and it is in his choice of candidates for both

---

11 Ronald Buick Knox (as note 2), p. 9.
12 R. Parr (as note 3), p. 9. For a discussion of this library – and Ussher's connection with it – see Elizabethanne Boran, 'Libraries and Learning: The Early History of Trinity College, Dublin from 1592 to 1641' TCD Ph. D. thesis 1995.
13 H.J. Monck Mason, *The Life of William Bedell*. London 1843, p. 127.
14 C.R. Elrington (ed.), *The Whole Works of the most reverend James Ussher D.D.* Dublin 1864, 17 Volumes.
15 C.R. Elrington (ed.) (as note 14), vol. 15, p. 389.
16 C.R. Elrington (ed.) (as note 14), vol. 16, p. 474.

important posts, such as the provostship and the professorship of theological controversies, and also for lesser positions, that we begin to glimpse a pattern of a moderate Puritan network. Even before the death of Temple, Ussher was quick to suggest Richard Sibbes as a possible candidate for the post of provost. His letter on the subject to Abbot, archbishop of Canterbury in 1626 reads like a panegyric:

> I then recommend unto you Mr Sibbes, the preacher of Gray's Inn, with whose learning, soundness of judgement, and uprightness of life I was well acquainted

an acclamation he reiterated on the death of Temple.[17] Richard Sibbes (1577-1635) had been educated at St John's, Cambridge where he was converted by Paul Baynes.[18] In 1618 he was chosen preacher of Gray's Inn 'where', according to Benjamin Brook, 'he became remarkably popular and useful'.[19] Indeed, his presence there may explain the seemingly extraordinary selection of an unknown Mr Gibbs, as a possible candidate for the professorship of theological controversies in 1621.[20] Sibbes's refusal of the TCD provostship owed much to his elevation to the mastership of St Katherine's Hall in Cambridge in 1625, which, like Gray's Inn, was immensely popular among the Puritan gentry. Indeed, from 1626 to 1642, most of the fellows of the Hall were Puritans, and under Sibbes's leadership there was an influx of Puritan gentry.[21] This may have something to do with the fact that, as Samuel Clarke relates:

> He used sometimes in the sommertime, to go abroad to the houses of some worthy Personages, where he was an Instrument of much good, not only by his private labours, but by his prudent council and advice, that upon every occasion he was ready to minister unto them.[22]

Earlier in his career Sibbes had been summoned before the High Commission, and deprived of his fellowship of St John's, on account of his nonconformity.[23]

On Sibbes's refusal of the office of provost, Ussher's mind turned to Joseph Mede, whom he duly recommended to the fellows and, though Mede

---

17 C.R. Elrington (ed.) (as note 14), vol. 15, p. 361.
18 B. Brook, *The Lives of the Puritans*. London 1813, vol. 2, p. 417.
19 B.Brook (as note 18), p. 417.
20 Gilbert MS 169, p.124; see Joseph Foster (ed.) *The Register of Gray's Inn 1521-1889*. London 1889, p. 148.
21 J.T. Cliffe, *The Puritan Gentry*. London 1984; see also W.J. Sheils, *The Puritans in the Diocese of Peterborough 1558-1610*. Northhampton 1979, p. 116.
22 Samuel Clarke, *A Generall Martyrologie*. London 1650, p. 168.
23 B. Brook (as note 18), p. 417.

declined on this occasion, Ussher saw fit to reconsider him on the elevation of Bedell to the bishopric of Kilmore, and, indeed after Chappel's provostship, describing Mede as 'a single man, very eminent for learning'.[24] Joseph Mede (1586-1638) had been educated at Christ's Cambridge where he had been a pupil of the renowned Puritan, Daniel Rogers.[25] A close correspondent of Ussher's, sharing an interest in eschatological and chronological matters, he is described by Brook as follows:

> He was suspected of Puritanism; and having united himself with the Puritans in the university he is justly denominated one of them. He maintained a constant friendship with several eminent nonconformists and kept up a regular correspondence with them[26]

a comment which fits Ussher just as well. However, Mede like Sibbes, proved reluctant to leave England for uncertain honours in Dublin, and so Ussher's final choice fell on Bedell, again one of this group of moderate Puritans.

Yet another member of the group was John Preston, who along with Sibbes is described by Ussher's earliest biographer as one of the most eminent divines in London 'between whom and Ussher there was a most entire affection'.[27] Circa 1619 Ussher had offered a post to Preston who, like Sibbes and Mede, declined to join Ussher in Dublin.[28] 'Converted' by John Cotton, then a fellow of Emmanuel, during his undergraduate days in Cambridge, he was connected with other eminent Puritan divines, such as John Dod, who later preached his funeral sermon.[29] Brook carefully defines him as 'having inclinations to Puritanism', and outlines his career as an attempt to use his influence both at court and Cambridge to shield Puritans.[30] Other writers are more outspoken: Echard calls him 'the most celebrated of the Puritans, an exquisite preacher, a subtle disputant, and a deep politician,' while a contemporary, Bishop Andrews, is reported as saying to the king that 'if Mr Preston were not for this expelled the university, Lord Bishops would not long continue'.[31]

Ussher's habit of suggesting preachers with at least a moderate Puritan background is likewise mirrored in his suggestions for candidates for lesser

---

24 C.R. Elrington (ed.) (as note 14), vol. 16, p. 453.
25 B. Brook (as note 18), vol. 2, p. 429.
26 B. Brook (as note 18), vol. 2, p. 431.
27 Nicholas Bernard, *The Life and Death of the Most Reverend and Learned Father of our Church, Dr James Ussher*. London 1656, p. 83.
28 C.R. Elrington (ed.) (as note 14), vol. 16, p. 371.
29 B. Brook (as note 18), vol. 2, p. 360.
30 B. Brook (as note 18), p. 353.
31 B. Brook (as note 18), p. 360 and S. Clarke (as note 22), p. 109.

appointments, both within the College and in the affiliated ministries in Dublin City. A close friend of his, Samuel Ward of Emmanuel College and later Master of Sidney Sussex College in Cambridge, was offered a post by Provost Alvey in 1608, which he regretfully declined but, just as Preston in a similar situation suggested Cotton, Thomas Hooker, Ward himself and Slaughton of Emmanuel as other possibilities, Ward in turn suggested William Eyre, like himself a fellow of Emmanuel, who was already known to Ussher.[32]

Ussher followed up this suggestion by writing to Thomas Lydiat (the well-known mathematician) to contact Eyre about the ministry of St Werburghs – a ministry in the city of Dublin connected with the college. Yet another letter of Ussher to Lydiat exhibits an interest in calling forth preachers from England to serve the city of Dublin:

> I would hear also willingly, whether you have proceeded further with Mr Web, and what hope we may conceive of his coming. Because you have met not with himself, and we have no certainty from to pitch upon, Dr Chaloner thought good, at Mr Bernard's departure, to try whether Mr Storer, a worthy preacher, might be drawn over to the place.[33]

Unfortunately, no positive identification may be made concerning Mr Web and Storer, but the Mr Bernard alluded to may well be Richard Bernard, born in 1567, educated at Christ's, Cambridge and later vicar of Worksop in Nottinghamshire until 1605. Brook gives no information as to his subsequent career until *c*.1613 when he attained the living at Batcombe in Somersetshire, so it is possible that at some stage in the intervening period he may have been in Dublin.[34] Perhaps best known for his attack on episcopacy in 1641, he was considered a staunch opponent of separatism: a tendency also prevalent in TCD.

Ussher and his father-in-law, Luke Challoner, took a keen interest in the provision of livings in the city of Dublin. Challoner, a dominant force in the college, chose an even more prominent Puritan to fill a living in 1612. Ussher, writing to Challoner in 1612 declared that 'I signified unto you, how Mr Dike would in no wise present himself before my Lord of Canterbury, but otherwise if you could procure his liberty here, he offered willingly to come unto you.'[35] Daniel Dyke came from a nonconformist family; his father had been silenced for the offence. Educated at Cambridge, he was minister

32 C.R. Elrington (ed.) (as note 14), vol. 15, p. 55 see also vol. 16, p. 371.
33 C.R. Elrington (ed.) (as note 14), vol. 15, p. 70.
34 B. Brook (as note 18), vol. 2, p. 460.
35 C.R. Elrington (ed.) (as note 14), vol. 16, p. 315.

of Coggeshall in Essex. Daniel Dyke had been suspended for nonconformity on two occasions, and not even the patronage of Burleigh had helped him in his career within the church.[36] As Ussher relates no christian name, we are either dealing with Daniel, or his brother Jeremiah Dyke, 'another excellent Puritan'.[37]

Another possible Puritan connection is that of John Hill. Ussher in a letter to Challoner in 1613 mentions a Mr Hill as being placed at St Werburghs, while the lord deputy in a 1620 letter to Ussher writes, 'concerning the chancellorship of St Patrick's , I have destined it to Mr Hill of St John's; according to the several desire of the best affected here'.[38] John Hill had been a minister of Bury St Edmunds, but was suspended for omitting the cross in baptism.[39] A more certain identification is of Mr Howlett, a minister suggested by both Ussher and the bishop of Derry as a suitable replacement for Chappel if Joseph Mede should refuse. Howlet belonged to the TCD – Emmanuel – Sidney Sussex nexus.[40]

Ussher's correspondence also demonstrates the interconnectedness of some of these links. John Dod is a case in point, being connected to Ussher, Challoner, Sibbes and Preston. Ussher writing to Challoner in 1612, mentions that at the funeral of Prince Henry 'Good Mr Dod, and Mr Culverwell and myself spent that day together, in humbling ourselves before God'.[41] Dod had been educated at Jesus College, Cambridge and had been a friend of some of the most noted Puritans of his day – Fulke, Whitaker, Chaderton and Gouge – having in common with them an abiding interest in practical divinity.[42] He was suspended by the High Commission on a number of occasions, yet despite this Ussher was happy to assert that 'whatever some may affirm of Mr Dod's strictness, and scrupling some ceremonies, I desire that when I die my soul may rest with his.'[43] This affection was reciprocated, if one is to believe Richard Sibbes' letter of 1622, when he states that 'Mrs More, Mr Drake and his wife, Mr Dod, with others that love you heartily in the Lord, are in good health'.[44]

The other divine whom Ussher met with Dod was Ezechiel Culverwell, yet another well-known Puritan. Educated at Cambridge, and rector of Stambridge in Essex, he later became vicar of Felsted in the same county. In 1583 he had been suspended for his neglect of the surplice. He had been

36 B. Brook (as note 18), pp. 235-237.
37 B. Brook (as note 18), p. 257.
38 C.R. Elrington (ed.) (as note 14), vol. 15, p. 74; see also vol. 16, p. 374.
39 B. Brook, Lives (as note 18) vol. 1. p. 274.
40 C.R. Elrington (ed.) (as note 14), vol. 16, p. 37 and *Cal. S.P.Ir. 1633-1647*, p. 198.
41 C.R. Elrington (ed.) (as note 14), vol. 16, p. 320.
42 B. Brook (as note 18), vol. 3, p. 1.
43 B. Brook (as note 18), vol. 3, p. 1.
44 C.R. Elrington (ed.) (as note 14), vol. 16, p. 395.

instrumental in the conversion of Dod's friend, William Gouge, another of the same circle.[45] Both Dod and Culverwell were acquainted with yet another correspondent of Ussher's, a certain Mr Heartwell whose letters to Ussher demonstrate Ussher's links with a number of Essex Puritans.[46] His letter of 1616 mentions both Dod, Culverwell and a Mr Rogers, and is of particular interest as it seems to suggest some reluctance on Ussher's part to publish papers of his, with which these Puritans were in agreement:

> As concering those **** of yours, which you are so loath should see the press, would one would do you of purpose a shrewd turn as may be. Before I answer you I must lay divers conclusions; I am sure you tender the good of many poor souls, who are ignorant of Christ, therefore to stop that help which might further their peace, I see not how it can be answered, since both Mr Smith of Cla. Mr Culverwell and diverse godly preachers affirm them, even as they are, as to be worthy or more of the press than any which are now in print. 2. That that which hath already passed in many copies, now being in I know not how many hands, it seems impossible but that someone or another will, on a sudden, thrust them to the press, though without your name. 3. That, those things duly considered, I would think it very expedient that you would receive a copy (of them) yourself, correcting it so that it might pass the press before any other copies can, lest, they coming forth otherwise, you be forced too late to put your hand to mend them.[47]

Heartwell, though not a minister, was undoubtedly a Puritan sympathiser, a fact not only demonstrated in his friendships, but also in his opinions on church matters. In a letter to Ussher he declares that 'the affairs of the Church here are much after one style, the better sort of preachers, some stand and are hid or winked at, and some go down the wind.'[48] From the same letter it transpires that Ussher had begun to distance himself from such a potential source of trouble, for Heartwell refers to Ussher's brevity in his letters and the fact that mutual friends 'wonder they cannot hear from you'.[49] Possibly Ussher may have wished to play down his Puritan connections while he was trying to find favour at the court of James I.

Other direct connections between Ussher and Puritan ministers include those of Thomas Gataker the younger, and Arthur Hildersham. Gataker was a friend of Samuel Ward, and a Fellow of Sidney Sussex College. Whether

45 B. Brook (as note 18), vol. 3, p. 512.
46 C.R. Elrington (ed.) (as note 14), vol. 16, pp. 333-334.
47 C.R. Elrington (ed.) (as note 14), vol. 16, p. 332.
48 C.R. Elrington (ed.) (as note 14), vol. 16, p. 355
49 C.R. Elrington (ed.) (as note 14), vol. 16, p. 356.

by this connection, or by the fact that he had been educated at St John's by Alvey and had preached with Bedell, he became a correspondent of Ussher's.[50] Undoubtedly what Ussher and he had in common was their fascination for ancient history, and certainly their correspondence is devoted more to such matters than theological controversies. Hildersham, that 'Hammer of Schismatics', was evidently known to Challoner and was a friend of John Cotton.[51] Like many another Puritan he was, in the words of Clarke, 'cast aside like a broken vessel' as a result of his nonconformity.[52]

Yet Ussher did not limit his Puritan connections to this circle of ministers; perhaps more importantly his network extended to some of the principal members of the Puritan gentry, particularly in the area of Essex and Herefordshire. His closest Essex connection were the Barringtons of Hatfield Broad Oak. No direct correspondence is referred to by Elrington in his edition of Ussher's works, but a letter of 1637 written by a certain J.G. to Ussher related the following: 'Once again, I pray your Grace's answer to my former letters, concering my MS for since I wrote them outwards, both Sir Thomas and the Lady Barrington desired me to put you in mind, and withal to remember their own and their services to you.'[53] The Barringtons were an ancient and prominant family in Essex.[54] Sir Francis, Sir Thomas' father, had succeeded his father in 1583. His nickname of a 'Second Nehemiah' gives some indication of his popularity among the godly.[55] His career in parliament, ably aided by the Rich family, and ministers such as Hildersham, exhibited most of the preoccupations of Puritan M.P.s; he was an active supporter of legislation which underpinned what Hunt calls 'the culture of discipline'.[56] Imprisoned for his opposition to the Forced Loan, he died soon after his release, his death provoking a veritable storm of elegies from Puritans for this 'lay patriarch of the godly party in Essex'.[57] As such he had been the recipient of dedications of books by Puritans such as Samuel Hieron and Jeremiah Dyke, while Ezechiel Rogers, another famous Puritan, had been the family chaplain for twelve years.[58] Francis Barrington's connections to Ussher illustrate a vital point about Puritans, namely that not all were dogmatic Presbyterians, and were in the main happy to distinguish between bish-

---

50 B. Brook (as note 18), vol. 3, p. 200.
51 S. Clarke (as note 22), p. 151.
52 S. Clarke (as note 22), p. 153.
53 C.R. Elrington (ed.) (as note 14), vol. 16, p. 534.
54 William Hunt, *The Puritan Moment. The coming of Revolution in an English County.* Harvard 1983, p. 15. Much of the following discussion of Ussher's links with Essex Puritans is based on this valuable work.
55 William Hunt (as note 54), p. 104.
56 William Hunt (as note 54), p. 166.
57 William Hunt (as note 54), p. 215.
58 William Hunt (as note 54), p. 215. See also J.T. Cliffe, *Puritan Gentry* (as note 21), p. 44.

ops like Ussher, and, from a Puritan point of view, their more unsavoury counterparts such as Alymer and Bancroft. By now it should not be surprising to learn that Ussher and Preston both preached at Barrington Hall in Hatfield Broad Oak in December 1625, a meeting which Hunt suggests, contained more than the family as an audience, and which may even have served as a sort of regional synod of the godly, preparing their struggle against the Arminians, who held diverging views from mainstream Calvinists on the issue of predestination and free will.[59]

The real power in Essex was in the hands of the Rich family, particularly those of the second earl of Warwick, Robert Rich, described by Edmund Calamy as a 'Maecenas to the pious and religious ministry', a tradition he taken over from his father.[60] The Barringtons had purchased Hatfield Priory from Richard Rich in 1564, and this was to prove the start of 'a beautiful relationship', Barringtons standing as Rich candidates in parliamentary elections on more than one occasion.[61] Hunt describes both the first and second earl as Essex's 'premier noble professor', a position in which the Riches were no doubt aided by their acquisition of twenty-two advowsons and phenomenal wealth.[62] Indeed, the connection between the Puritan cause and the earls of Warwick was considered so incestuous that Richard Rogers, a famous Essex Puritan, was described in local folklore as a son of the family steward.[63]

Certainly Robert Rich, the second Earl, had direct connections to a number of prominent Puritans, having been educated at Cambridge with William Gouge, a leading Puritan preacher.[64] Both had gone to Emmanuel College, Cambridge. Warwick presented a number of Puritan preachers to livings, for example Thomas Barnes.[65] He was connected with others such as Preston, Hooker, Stephan Marshall and Sibbes, to name but a few of an ever-increasing patronage network. Hunt goes so far as to suggest that at Leighs Priory Warwick 'maintained a veritable seminary of unbenificed divines'.[66] Pemberton, writing in 1613, described the second Earl as 'a faithfull doorkeeper in the House of God' and Rich certainly played a dominant role as a centre of Puritan discontent in parliament, relying on his political allies such as the aforesaid Barringtons, Edward Lewkenor and Sir Francis Harvy; the last being another possible acquaintance of Ussher's.[67]

59 William Hunt (as note 54), p. 193.
60 William Hunt (as note 54), p. 164.
61 William Hunt (as note 54), p. 166. See Hunt for a more detailed discussion.
62 William Hunt (as note 54), p. 104.
63 William Hunt (as note 54), p. 104.
64 William Hunt (as note 54), p. 163.
65 William Hunt (as note 54), p. 176.
66 William Hunt (as note 54), p. 203.
67 William Hunt (as note 54), p. 259; for Ussher's connection with the Harvy family see C.R. Elrington (ed.) (as note 14), vol. 15, p. 269.

Ussher's own connection with Rich was indirect; his dealings were with Nathaniel Rich, a first cousin of the second Earl and educated with him at Emmanuel. He played an important role in parliaments, practising Rich's policies. In the 1620 parliament, as M.P. for Harwich, he had denounced the harassment of Calvinist lecturers and was quick to promote godly preachers such as Nathaniel Ward to his livings.[68] A supporter of Mede's elevation to the TCD provostship (a support little appreciated by Mede), Nathaniel Rich had been recommended to Ussher by Richard Sibbes in 1622, who considered him full of 'sincerity, wisdom, and right judgement, worthy of your inward acquaintance'.[69]

Both Nathaniel Rich's and Francis Barrington's careers ultimately proved unsatisfactory. Discouraged by their lack of political success, Warwick, Rich, Barrington and Pym decided to try another avenue. By setting up a corporation to settle the West Indian island of Catalina they started a venture which brought forth the Providence Island Company, whose membership role reads like a list of prominent Puritan gentry.[70] This interest in emigration to America no doubt explains both Nathaniel Rich's and Francis Barrington's connections with the Winthrop family, and it is this friendship network in particular, which sheds valuable light on the ethos of Trinity College, Dublin during this period.

John Winthrop the elder was born in 1588 and was educated at Trinity College, Cambridge.[71] His father had been a keen supporter of the prophesying movement, and Winthrop quickly came under Puritan influence. Married by Ezechiel Culverwell, he decided to move to Culverwell's parish, so highly did he favour this Puritan, and on the death of his first wife he married Thomasine Clopton, again of Puritan persuasion.[72] Marriage — one of the key methods by which any friendship network could be established — could not only be utilised by the Puritan laity but also by Puritan ministers to establish circles of friends at this time. In this the ministers definitely had an advantage over their Roman Catholic counterparts! Connected with other members of the Essex Puritan network, among them the Mildmays, Winthrop, the future governor of Massachusetts, decided in 1622 to send his son, John junior, not to Oxford or Trinity College Cambridge, but to TCD.[73]

68 William Hunt (as note 54), p. 179.
69 C.R. Elrington (ed.) (as note 14), vol. 16, p. 395. Hunt seems a little confused about who introduced whom — see p. 169.
70 William Hunt (as note 54), p. 263.
71 See *DNB*.
72 R.C. Black, *The Younger John Winthrop*. London 1966, p. 6 and p. 11.
73 S.E. Morison, *English University Men who emigrated to New England before 1646*. Harvard 1932, p. 253. For links with the Mildmays see R.C. Winthrop Jr, *Evidences of the Winthrops of Groton, co. Suffolk, England*. Boston 1894-1896, p. 47.

Robert Black, the biographer of the younger Winthrop, states that at this time, in 1622, there was 'a good deal of family discussion as to the feasibility of establishing a Puritan colony overseas in Ireland', a plan later put into effect in America by the Winthrops.[74] The Winthrops had some connections in Ireland already, in Cork and Dublin, the latter being a tangential link – Winthrop senior's brother-in-law, Emmanuel Downing's first wife was the daughter of Sir James Ware, also connected to TCD.[75] Undoubtedly one reason for Winthrop's choosing to send his eldest son to TCD lay in the fact that his sister and brother-in-law, Lucy and Emmanuel Downing, another Puritan, were just about to depart for Ireland in 1622, but it certainly implies that TCD was considered a fit place for a son of this 'great lover of Saints, especially ministers of the Gospel', to send his son.[76]

In this context, it is interesting to note that Winthrop's was not the only connection between Puritans, TCD, and the American venture. John Cotton, that 'Puritan of Puritans', was also part of Ussher's network, and Increase Nowel is referred to in a letter of Ussher's to Challoner in 1613: 'Mr Sherwood has written to the provost for one Increase Nowel, of the age of nineteen years, of good sufficiency in learning, and religious; he looketh to have your furtherance also in his admitting.'[77] Nowel later played an active role in the company of Massachusetts Bay, and he travelled with Winthrop the Elder to America in 1630, where he played an important role in the Massachusetts colony.[78] Both Winthrop and Cotton had been overseers on the board of Harvard College, and certain other links may be traced between Harvard and TCD. The second president of Harvard, Charles Chauncey, had been offered a post by Ussher in Ireland, judging by his letter to Bedell in 1627 while Thomas Parker, a son of the noted Puritan Robert Parker, had matriculated as a sizar in TCD in 1610.[79] His later career took him even further afield from his native Berkshire, to Leyden, Franeker, and eventually Newbury in America.[80]

Ussher's lay Puritan connections spread beyond the county of Essex. Following his accession to the bishopric of Meath in 1621 Ussher wrote to Lady Mary Vere, thanking her for the 'effectual means' which she had employed in order to support his elevation.[81] This connection is particularly interesting since Lady Vere was noted for her Puritan views and was in con-

---

74 R.C. Black (as note 72), p. 22.
75 R.C. Winthrop (as note 73), p. 18 and p. 99.
76 See *DNB*.
77 C.R. Elrington (ed.) (as note 14), vol. 15, p. 74.
78 See *DNB*.
79 TCD MUN/P/1/194; for Parker see S.E. Morison (as note 73), p. 37.
80 S.E. Morison (as note 73), p. 37.
81 Jacqueline Eales, *Puritans and Roundheads. The Harleys of Brampton Bryan and the outbreak of the English Civil War*. Cambridge 1990, p. 65.

tact with a circle of Puritan ministers, men like John Dod, with whom as we have seen, Ussher was also in communication.[82] Lady Vere's husband, Sir Horace Vere, himself an Essex man and no doubt in contact with the Barringtons and the Rich families, had been commander of the abortive expedition in 1623 to the Palatinate.[83] No doubt it was through the Vere link that Ussher came into contact with the Harleys of Brampton Bryan, Herefordshire. Lady Vere's niece, Brilliana Conway, had married Robert Harley of Brampton Bryan, who as Jacqueline Eales has demonstrated, developed a Puritan network in Herefordshire.[84] Robert Harley was also in contact with Thomas Gattaker, another connection of Ussher's, but an even more direct link exists between the two men, since a chaplain of Ussher's, Stanley Gower, later became chaplain to the Harleys, and, indeed, made a name for himself on account of his non-conformity.[85] In January 1636, two years after Gower had become Robert Harley's chaplain, Harley wrote to Ussher concerning Gower, stating that Ussher had sent Gower to them in order to 'hold out his holy light againe amonge us'.[86]

In connection with these links of Ussher's to English Puritan gentry it is noteworthy that yet another member of the Puritan gentry, this time from the diocese of Peterborough, was none other than Sir William Fitzwilliam, Lord Deputy of Ireland at the time of the foundation of TCD, and, judging by his personal benefaction, an ardent supporter of the new institution.[87] He is known to have favoured nonconformists such as Michael Cuthbert, at his parish of Etton.[88] Fitzwilliam draws together many of the factors in the Puritan gentry connections already touched on: his conversion at Gray's Inn, his Essex links, among them a connection with the Mildmay family, and his interest in supporting Colleges. Clearly, Fitzwilliam's generosity to the college was much appreciated, if we are to believe an account which declares that his coat of arms was hung at the entrance to the new college.[89] Possibly Fitzwilliam saw himself as another Walter Mildmay, this time nurturing a Puritan foundation in Dublin rather than the Puritan Emmanuel College in Cambridge.

Ussher's correspondence is not the only indicator of a Puritan friendship network and, indeed, of a Puritan self perception in TCD. On Ussher's first trip to England to buy books for the college library he stopped at Chester,

---

82 Jacqueline Eales (as note 81), p. 42.
83 William Hunt (as note 54).
84 Jacqueline Eales (as note 81), p. 19.
85 Jacqueline Eales (as note 81), p. 56.
86 J.T. Cliffe (as note 21), p. 189.
87 TCD MS 571, fol 2r.
88 W.J. Sheils (as note 21), p. 40.
89 Thomas Fuller, Thomas, *The Church History of Great Britain*. London 1655, Book 9, p. 212; J.P. Mahaffy, *An Epoch. in Irish History*. Dublin 1903, p. 66. Mahaffy disagrees with Fuller.

to meet none other than the nonconformist Christopher Goodman, who, despite his refusal to subscribe to the Prayer Book and Articles, had been considered by Loftus as a possible candidate for the archbishopric of Armagh.[90] Carr notes that Ussher 'had a desire to deal gently with the Presbyterian party', and emphasises that when the English Articles were ratified in Ireland Ussher was careful not to reject the 1615 Irish Articles; and, indeed, he put up a strong fight against the adoption of the 1604 Canons.[91]

The issue of the 1615 Articles and Ussher's role in their compilation has been much debated. Buick Knox, in his attempt to portray Ussher as an 'Anglican' bishop, desperately tries to deny any Puritan overtones to the Irish Articles, while others have gone further and suggested that Ussher did not play a major role in their formulation.[92] This last argument has little to recommend it as it is highly unlikely that Ussher, at that time professor of theological controversies at TCD, and thus the holder of the most distinguished post in that College, should not have been consulted. Indeed, a seventeenth century historian, Peter Heylyn, was one of the first to question this view, by emphasising Ussher's role in the formulation of the Irish Articles of 1615, articles which fullfilled many of the criteria favoured by Puritans. Speaking of the Irish Articles he wrote:

> For Calvinism by degrees had taken such deep root amongst them, that at last it was received and countenanced as the only Doctrine which was to be defended in the Church of Ireland. For not contented with the articles of the Church of England, they were resolved to frame a Confession of their own; the drawing up whereof was referred to Doctor James Ussher, then provost of the College of Dublin, and afterwards archbishop of Armagh, amd Lord Primate of Ireland: By whom the Book was so contrived, that all the Sabbatian and Calvinian Rigors were declared theirin to be the Doctrines of the Church. For first the articles of Lambeth rejected at the conference of Hampton Court, must be inserted into this confession, as the chief parts of it. And secondly an Article must be made of purpose to justify the morality of the Lord's day, Sabbath, and to require the spending of it wholly in Religious exercises ... All which being Ussher's own private opinions were dispersed in several places of the Articles for the Church of Ireland.[93]

---

90 J.A. Carr, *The Life and Times of Archbishop James Ussher*. London 1985, p. 94
91 J.A. Carr (as note 90), pp. 300-301.
92 See Ronald Buick Knox (as note 1), pp. 16ff. and Alan Ford, *The Protestant Reformation in Ireland, 1590-1641*. Frankfurt 1985, reprinted Dublin 1996, pp. 196-197.
93 Peter Heylyn, *Aerius Redivivus: or the History of the Presbyterians*. London 1672, p. 388.

Heylyn, as a source, must be treated with caution; the one or two obvious errors in this piece, such as his designation of Ussher as provost of TCD, and the overestimation of Ussher's influence on the formation of the Irish articles, are not negligible, but his view is not entirely without foundation. Later apologists for Ussher, such as his biographer Richard Parr, have stoutly denied Heylyn's imputation, and have underlined errors like his ascription of the provostship to Ussher. However, even Parr concludes:

> Of it after all I can say, the Reader shall happen to think otherwise, I desire him not to censure too hardly, but to pass it by, since such difference (if any be) was not in the fundamental Doctrine of our Religion, but only some Points of lesser moment; or in which the Church itself has not led men either to this or that sense; and that the lord Primate held these opinions, not out of contradiction or singularity but only because he thought them more agreeable to Scripture and Reason.[94]

Parr's comment might well describe other Puritans. Certainly an examination of the Irish Articles, particularly article 80, and even more especially the startling absence of any reference to the episcopacy, suggests an adherence to Puritan values in the originators, while Parr's attempt to mitigate Ussher's role by denying him any influence in the compliation must be seen for what it was: a desperate attempt to explain a seeming contradiction between Ussher's earlier views and his mature reappraisal of his theological opinions.[95] As Carr, another biographer of Ussher, states:

> The Archbishop seem afterwards to have considerably modified his theological opinions. Having begun as an extreme Calvinist, under the training of men like Travers and Alvey, he ended as a man of more reasonable views on such subjects as the extent of Christ's atonement, election, reprobation etc.[96]

Thus Ussher's later avowals of conformity must not overshadow earlier, more Puritan, preoccupations.

Ussher's early Puritan connections should be viewed in the light of the Puritan affiliations of Trinity College, Dublin, Ussher's most immediate friendship circle. Carr states that TCD had a rival in Emmanuel College, Cambridge, a Puritan foundation of 1584.[97] This is true if one is talking about

---

94 Richard Parr (as note 2), p. 1.
95 Richard Parr (as note 2), p. 30; for a more modern version of this argument see Alan Ford, *The Protestant Reformation in Ireland, 1590-1641*. Frankfurt 1985, p. 196.
96 J.A. Carr (as note 90), p. 203.
97 J.A. Carr (as note 90), p. 77.

appealing to a Puritan market, but Carr's statement both exaggerates TCD's role and confuses the nature of the relationship between the two colleges, for members of TCD would almost certainly not have considered themselves at odds with their sister foundation, but supported by it. Though Mahaffy casts doubt on the extent to which Trinity's statutes drawn up by Bedell devolved from those of Emmanuel College, it is clear that Bedell, as a graduate and fellow of Emmanuel intended the statutes of TCD to be modelled on those of his former college.[98] Writing to James Ussher in 1628, he admitted his design to use Emmanuel's statutes as a model, and indeed Ussher commented on this fact in a later letter to Laud, saying that Bedell, now bishop of Kilmore 'while he was provost there, composed statutes for the good of the house, conformable to those of Emmanuel College in Cambridge, where he himself in former time lived.'[99] Differences in detail obviously occurred, but in crucial matters – such as the length of tenure – TCD continued the spirit of the *De mora sociorum* statute of Emmanuel. The Bedell statutes also, naturally enough, included Puritan preoccupations with the tyrannical rule of the Antichrist, and certain phrases were omitted by the Laudian statutes as conveying a Puritan ethos.[100] The earlier statutes of Trinity College, Dublin, compiled by Provost Temple, likewise demonstrate strains of Puritan thought, particularly in their attitude to such matters as the use of surplices.[101]

It was in their choice of provosts, that the members of TCD really demonstrated their self perception as a Puritan foundation. Loftus, their first provost, described by Carr as 'a strong Puritan', had had the famous Puritan Thomas Cartwright as his chaplain, and had even suggested him as a possible replacement in the archbishopric of Armagh, while the Puritan career of Walter Travers, one of the foremost leaders of the Presbyterian movement, is too well known to need repetition here.[102] The fact that the early provosts of the Dublin College did not continue their more vociferous demands during their tenure there should not be misinterpreted as a sign that they had turned their backs on their earlier concerns. For example, Loftus's speech to the second provost Travers on the latter's accession, has sometimes been evaluated as evidence that Loftus should not be termed a Puritan. Though

---

98 Frank Stubbings, *The Statutes of Sir Walter Mildmay for Emmanuel College*. Cambridge 1983, p. 95.
99 C.R. Elrington (ed.), (as note 14), vol. 15, p. 575.
100 J.P. Mahaffy (as note 89), p. 334.
101 TCD MUN/P/1/168.
102 J.A. Carr (as note 90), p. 70; for Loftus's links to Cartwright see William Urwick, *The Early History of Trinity College Dublin 1591-1660*. London 1892, p. 15; for more information concerning Walter Travers see S.J. Knox, 'Walter Travers and the Presbyterian movement prior to the Westminster Assembly' TCD Ph.D. 1958, note 86; see also H. Robinson-Hammerstein's contribution above.

the speech starts with a commendation of Travers as the fittest person for the post, Loftus continues to elaborate on a stringent warning for Travers to avoid all theological controversy:

> You are to remember that this place requires a person of exemplary conformity to the doctrine and discipline of this Church as they are established by law, and as you have hitherto lived in a venerable esteeme above the corruption of bad examples, soe it is expected that your good examples shall now have the greatest influence on the regulation of their behavious whom you are to govern both in doctrine, discipline, and morall course of life, for your actions are to be the transcript of your doctrine. You are therefore to hold out the lamp of a godly and holy profession to the eyes of the world.[103]

Yet the real stress in Loftus's speech lies not in any abhorrence of Puritan values, but in a keen aversion to Papists and separatists, while at the same time Loftus could warn Travers that his Presbyterian principles might prove as unfortunate for his career in Dublin, as they had in London. Such reasoning was merely common sense, given the backlash against the Presbyterian movement in the late 1590s.

Another factor connected with Loftus's advice was that in Ireland the audience was composed of different elements, and therefore had to be treated differently. Roman Catholics thinking of converting might well be put off by internal tension in the Church of England and Ireland, and therefore, from an evangelical point of view, it seemed better sense to divert Puritan zeal into godly preaching.[104] That Travers saw the justice of this argument, and had read the signs of the times in England, may be deduced from Sir Geoffrey Fenton's analysis of his sojourn in Ireland:

> he hath governed his ministry so wisely and learnedly during his stay here, as by the same he hath not only made the word fruitful in the hearts of many, but also hath added much to the credit and reverence of the Gospel amongst these backward people. And specially I have noted him always to proceed sincerely in a sound exposition of the word, nor diverting at any time to contentions, whereby the hearers might be rather led into doubts than truly edified.[105]

The third provost, Henry Alvey, listed by Benjamin Brook as 'this zealous Puritan', as a fellow of St John's College Cambridge, had been a tutor

---

103 J.W. Stubbs, *The History of the University of Dublin from its foundation to the end of the eighteenth century*. London 1889, App. p. 16.
104 TCD MUN/P/1/72.
105 *Cal. S.P. Ir. 1598-1599*, p. 283.

to Thomas Gattaker Junior.[106] His antipathy to Barrett's views was well known, and Brook concludes that, though we have little knowledge of any specific persecution for his views, he probably left Cambridge for Dublin as a result of some intimidation.[107] Temple, the fourth provost, and the incumbent from 1609 to 1627, was less ostentatiously Puritan, though Carr declared him 'a pronounced Puritan'.[108] That he was of Puritan persuasion was to become clearer in his tenure of office than in the prologue to his advancement. The fifth provost, Bedell may be considered yet a more moderate Puritan, heavily influenced by the Emmanuel College ethos, while later provosts, such as Robert Ussher were to break the stranglehold Cambridge had on the College, by the appointment of one of its own. Undoubtedly Ussher was influenced by the moderate Puritan ethos of Trinity College Dublin.

This brief investigation of James Ussher's early connections with Puritans is not intended to be read as an argument for seeing Ussher as solely of a Puritan persuasion. Rather it is offered as a corrective to views which too hastily deny any Puritan tendencies in Ussher. Ussher's role, as first bishop and then archbishop, was not seen as inimical to the pursuit of a Godly life, a fact that was accepted by Ussher's Essex network of friends.[109] Clearly, however, though Ussher maintained some of his connections, his theological views changed over the succeeding decades, just as he widened his friendship circle. However, an investigation of this early network is instructive, for it can not only shed light on Ussher's personal connections but also can augment our knowledge of the early ethos of Trinity College, Dublin at this time.

106 B. Brook (as note 18), vol. 2, p. 85.
107 B. Brook (as note 18), vol. 2, p. 85.
108 J.A. Carr (as note 90), p. 75.
109 William Hunt (as note 54), p. 252; for Ussher's links with the Barringtons see Essex Record Office, Chelmsford, E R O Barrington papers D/DBa/F5 11.

Aristotle and the English universities in the seventeenth century: A re-evaluation[1]

Mordechai Feingold

In 1654 the German traveller Christoph Arnold visited Oxford. With a mixture of amazement and contempt, he recorded in his diary that 'it is said that in the Oxford colleges in private discussions the authority of Aristotle is so great that whoever keeps on opposing this authority, or speaks denigratingly about it, is expected to pay the huge sum of five shillings.' If, he concluded, 'in England the Holy Scripture had the same weight as Aristotle, it would not be attacked by so many sectarian slanderers.' Were this entry more widely known, historians would undoubtedly have seized upon it as yet another indication of the iron grip of Aristotelianism over the course of studies at the English universities. As things stand, it is the statutes of the universities that are often regarded as the key witnesses for such an interpretation. Take, for example, the Laudian statutes at Oxford which stipulated that the university lecturer in logic explicate 'some part of Aristotle's logic', the White Professor of moral philosophy discuss Aristotle's ethics, politics, and economics, and the Sedleian professor of natural philosophy handle the entire corpus of Aristotle's scientific writings, from the *Physica* and *De caelo*, through *De generatione et corruptione* and the *Meteorologia*, concluding with *De anima*. Likewise, the Laudian ordinances regulating disputations and ceremonies also emphasized the centrality of Aristotle to the corporate identity of the university; the section on 'the form of creating general sophists', for example, stipulated that one of the four regent masters exhort the candidates to pursue polite literature and then 'recount the merits and advantages' of Aristotelian dialectics. This was to be followed by the bestowal of a copy of Aristotle's *Logic* upon each undergraduate. Finally, the rules regulating disputations specifically charged that the determining bachelors who 'propounded questions in logic for discussion' defend these accord-

---

[1] The material for this paper is extracted, for the most part, from my chapter on the mathematical sciences and the new philosophies in Nicholas Tyacke (ed.), *The History of the University of Oxford: The Seventeenth Century*. Oxford 1997.

ing to Aristotle, 'whose authority is paramount'. In disputing questions in rhetoric, moral philosophy, and politics, Aristotle 'and the entire doctrine of the peripatetics' was to be followed as well, under penalty of a fine.[2]

Under closer examination, however, this over-worked exercise of citing the statutes as proof of the Aristotelian yoke under which the universities laboured is misleading. For all their quotability, the statutes are not indicative of the actual course of studies during the early modern period. At most, the Aristotelian framework served as the old skin into which the new wine was poured.[3] A scrutiny of actual practices reveals that contemporaries were quite capable of distinguishing, correctly, between those writings of Aristotle that retained their relevance and those that had served their purpose. As a consummate expert on moral, political and literary issues, Aristotle was justly studied; as a natural philosopher, however, Aristotle was regarded by Oxford professors and tutors simply as a past master with whom they openly reserved the right to differ. In his polemic with John Webster and other sectarian opponents of the universities during the Interregnum, Seth Ward made this point clear. After praising Aristotle's contribution to humanist studies and to the 'historicall parts of nature', Ward continued:

> only his physicks is to be eliminated, it being founded upon either false, or not intelligible principles, referring all things to that system, and modell of the world, which time and observation have manifested to be untrue. The astronomy depending thereon (upon that system of foure elements, and a quintessentiall solid heaven) falls necessarily upon the removall of his physicks, or rather the physicall part of that astronomy.[4]

Ward's position was not that of a hack defender of university privilege and learning against its detractors. Robert Boyle, who was a severe critic of Aristotelian natural philosophy and metaphysics, reiterated more fully Ward's important distinction in the preface to his *Origine of Formes and Qualities* a

---

2 F. Blom, *Christoph and Andreas Arnold and England*. Nuremberg 1982, pp. 83-84; G.R.M. Ward, trans. *Oxford University Statutes*. 2 vols. Oxford 1845, vol. 1, pp. 20-23, 34-35, 43-44.

3 Fuller discussion of these two issues are available in my *The Mathematicians' Apprenticeship: Science, Universities, and Society in England, 1560-1640*. Cambridge 1984 and in my chapters in vol. 4 of the *History of Oxford University*.

4 John Wilkins and Seth Ward, *Vindiciae academiarum*. Oxford 1654, pp. 29-30 (repr. in A.G. Debus, *Science and Education in the Seventeenth Century: The Webster-Ward Debate*. London 1970, pp. 45-46). Ward concluded 'when these things are laid aside, that which remains deserves for him [Aristotle] the honour that ought to be given to one of the greatest wits, and most usefull that ever the world enjoyed'. More than three decades earlier John Bainbridge referred to Aristotle as 'that great and witty, but often misleading peripateticke' in *An Astronomical Description of the Late Comet*. London 1619, p. 12.

decade later. Wishing to articulate the precise nature and scope of his criticism of Aristotle, Boyle continued:

> By which nevertheless I would not be understood to censure or decry the whole peripatetick philosophy, much less to despise Aristotle himself ... For I look upon Aristotle as one (though but as one amongst many) of those famed ancients, whose learning about Alexander's time enobled Greece; and I readily allow him most of the praises due to great wits ... And I here declare once for all, that, where in the following tract, or any other of my writings, I do indefinitely depreciate Aristotle's doctrine, I would be understood to speak of his physicks, or rather of the speculative part of them (for his historical writings concerning animals I much admire) nor do I say that even these may not have their use among scholars, and even in universities, if they be retained and studied with due cautions and limitations (of which I have elsewhere spoken).[5]

Ward and Boyle articulated this astute and generally acceptable position – save during polemical debates – concerning the 'worth' of Aristotle. The Cambridge champion of the new science, William Watts, stated the position plainly during the 1630s: 'Aristotle (it must be confessed) hath made all learning beholden to him; no man hath learned to confute him, but by him, and unless he hath plowed with his heifer'. His younger Oxford contemporary, Thomas Browne, who was generally favourable to the assault on Aristotle's natural philosophy, concurred: 'while much is lacking in Aristotle, much wrong, much self-contradictory, yet not a little is valuable. Do not then bid farewell to his entire work; but while you hardly touch the Physics and read the Metaphysics superficially, make much of all the rest and study them unweariyingly'.[6]

The ability to honour Aristotle and yet forsake him whenever he was in the wrong was, for many university men, testimony to a truly liberated mind and a direct consequence of the atmosphere of philosophical freedom at Oxford and Cambridge.[7] Such an atmosphere made possible not only the free

---

5 Thomas Birch (ed.), *The Works of the Honourable Robert Boyle*. 6 vols. London 1772, vol. 3, p. 9.
6 William Watts, 'To the venerable artists and younger students in divinity, in the famous university of Cambridge', reprinted in J. Churchil (ed.), *A Collection of Voyages and Travels*. 6 vols. London 1732, vol. 2, p. 464; G. Keynes (ed.), *The Works of Sir Thomas Browne*. 4 vols. Chicago 1964, vol 3, p. 206.
7 Already in the mid-1570s John Rainolds defended his criticism of Aristotle's ethical theory of the summum bonum by saying that he was 'enjoyned' as a 'publike teacher to deliver sound and true opinions, not errors in the expounding of authors': John Rainolds, *An Excellent Oration ... very usefull for all such as affect the studies of logick and philosophie*, trans. J. Leycester. London 1638, p. 3.

pursuit of all studies, but rendered superfluous rhetorical excesses against Aristotle. Wilkins and Ward used this two-pronged argument in their counter-attack on Webster – emphasizing the vigilance with which philosophical freedom was guarded at Oxford, while branding Webster's claims about the enslavement of the university to Aristotle as those of an ignorant enthusiast. All new systems of thought have their 'strenuous assertours', insisted Wilkins in the preface to the *Vindiciae academiarum*. Indeed, intellectual pluralism at Oxford had reached such a propitious state that 'there is not to be wished a more generall liberty in points of judgment or debate, then what is here allowed'. As for Aristotle, despite

> his profound judgment and universall learning, yet are we so farre from being tyed up to his opinions, that persons of all conditions amongst us take liberty to discent from him, and to declare against him, according as any contrary evidence doth ingage them, being ready to follow the banner of truth by whomsoever it shall be lifted up.

For his part, Ward repeatedly emphasized the supremacy of 'liberty and variety amongst us'.[8]

This response to the charge that philosophical studies at Oxford laboured under the yoke of Aristotle is significant not only for its forceful rebuttal of a hostile critic, but for its illustration of the pride with which university scholars, throughout the seventeenth century, championed philosophical freedom. An early example of such advocacy can be found in the publication at Oxford of Nathanael Carpenter's *Philosophia libera* in 1622. Carpenter, a fellow of Exeter college, designed the book to serve as a *primer* stressing the dignity and necessity of *libertas philosophandi*, and inviting his readers, students in particular, to cultivate such freedom. He emphasized the pitfalls of blind submission to the authority of the ancients and, by means of his ensuing discussion of specific instances, illustrated the need to apply sober judgment in philosophical studies. Thus, though he himself was not a proponent of Copernicanism, Carpenter nonetheless upheld an author's duty to present impartially the views of the 'moderns' as well as the ancients, thereby investing the reader with the ability to choose freely among alternatives. '*In nullius iuratus verba*', he spiritedly paraphrased Horace, emphatically denouncing servility to the ancients when dealing with 'the business of nature'. Carpenter restated his position three years later in his *Geography Delineated*, where he occasionally returned to the theme of *libertas philosophandi*, e.g. in discussing the heliocentric hypothesis. Again, though Carpenter rejected the theory on religious grounds, he nonetheless acted on his conviction that the reader be

---

8 Wilkins and Ward (as note 4), pp. 2, 32, 39, 48.

presented with a fair and complete account of even those views rejected by the author: 'I would not willingly mangle it in any part', he declared, 'but shew it whole and intire to the view of the judicious; who herein may use their philosophicall liberty, to imbrace or reject what they please'.

Indeed, Oxford authors often waved the banner of philosophical freedom – and sometimes in unexpected contexts. When Francis Potter published in 1642 *An Interpretation of the Number 666*, for example, he defended his advocacy of an original theory by quoting William Gilbert:

> I know how hard it is to impart the air of newness to what is old, trimness to what is gone out of fashion, to lighten what is dark, to make that grateful which excites disgust, to win belief for things doubtful. But far more difficult is it to win any standing for or to establish doctrines that are novel, unheard-of, and opposed to everybody's opinions.

'But all truths which are now old', added Potter, 'were once new, and have had their severall oppositions. New truths are like new friends, worthy to be tried, though not to be trusted, and I propose these things to the wise and learned, as Martiall proposed himselfe to his friend, to be tryed and examined first, and to be believed afterward'.[9]

On the eve of the Restoration, Edward Bagshaw, John Locke's predecessor as censor of moral philosophy at Christ Church, appended to a genuine encomium of Aristotle's contribution to ethics, a fiery denunciation of slavish adherence to authority, exhorting his young auditors to join him in resisting any infringment of philosophical freedom. Locke himself imbibed such principles during his student days, as becomes evident from one of his early letters:

> When did ever any truth settle it self in any ones minde by the strength and authority of its owne evidence? Truths gaine admittance to our thoughts as the philosopher did to the tyrant by their handsome dresse and pleasing aspect, they enter us by composition, and are entertained as they suite with our affections, and as they demeane themselves towards our imperious passions, [but] when an opinion hath wrought its self unto our approbation and is gott under the protection of our likeing tis not all the assaults of argument, and the battery of

---

9 Nathaniel Carpenter, *Philosophia libera*. Oxford 1622; Idem, *Geography Delineated*, vol. 1, p. 76. For further discussion see R.F. Jones, *Ancients and Moderns*. St Louis 1961, pp. 65-71, 288-289; Francis Potter, *An Interpretation of the Number 666*. Oxford 1642, 'The epistle to the reader', sig. **; William Gilbert, *On the Loadstone and Magnetic Bodies*, trans P.F. Mottelay. New York 1893, p. xlix.

dispute shall dislodge it? Men live upon trust and their knowledg is noething but opinion moulded up betweene custome and interest, the two great luminarys of the world, the only lights they walke by.

A few years later, Samuel Parker publicly expressed his gratitude to Ralph Bathurst, president of Trinity College, Oxford who 'first rescue[d] him from the chains and fetters of an unhappy education', and had introduced him into a society that valued most 'a true freedom and ingenuity of mind'.[10]

College disputations and other public exercises offered students a wealth of opportunities to express their own approving sentiments on the theme of philosophical freedom. At Merton College, for example, a long tradition – stretching back to the late sixteenth century – established the custom of explicitly requiring students to vary from the opinion of Aristotle. Joachim Hübner, who attended one such occasion in 1640, was full of admiration for what he had seen: 'One of the best exercises at Oxford', he told Samuel Hartlib, 'is their declamations contra Aristotle, which are kept yearly at a certain time. Their speeches for the most part are most accurately elaborated wherin Aristotel is mightily towsed'.[11]

At the same time, contemporaries, and especially those who had joined teaching with research, firmly believed that despite the undeniable contribution of various 'moderns' to the study of nature, none should be allowed to impose his views unchallenged to the exclusion of competing theories. After all, no matter how superior to the ancients a new theory might be, none thus far had managed to accommodate the totality of available knowledge; besides, to chain oneself to a new authority would undermine the very concept of philosophical freedom that had just been acquired. Contemporaries clearly recognized that while errors of fact and method within Aristotelian natural philosophy had become manifest, the shortcomings of the various new theories, though not yet apparent, might become so in the future. Consequently, to accept them wholeheartedly on faith alone would be a mistake. It was also recognized that the neoterics, such as Descartes, Hobbes and Locke, were in their own way quite dogmatic. They acknowledged neither the benefit they derived from their predecessors nor from competing modes of thought, demanding instead total and immediate acceptance of their ideas. And if the previous century had taught seventeenth-century savants anything, it was how transitory were all theories and systems. Only intellectual pluralism and the right to choose could accommodate and guide the search for truth.

10 Edward Bagshaw, *Exercitationes duae ... altera academica, de philosophia veterum, ejusque usu*. London 1661; R.F. Jones (as note 9), p. 141; E.S. de Beer (ed.), *The Correspondence of John Locke*. 8 vols. Oxford 1976-1989, vol. 1, p. 123; Samuel Parker, *A Free and Impartial Censure of the Platonick Philosophie*. Oxford 1666, sig. A3v.
11 Sheffield University Library, Hartlib Papers 30/4/61A.

Partly for this reason, Wilkins and Ward lashed out at Hobbes's presumptions in unambiguous terms. Wilkins's intimation that Hobbes was 'magisterial' in his writings[12] was further developed by Ward into a fully-fledged indictment: 'It appears that the end he proposes to himselfe', Ward wrote in reference to the prescriptions of the author of *Leviathan*, is 'that the world should be regulated exactly by that modell which he there exhibits, and that his reason should be the governing reason of mankind'.[13] Hobbes's criticism of the universities, therefore, was not only inaccurate but disingenuous, for he faulted them simply for not teaching his views: 'From whence it is manifest, that the only thing which paines him is the desire that Aristotelity may be changed into Hobbeity, and instead of the Stagyrite, the world may adore the great Malmesburian phylosopher'. Ward was pleased to inform Hobbes that at Oxford he and his colleagues 'enjoy a liberty of philosophizing'; and should Hobbes honour them with a visit, Ward was certain, 'he would hardly find any other fault with [them], except that great unpardonable one, that the publick reading of his *Leviathan*, is not by a sanction of the magistrate imposed upon [them]'.[14]

The sincerity with which these expressions of intellectual freedom were expressed and the light they shed on university learning are not diminished by the fact that the curriculum retained, at least superficially, its Aristotelian framework throughout much of the seventeenth century. After all, the durability of Aristotelianism, as Charles Schmitt has pointed out, was due in no small part to pedagogical convenience. If such sixteenth-century critics as Pico, Copernicus, Ramus, Telesio, and Bruno were able 'to show a few Aristotelian doctrines to be in error, they could in no way produce a comprehensive alternative system to replace the established one', and Aristotelianism, despite its many flaws, 'still covered such a wide range that no other system could challenge its cultural hegemony'.[15] Only during the first half of the seventeenth century did comprehensive alternatives to Aristotle become

---

12 Hobbes is 'a person of good ability and solid parts', wrote Wilkins, 'but otherwise highly magisteriall, and one that will be very angry with all that do not presently submit to his dictates. And for advancing the reputation of his own skill, cares not what unworthy reflexions he casts on others'. Wilkins and Ward (as note 4), pp. 6-7.
13 Ward referred to the passage where Hobbes, cognizant of the centrality of the universities in training the political and social elite, expressed the hope 'that one time or other, this writing of mine, may fall into the hands of a soveraign, who will consider it himselfe ... without the help of any interested, or envious interpreter; and by the exercise of entire soveraignty, in protecting the publique teaching of it, convert this truth of speculation, into the utility of practice'. Thomas Hobbes, *Leviathan* (ed. C.B. Macpherson). London 1976, p. 408, see also pp. 727-728.
14 Wilkins and Ward (as note 4), pp. 51-52, 58-59.
15 C.B. Schmitt, 'Philosophy and science in sixteenth-century universities: some preliminary comments' in J.E. Murdoch and E.D. Sylla (eds.), *The Cultural Context of Medieval Learning*. Dordrecht 1975, p. 489.

available – following the publications of the works of Bacon, Galileo, Kepler, Harvey, Hobbes, Gassendi, and Descartes. Yet although the new ideas were widely recognised as offering superior knowledge, another generation was to pass before they were digested into textbooks appropriate to neophytes. But even then, the old learning was not immediately rendered obsolete, both because of the pedagogical function of the university to impart old and new learning and because the new learning could hardly be made comprehensible without at least some grounding in what it sought to replace.[16] Seth Ward commented in 1654 on the continued utility of the Aristotelian structure of knowledge. No reading of 'modern' rhetoricians, moralists, and politicians, he argued, could replace Aristotle, for even if the writings of various innovators 'did conteine things better in their kind than Aristotle', these 'are not fit to be read in universities by way of institution'. The moderns, Ward continued,

> have written diffusedly *stilo oratorio* ... but have not given a briefe methodicall body of the things they handle. The businessse of such as have the institution of youth, is to give them, first a briefe and generall comprehension of the kinds and natures of those things, about which their studyes, and endeavours are to be employed, and so to excite and stirre them up to a deepe and more thorough consideration of them, to set them into a way of study and knowledge.

It is primarily for this reason that Aristotle is important and why he 'hath been universally received as *magister legitimus*' in the schools: 'the universallity of his enquiries, the brevity and method of them, fitting them for institutions, and not the truth or infallibility of his workes' have all rendered the teaching of Aristotle irreplaceable.[17] Thus speaking as an educator rather than as a professional scientist, the Savilian professor of astronomy advocated a position similar to one that Bartholomew Keckermann had expressed half a century earlier, when he frankly admitted that it was 'better to teach method-

---

16 A similar dilemma faced the Newtonians at the turn of the eighteenth century, as they were forced to convey the new ideas within the more traditional Cartesian text of Jacques Rohault until such time as proper textbooks became available. When Samuel Clarke asked William Whiston in 1697 whether he should publish a translation of Rohault, the latter replied: 'Since the youth of the university must have, at present, some system of natural philosophy for their studyes and exercises; and since the true system of Sir Isaac Newton's was not yet made easy enough for the purpose, it is not improper, for their sakes, yet to translate and use the system of Rohault ... but that as soon as Sir Isaac Newton's philosophy came to be better known, that only ought to be taught, and the other dropped'. William Whiston, *Historical Memoirs of the Life of Dr Samuel Clarke*. London 1730, pp. 5-6, quoted in M.A. Hoskin, ' "Mining all within": Clarke's notes to Rohault's *Traité de Physique*' in Thomist 24, 1961, p. 355.
17 Wilkins and and Ward (as note 4), p. 39.

ically ordered traditional positions, even if erroneous or questionable, rather than as-yet unmethodized new theories, even if true'.[18]

Moreover, whatever its shortcomings, the philosophy of Aristotle still provided an indispensable background for the comprehension of the more recent world views, just as the terminology utilized by Aristotle and his followers still remained an integral component of both new and old philosophy. In 1668 Ralph Bohun of New College articulated at length his method of education to John Evelyn, whose son was then under Bohun's care:

> I begin with the philosophy of the schooles, which though I make it not my creed, and have often declared to your selfe how insufficient I believe the peripatetic hypothesis to solve the phaenomenas of nature, with any tolerable consistency to it selfe, yet since Aristotle has so universally obtained in all the universitys of Christendome for so many ages [and] thus insensibly crept into all modern writers by the use of his terms, it's almost impossible, as things stand, to be either divine, physician, or lawyer without him ... how then can it be expected that we should understand the new philosophies without him, when the greatest part of their works consist only in confutation of his; so that I should advise Mr John to speak against Aristotle because he had read him, and not like the young gallants of the town that continually condemn his hypothesis only because they heard it censured in the last coffeehouse, or think it out of vogue in the Royal Society ... All that I admonish Mr John is that he should not be prejudiced too soon.[19]

Such efforts to avert early bias in the minds of youths further testify to the conscious attempt on the part of tutors and educators to inculcate among students the liberty of philosophizing by offering them a range of options. Gilbert Burnet's views were typical. After the young student completed his course of mathematics, he was to 'be acquainted with the hypotheses of philosophy'. However, cautioned Burnet, 'I would not allow so many moneths as we give yeeres; and the youth is only to be acquainted with the several sects, and their chieffe grounds; but must not be byassed to any; but left at liberty to chuse, in a riper age, what shall seem most sutable to nature's operations, and not to poor pedantick sophistry'. Interestingly, the views expressed by Bohun and Burnet were basically those that informed Locke in his recommendation of the proper course of natural philosophy. In the company of contemporaries, Locke was convinced that none of the available systems offered either total or certain knowledge. Yet

---

18 P. Reif, 'The textbook tradition in natural philosophy, 1600-1650' in *Journal of the History of Ideas* 30, 1969, p. 29.
19 Christ Church, Oxford, Evelyn Letters, no. 301.

it is necessary for a gentleman in this learned age to look into some of them, to fit himself for conversation. But whether that of Des Cartes be put into his hands, as that which is most in fashion, or it be thought fit to give him a short view of that and several others also, I think the systems of natural philosophy, that have obtained in this part of the world, are to be read, more to know the hypotheses, and to understand the terms and ways of talking of the several sects, than with hopes to gain thereby a comprehensive, scientifical, and satisfactory knowledge of the works of nature. Only this may be said, that the modern corpuscularians talk, in most things, more intelligibly that the peripateticks, who possessed the schools immediately before them.

Burnet and Locke also agreed that, in the words of the latter, the writings of the chief experimental authors 'may be fit for a gentleman, when he has a little acquainted himself with some of the systems of the natural philosophy in fashion'.[20]

The conviction that the correct method of teaching philosophy necessitated a proper blend of old and new learning – and that the terminology of the former was indispensable for the comprehension of the latter – resulted in their study in tandem by all students, irrespective of social origins or career choices. Stephen Penton, for example, cautioned the well-born youth coming up to the university not to expect that 'the taylor should put on him philosophy with his gown'. Rather, at 'his first coming to Oxford, it is fit he should be made acquainted with some general knowledge of philosophy, of the original design, and several parts of it'. This meant familiarizing himself with the terms of art and, though such course 'may be thought dry diet for a gentleman', yet no philosophical argument or learned conversation could be understood without it. 'After a short system of physick, in the old way', concluded Penton, 'a taste of the new philosophy would relish well, to understand the differing principles upon which it proceeds'.[21]

The guiding principles that animated scholars in educating youth were clearly spelled out by Edward Reynolds in 1647:

> I consider a double estate of the learned: inchoation and progresse. And though in this latter there be requisite a discerning judgement, and liberty of dissent, yet for the other, Aristotle's speech is true ... beginners must believe. For as in the generation of man, he receiveth his first life and nourishment from one wombe, and after takes onely those things, which are by the nurse or mother given to him; but when

---

20 J. Clarke, *Bishop Gilbert Burnet as Educationist*. Aberdeen 1914, pp. 61, 63; TJ.L. Axtell (ed.), *The Educational Writings of John Locke*. Cambridge 1968, pp. 304-306.
21 Stephen Penton, *New Instructions to the Guardian*. London 1694, pp. 94-96.

> he is growne unto strength and yeares, he then receiveth nourishment not from milke onely, but from all variety of meats, and with the freedom of his own choise or dislike; so in the generation of knowledge, the first knitting of the joynts and members of it into one body is best affected by the authority and learning of some able teacher (though even of his tutors, Cato being a childe, was wont to require a reason) but being growne thereby to some stature and maturity, not to give it the liberty of its owne judgement, were to confine it still to its nurse or cradle.

Reynolds, indeed, revered the ancients. Yet, he continued, 'there is a difference between reverence and superstition; we may assent to them as antients, but not as oracles ... and where I finde expresse reason of dissenting, I will rather speak truth with my mistresse nature, then maintain an error with my master Aristotle. As there may be friendship, so there may be honour with diversity of opinions'.[22]

Such advice was equally applicable to the domains of natural philosophy and of metaphysics. Henry Dodwell recommended the study of Aristotelian philosophy because it served as a foundation to more recent philosophies as well as because such historical method would familiarize students with those concepts and terminology without which one could scarcely understand either old or new philosophy: 'Notwithstanding you are not now to be confined to the peripatetick principles, but may more ingenuously examine others, and accept what you your self shall conceive most satisfactory ... the investigation of the particular divine attributes will be best performed by metaphysicks, wherein all the terms requisite to this way of arguing are professedly handled'. In his usual convoluted manner, John Norris was even more explicit:

> However the physicks, or natural philosophy of the schools does not please me, as partly proceeding too much upon the false and confused ideas of sense, and partly as explaining the particular effects of nature, by the general and indeterminate notions of pure logick, yet I have a great value and esteem for their metaphysicks, and for theology ... And indeed I am pretty much of opinion, that nothing of any moment, either in philosophy, or in religion, can be either distinctly stated, or well understood, without the help of their useful, I might say, necessary distinctions: Which, whosoever is well instructed in, has a great advantage over him that has not, tho' otherwise ever so ingenious.[23]

---

22 Edward Reynolds, *A Treatise of the Passions and Faculties of the Soul of Man*. London 1647, pp. 491-493.
23 Henry Dodwell, *Two Letters of Advice*. 3rd ed. London 1691, p. 163; Norris, *An Essay Towards the Theory of the Ideal or Intelligible World*, vol. 2, sig. A6-A6v.

Constraints of space prevent me from demonstrating the manner in which the undergraduate curriculum was consciously balanced in order to acquaint the student with the divergent versions of natural philosophy, both ancient and modern. Suffice it to say that if the university authorities were guilty of anything, it was their seemingly excessive veneration for the wording of the statutes rather than for any attempt to enforce submission to Aristotle.[24]

The finest testimony to the prevalence of English academic freedom is that, in sharp contrast to what occurred elsewhere, there are no instances of official condemnation of new scientific ideas. While all Catholic, and most Protestant, universities either banned or imposed severe restrictions on the teaching of Copernicanism, in England such an option was never a consideration. And whereas at Leiden and Utrecht, at Paris, Geneva, Louvain, Uppsala and the Italian universities, the teachings of Descartes were condemned at various times from the 1640s onward, at Oxford and Cambridge no official attempt to curb the rapid dissemination of such ideas was ever felt necessary. Not that everyone was receptive. Certain dons expressed an aversion to the new ideas – invariably motivated by their perceived religious implications – and even cautioned their charges against them. Nevertheless, the tradition of intellectual freedom was too firmly embedded in English academic institutions to be uprooted by anxiety over the possible subversive implications of natural philosophy. At most, during the strife between the universities and the Royal Society in the late 1660s, the vice-chancellor posted a flyer reminding students of their duties to defend Aristotle. But the intention was to calm hot spirits. Certainly no effort was ever made to enforce such advice.

It is not surprising, therefore, that contemporary observers often commented on the intellectual freedom enjoyed by the English. John Barclay summarized this perception in 1612: 'In philosophy, and the mathematicks, in geography, and astronomy, there is noe opinion soe prodigious and strange, but in that island was eyther invented, or has found many followers, and subtile maintainers'. Three years later the vicissitudes of Johannes Drusius, who taught Hebrew in Elizabethan Oxford, drove him to contrast the persecution he suffered at home in the Netherlands with the freedom enjoyed by the English in their cultivation of all good learning. Accustomed to the freedom of thought at Oxford, John Locke was surprised to find, when he visited France in 1676, that 'the new philosophie [was] prohibited to be

---

24 They had little choice in the matter anyway for the Laudian Code intended to bind the university 'in perpetuity'. 'Not only was the university itself precluded from altering [the statutes], but it seems that neither did the crown intend under normal circumstances to intervene further': L. Sutherland, 'The Laudian statutes in the eighteenth century' in L.S. Sutherland and L.G. Mitchell (eds.), *The History of the University of Oxford: The Eighteenth Century*. Oxford 1986, p. 190.

taught in universitys, schooles and academies', while Newton reflected in the early eighteenth century on 'the happiness of [his] being born in a land of liberty where he could speak his mind – not afraid of [the] Inquisition as Galileo ... not obliged as Des Cartes was to go into a strange country and to say he proved transubstantiation by his philosophy'.[25]

Not that authorities were indifferent to university teachings. In 1622, for example, following a sermon by the Oxford scholar William Knight that seemed to condone tyrannicide, James I admonished divinity students to 'apply themselves in the first place to the reading of the Scriptures, next to the Councells and ancient Fathers, and then the Schoolmen, excluding those neotericks, both Jesuits and puritans, who are knowne to be medlers in matter of State and monarchy.' Both universities immediately proceeded to condemn and burn the writings of David Pareus, whose doctrine of passive obedience Knight claimed to have plaigarized.[26] Similarly, as a consequence of the boisterous Arminian disputes of the mid 1620s, Charles I prohibited in 1628, at both Oxford and Cambridge, the teaching and disputing of any theological issue contrary to the existing formularies of religion – a ruling that effectively banned predestinarian teaching at the universities. But what is striking in the case of Oxford and Cambridge is the (by and large) *irrelevance* of scientific and philosophical issues to the various religious and political changes that transpired in early modern England. Hence, the ability and willingness to distinguish between what was useful in Aristotle and what could at least be silently discarded went hand-in-hand with a more general tolerance of new modes of thought. And it is this aspect that not only differentiates the English universities from their continental counterparts, but also helps explain the meteoric rise of England to a position of European prominence in scientific studies – a development commented upon by a growing chorus of continental observers. Thus, in 1666 we find Jean Daillé writing from Paris to Leonard Holzhalb in Zurich: 'scarcely anything new is done in this city in the mathematics and philosophy, and it seems that today these noble sciences have crossed the seas to establish themselves in England

---

25 *The Mirrour of Mindes*, or, *Barclay's Icon Animorum*, trans. Thomas May. London 1635, pp. 117-118 quoted in F.R. Johnson, *Astronomical Thought in Renaissance England*. Repr. New York 1968, p. 248; J.E. Platt, 'Sixtinus Amama (1593-1629): Franeker professor and citizen of the republic of letters' in G. Th. Jensme, F.R.H. Smit and F. Westra (eds.), *Universiteit te Franeker, 1585-1811*. Leeuwarden 1985, p. 242; John Locke, *Travels in France 1675-1679* (ed. J. Lough). Cambridge 1953, p. 60; F.E. Manuel, *A Portrait of Isaac Newton*. Cambridge Mass. 1968, p. 267.

26 J.B. Mullinger, *The University of Cambridge*. 3 vols. Cambridge 1873-1911, vol. 2, p. 567; Anthony Wood, *The History and Antiquities of the University of Oxford* (ed. John Gutch). 2 vols in 3. London 1792-1796, vol. 2, p. 343; Peter O.G. White, *Predestination, Policy, and Polemic: Conflict and Concensus in the English Church from the Reformation to the Civil War*. Cambridge 1992.

where they are cultivated with great care.' That which distinguished the English, pronounced Pierre Bayle in 1685, 'was the strength and profundity of their speculations.' One of his correspondents, Daniel Laroque, concurred: 'The more I see of the English, the more I admire them; generally speaking, they surpass us in everything.' Even La Fontaine found occasion to introduce the following moral into one of his fables: 'The English think deeply; in that their mind is one with their character; delving deeply into things, and rich in experience they extend far and wide the empire of the sciences.'[27]

---

27 Harcourt Brown, *Scientific Organizations in Seventeenth Century France*. Repr. New York 1967, p. 192; Paul Hazard, *The European Mind*. New Haven 1953, pp. 79, 64.

What is an early modern university? The conflict between Leiden and Amsterdam in 1631

Willem Frijhoff

THE EARLY MODERN UNIVERSITY:
A VANISHING TRANSPARENCY

What is an early modern university? The question is much less rhetorical than it may seem at first sight. Somewhere between the Middle Ages and the Early Modern period the university lost its transparency. Although late medieval universities were more diverse than is generally assumed, they were recognisable by the feature they all shared, that of being a *studium generale* of papal or imperial foundation (or at least confirmation) bestowed with the right to grant the *licentia docendi*, that is, to award degrees.[1] Differences between the universities were mainly due to historical or geographical factors. They did not involve the definition of the institution itself but concerned merely the organisation of the university, not its triple institutional function: teaching, learning, graduating. Of course, there might be some hesitation about the university character of individual *studia*, set up by the initiative of minor princes or even local municipalities and issued with charters by contested authorities, but in general the picture was quite clear.

Ever since the sixteenth century, however, the university system became less self-evident.[2] Beginning with Alcalà de Henares (1499, opened 1508), major universities were still founded according to the old rules – but something had changed. Alcalà, with its trinlingual college, was already marked by

---

1 Jacques Verger, 'Patterns', in H. de Ridder-Symoens (ed.), *A History of the University in Europe, vol. I: Universities in the Middle Ages.* Cambridge 1992, pp. 35-74.
2 Willem Frijhoff, 'Patterns', (as note 1) vol. II. Cambridge 1996; P.S. Allen, 'The Trilingual Colleges of the Early Sixteenth Century' in P.S. Allen, *Erasmus, Lectures and Wayfaring Sketches.* Oxford 1934, pp. 138-163; H. de Vocht, *History of the Foundation and the Rise of the Collegium Trilingue Louvaniense, 1417-1530,* 4 vols. Louvain 1961-1965; Walter Rüegg, 'Humanistische Elitenbildung in der Eidgenossenschaft zur Zeit der Renaissance' in W. Rüegg, *Die Renaissance im Blick der Nationen Europas.* Wiesbaden 1991, pp. 95-133, especially pp. 126-131.

the new philology. In 1527, however, the foundation of Marburg as a Lutheran *studium generale* by the landgrave of Hesse, Philip the Magnanimous, without papal or imperial approval (although the Emperor approved the foundation in 1541), made the first breach in the hitherto universally observed system.[3] Henceforth, the territorial and religious disintegration of the German Empire made sovereignty a hotly contested, indeed a crucial question, and this involved more specifically the pursuit of the *jus regale* to charter a university.

Another powerful reason for the dilution of the institutional norms was the evolution of the educational system itself, as related to the expectations of society at large. The need for a more widespread general education led, at least from the fourteenth century onwards, to the creation of grammar schools with a teaching programme that overlapped the traditional arts faculties. During the sixteenth century, under the convergent pressures of municipalities, administrations, emerging professions and church requirements, an autonomous network of grammar schools (Latin schools, *colléges*) came into being; they formed the bridge between the schools which taught in the vernacular on the one side and the universities and the use of the Latin tongue on the other.[4] At the same time, the ever more intricate ramification of the educational network together with the tendency to territorial restraint or at least protection prompted the creation of institutions that formally overlapped the traditional universities: grammar schools with a superstructure of chairs of philosophy and theology, which would be adequate for most of the educational needs of the territory or the town. Institutions such as the Lutheran municipal gymnasium organised in 1538 at Strasbourg by John Sturm, or its Calvinist counterpart under the direction of Claude Baduel at Nîmes (1540); and the whole range of 'colléges de plain exercise' or *gymnasia* (*academia illustria*) derived from this formula. The needs of apologetics and the religious and cultural offensives of Protestants and Catholics against each other, but also against the heretics or unbelievers on the frontiers of Christian Europe (Arabs in the south, Turks in the southeast, Orthodox believers in the east, perhaps still some pagans in the north, and at any rate, the mass of unbelievers in the ever growing colonial empires) justified any substantial investment in schools for philosophy and theology: seminaries, convents, small universities run by old orders or new congregations, but always adapted to the local or regional conditions.

All these factors explain why the university system as such suffered an unmistakable crisis of identity. Other reasons can easily be added, such as the

---

3 W. von Bredow (ed.), *450 Jahre Philipps-Universität Marburg*. Marburg 1979.
4 See the various contributions in Domenico Maffei & Hilde de Ridder-Symoens (eds.), *I collegi universitari in Europa tra il XIVe il XVIII secolo*. Milan 1991.

changes in the paradigms of science or in the university curriculum itself.[5] In this article, however, I shall restrict myself mainly to the institutional level. In fact, ever since the end of the Middle Ages university or semi-university level institutions sprang up and flourished, whereas the attendance at the old universities themselves dramatically declined, as Laurence Brockliss has strikingly shown in his study on the university of Paris.[6] To be sure, individual universities remained very proud of their university status, and new institutions claiming that position surpassed each other in boasting their conformity to the old university models. They created senates, colleges, faculties, and were first in the field of copying or 're-inventing' all the symbolic marks of the full universities: beadles, maces, gowns, seals, privileges, rituals and auditoria. It was not the self-confidence of individual institutions that suffered from the changing conditions, but the transparency of the system as a whole. If every teaching institution claimed the same status, how is one to make a responsible choice between real and fake universities, between institutions of true learning and second-rate schools? In other words, institutional requirements may still have existed for the foundation and confirmation of a university, but henceforth their application was spoiled by problems of interpretation due to the lack of a political and juridical consensus, added to ancient social and cultural rivalries.

UNIVERSITY CATALOGUES

The awareness – more or less acute – of this general problem accounts at least partially for the publication, from the second half of the sixteenth century, of a long chain of European university catalogues, especially in those regions of Europe where the university had to cope with fierce competitors. One of the first of such catalogues was the *Tractatus de academiis et scholis in Europa*, published by W. Jobst (Justus) at Frankfurt-on-Oder in 1554. It was followed by a long series of similar catalogues such as those written by M. Cholinus (Cologne, 1572), J. Middendorpius (Cologne, 1567, second edition 1602), Franciscus Junius or du Jon (Heidelberg, 1587), A. Burchardus (Magdeburg, 1615), Hermann Conring (Helmstedt, 1651), J. M. Schwimmer (Jena, 1672), S. Parchitius (Frankfurt-on-Oder, 1692), Franciscus Lucae (Frankfurt-on-Oder, 1711), Jean de Launoy (Hamburg, 1717), J.G.

---

5 For an overview see John M. Fletcher, 'Change and resistance to change: a consideration of the development of English and German universities during the sixteenth century' in *History of Universities* 1, 1981, pp. 1-36.
6 L.W.B. Brockliss, 'Patterns of attendance at the University of Paris, 1480-1800' in Dominique Julia & Jacques Revel (eds.), *Les universités européennes du XVIe au XVIIIe siècle. Histoire sociale des populations étudiantes*, vol. 2. Paris 1989, pp. 487-526.

Hagelganss (Frankfurt-on-Main, 1737) and many others. Of course, university catalogues were useful as pocket-guides for the academic traveller abroad. However, at the same time they satisfied another need, that of recognizing in the exponentially growing field of the educational institutions those schools of higher learning which claimed deservedly, both on institutional grounds and for reasons of quality, the title of a 'university' in the full sense of the word, that is, an institution of higher education founded or recognized as of university level by the public authorities of the territory concerned and endowed with the right to confer proper degrees. Only such universities could be profitably attended by future theologians, physicians, law-students and other men of letters, without running the risk of a ridiculous curriculum, a heterodox reputation or a worthless degree.

The utility of those catalogues is quite evident for those wishing to take a closer look at the early modern university system, although the entries are not free from error. I wish to concentrate on an example that may at the same time illuminate the conflict which will be dealt with in the second part of this essay. In his inaugural lecture delivered on 15 May 1636 at the opening of the new chartered university of Utrecht in the United Provinces – the institution itself had been founded four years earlier as a civic illustrious school with the right to grant degrees – the famous Calvinist theologian Gisbertus Voetius (1589-1676) outlined systematically the whole range of the sciences and skills to be taught at a fully-fledged university, from theology, the central and basic science, to such arts as *optica*, *gnomica* or *scioterica* (the arts of refraction and perspective which were of such importance in Dutch arts and crafts at that very moment),[7] and mere technical skills as *castrametatio*, *hydrographica* and *nautica*, which as a matter of fact remained with very few exceptions outside the formal scope of university teaching until far into the eighteenth century.[8] For Voetius, clearly, the university remained a *studium* truly '*generale*' defined by its teaching function more than by its structure. Hence his attempt to put on the same footing all the institutions of academic learning, whether universities or simply higher schools, *athenaea* or *gymnasium*. It is surely no coincidence that at the beginning of his lecture he refers explicitly to the example of Christ attending at the age of twelve the – in his perception – 'Higher School' at Jerusalem's temple (Luke 2, 46). Deliberately, Voetius speaks of academies and schools, not of universities. It is true learning he looks for, wherever that may be found, not its formal recognition by means of a degree.

It is therefore quite natural that at the end of his lecture Voetius lists the higher schools where true learning may be acquired. He gives the names of

---

7 Svetlana Alpers, *The art of describing: Dutch art in the seventeenth century*. Chicago 1983.
8 Gisbertus Voetius, *Sermoen van de nutticheydt der Academien ende scholen, mitsgader der wetenschappen ende consten die in de selve gheleert werden*. Utrecht 1636.

famous professors and a judgement about the present situation and the fame of individual institutions. Here, however, he makes a distinction between the universities and the 'illustrious schools', not referring to a difference in quality but along formal lines: only universities guarantee the civil effect of a period of study that is symbolized in and obtained by a degree. Among the universities listed by Voetius we find the Huguenot 'académies' of the kingdom of France and Navarre – Nîmes, Montauban, Die, Saumur, Sedan, Orthez – and at least five other examples of the growing opacity of the university system. Voetius mentions, for example, phantom universities at Lyons in France ('founded in 830'), Bergamo in Italy and Braga in Portugal. He might have inferred the existence of the latter ('an old academy, not very famous') from the correspondence of the famous grammarian Nicolaus Clenardus (1493-1542) who in 1537/1538 assisted Prince Henry of Portugal in the foundation of a new college at Braga, apparently of the trilingual kind.[9] Voetius considers as an independent university the school of Poznan. It is not clear whether he means the Poznan outpost of Cracow university (which enjoyed a graduation monopoly in the kingdom of Poland) founded by Bishop John Lubrianski in 1519, or the Jesuit college of 1573, bestowed with a university charter by the Polish parliament in 1611 but forced to drop its ambitions as early as 1613 by order of the pope.[10] Voetius also places the Academy of Nobles at Sorø (Denmark) on a full university footing. This is interesting, since the academy of Sorø had been founded a dozen years earlier by King Christian IV as a new, socially restricted alternative to the University of Copenhagen and had, as such, earned itself some fame in the Netherlands.[11] Finally, Voetius is aware of the existence of a university in Mexico, mistakenly called a 'Jesuit' foundation, perhaps because all monks were easily reduced to the status of Jesuit educators by their Calvinist opponents. On the other hand, Voetius ignores several smaller universities and colleges in Spain. The Iberian peninsula and the Spanish colonies were clearly becoming *terra incognita* for the oldest extraterritorial subjects of the king of Spain.

Still more interesting is Voetius's list of illustrious schools, that is, higher schools without the right to award degrees but famous enough to be recommended for their learning. Besides the illustrious schools of the United Provinces (Harderwijk – soon to be made a full university – Middelburg, Amsterdam, Deventer and Dordrecht, the latter three founded less than a decade before), he mentions 55 other institutions of higher education, half of

9   Gisbertus Voetius, *Sermoen van de nutticheydt* (as note 8).
10 Karlheinz Goldmann, *Verzeichnis der Hochschulen*. Neustadt an der Aisch 1967, pp. 293-294.
11 William Norwin, 'Christian IVs Ridderakademi og Skolen 1623-1665' in M. Mackeprung (ed.), *Sorø, Klostret, Akademiet giennem tiderne*, vol. 1. Sorø 1923, pp. 374-632.

them (26) situated in the German Empire. London is mentioned as an 'illustrious school' founded in 1489; its reputation had, according to Voetius, been established by John Colet. For Scotland the list contains only the school of Edinburgh, apart from the universities of St Andrews, Glasgow and Aberdeen; Voetius seems to have been ignorant of the fact that there were two separate colleges at Aberdeen. There is another mystery here, since Edinburgh had received full university status in the late sixteenth century. Although Geneva was not a university in the formal sense of the word, because the emperor refused to recognise universities in the Calvinist mode, its degrees were *de facto* accepted by the Dutch universities. The mutual recognition of each others degrees had even been used as an argument for granting the formal university status of the Dutch universities themselves – founded, as is well known, by the rebellious government whose sovereignty was not recognized by the two political powers involved, the king of Spain and the German emperor, not to mention the pope, before the Peace of Westphalia (1648). It is therefore somewhat peculiar to find Geneva on the same footing as the Zurich, Bern and Lausanne theological schools, the *gymnasia academica* of Thorn (Torun), Elbing (Elblag) and Danzig (Gdan'sk), or the Protestant and Catholic colleges on the frontiers of Christianity at Tyrnau (Trnava; in fact raised to university status the year before), Debrecen, Patach (Sárospatak), Weissenburg (Alba Iulia), Clausenburg (Cluj), Cronstadt (Brasov), Besterce or Waradin, some of which were no more than somewhat large grammar schools. Rather surprisingly at first sight, Voetius seems better informed about Hungary and Transylvania than about France and Italy. However, Hungarian and Transylvanian Calvinist students came to study theology at Utrecht, indeed under Voetius's supervision, and may well have informed him.[12]

Outside this mainly Protestant world, however, Voetius's perception of higher education dissolves into a blurred image of grammar schools with an initial university level superstructure of more or less illustrious standing: one such case is the 'collège de plain exercise' at Annecy, run by the Barnabite Fathers since 1614 and perhaps known to Voetius because of its proximity to and competition with Geneva. Or was it because this college, founded in 1549/1553 by Eustace Chapuis, canon of Geneva and ambassador of the Emperor Charles V, was considered a twin ('plustot un mesme collège en deux endroits') to the College of Savoy, founded at Louvain in 1551 by the same canon who on that occasion put the school of Annecy under the authority of Louvain university?[13] On the other hand, he is uncertain about the

12   G.W. Kernkamp, 'Buitenlandsche studenten aan de Utrechtsche Akademie in vroeger eeuwen' in *Historia*, 2, 1936, pp. 128-132.
13   M.M. Compère & D. Julia (eds.), *Les collèges français 16e-18e siècles. Répertoire: I: France du Midi*. Paris 1984, pp. 52-63; Marina Roggero, 'I collegi universitari in età moderna' in

existence of a school at Asti in Piedmont, and he identifies as an illustrious school erected around 1480 the newly founded university of Mantova (1625) that had already been closed down because of the harshness of the times (1627), and he thinks that there still exists such a school at Besançon where, in fact, the papal privilege had been revoked as early as 1567. Apart from the school at La Rochelle (is this the memory of the Huguenot academy suppressed after the siege of 1627-1628, or the new Jesuit college of 1629?),[14] the Protestant grammar schools of Nérac and Castre in France deserve special mention in Voetius's estimation, but he is apparently unaware that both had been recently subjected to a mixed regime of Protestant and Catholic teachers.[15] Finally, his selection among the illustrious schools of the German Empire appears a rather personal one: only three Catholic institutions (the Jesuit *gymnasia* of Augsburg, Münster and Osnabrück) seem to reach the level of no less than twenty-three Lutheran or Calvinist schools. He lists not only the outstanding ones that one might expect to find here (such as Herborn, Steinfurt or Bremen which lacked only formal recognition by the emperor and achieved incidentally a quality level superior to that of many full universities), but spurious *gymnasia* such as the schools of Merseburg, Heilbronn, Goldberg, Görlitz, Korbach, Stettin or Meissen, and some genuine 'illustrious' schools, either Lutheran (Coburg, Stade) or Calvinist (Zerbst, a school of real educational importance that had earned a truly international reputation).[16]

Naturally, the question arises where Voetius got his information from and how he assessed the reputation of the schools. A close look at the composition of the lists strongly suggests his use of three different sources: firstly, the existing catalogues of universities which Voetius copied including their errors or uncertainties, as we see in the cases of Geneva and Besançon; secondly on hearsay which seems to be his source in the case of Mantova and certain 'illustrious' schools of Germany whose reputation he may have inferred from the *peregrinatio academica* of Calvinist or even Lutheran ministers of his acquaintance; thirdly, the actual Calvinist network around him – giving them an inflated significance – which he knew through the reputation of the institutions themselves, their professors and students. In his youth (1611), Voetius himself, the son of an impoverished nobleman, had made a vain attempt to obtain funds towards an extensive *peregrinatio academica* to all the Protestant academies worthy of the attention of a newly ordained minister, i.e. Heidelberg, Herborn, Basel, Zurich, Geneva, Saumur, Sedan,

---

Gian Paolo Brizzi & Angelo Varni (eds.), *L'università in Italia fra età moderna e contemporanea. Aspetti e momenti.* Bologna 1991, p. 123.
14   Compère & Julia (as note 13), pp. 337-339.
15   Compère & Julia (as note 13), pp. 206-209 & 487-488.
16   Goldmann (as note 10), *passim*.

Oxford and Cambridge.[17] The 1636 list reveals the continuities but also the shifts in his perception.

UNIVERSITIES VERSUS ILLUSTRIOUS SCHOOL

The academic landscape as designed by Voetius makes no clear distinction between universities and 'illustrious' or other higher schools. In fact, to a Protestant minister this distinction did not really matter. In the Calvinist perception of the ministry a university degree was of no real use to an ordinary minister, the service of the doctor of theology being an office in itself.[18] It was the church that judged the capability of a minister, whether educated at an institution of higher learning or not. Yet seen from the other side, not from the position of the user but from that of the university itself, the distinction was of crucial importance. Indeed, how important the distinction was and how intricate the higher education system had become, is clearly seen in the documents relating to the conflict of 1631 between the university of Leiden and the city of Amsterdam concerning the right of Amsterdam to found a proper institution of higher learning. Amsterdam won the lawsuit and it is partly the consequence of this successful plea that Utrecht could plan its own provincial university which was opened, five years later, by the solemn lecture of Gisbertus Voetius analysed in the first part of this essay.

We may recall that Leiden university had been founded in the first days of the year 1575 (January 6) by the self-styled authorities of the Northern Netherlands, by means of a charter fictitiously attributed to the legal sovereign King Philipp II of Spain, but in fact drafted and issued by the Stadtholder William of Orange together with the rebel Estates of the Provinces of Holland and Zealand.[19] Apparently the choice of Leiden was a reward for the long siege which the town had courageously sustained during the two preceding years 1573 and 1574. This is at least the interpretation the town of Leiden adhered to in later times and of which it was particularly proud. The point at issue, however, is not the location of the university but its monopoly of higher learning in Holland – and, according to a subsequent political interpretation launched by Leiden, in the whole Dutch Republic of which Holland had to be regarded the chief, indeed the head of the political body.

The foundation charter of Leiden university, drafted in Dutch, pointed out that reasons of war, religion, public finance and morality made study at

---

17 A.C. Duker, *Gisbertus Voetius*, 3 vols. Leiden 1897-1915.
18 H.H. Kuyper, *De opleiding tot den dienst des woords bij de gereformeeden*. The Hague 1891.
19 M.W. Jurriaanse, *The founding of Leyden University*. Leiden 1965. The text of the foundation charter has been published by P.C. Molhuysen (ed.), *Bronnen tot de geschiedenis der Leidsche universiteit*, vol. 1. The Hague 1913, pp. 1*-9*.

foreign universities undesirable. It created, therefore, within the city of Leiden a 'free, public school and university' ('vrye openbaere schole ende universiteyt')[20] with four faculties and the right to award doctoral and magisterial degrees. Besides, it stipulated explicitly that 'no other similar school may ever be founded and erected in Holland or Zealand'. The self-conferred graduation rights were not universally recognised in Europe until far into the seventeenth century and beyond. The recognition of the Leiden degrees by the French King Henry IV (January 1597) and Louis XIII (June 1624, 22 April 1635) solved this problem in the eyes of the Dutch law students.[21] However, the legitimacy of Leiden university was never seriously questioned among the intellectuals and administrators of the Dutch Republic, nor its location in the city of Leiden. Leiden was a prosperous industrial centre with an old history. With perhaps some 70,000 inhabitants at its zenith in the seventeenth century it was for a time the second city of the Dutch Republic.[22]

Amsterdam's position, already strong during the first years of the Revolt, was consolidated after the fall of Antwerp in 1585. With the merchants, bankers and entrepreneurs came the rhetoricians and artists, the poets and playwrights, the painters and engravers.[23] In fact, Amsterdam reinforced not only its position as the commercial capital of the United Provinces but became also the main cultural centre and the art market of the new republic. By contrast with the concentration of the traditional Latin-based scholarship at the university of Leiden, Amsterdam was the city of vernacular arts, of theatre and social life, of music and painting, of cartography, navigation and other technical skills. As early as August 1617 private initiative had founded at Amsterdam a 'Nederduytsche Academie' (Low German Academy) that aimed at public instruction in arts and sciences seen as useful for citizenship: instruction in Hebrew (by Johannes Antonides),[24] history, mathematics, navigation (by Sybrand Cardinael)[25] and astronomy was given in Dutch, not Latin.[26] However, except for the two Latin schools (grammar

20 Molhuysen (as note 19), p. 8*.
21 G.N.P. Hasselaer, *Dissertatio inauguralis de jruibus quibusdam singularibus Academiae Lugduno-Batavae*. Leiden 1776, pp. 12-18.
22 N.W. Posthumus, *Geschiedenis van de Leidsche lakenindustrie*. The Hague 1939, vol. 3, pp. 882, 1038, 1097-1200.
23 Deric Regin, *Traders, artists, burghers. A cultural history of Amsterdam in the seventeenth century*. Assen/Amsterdam 1976, on the Athenaeum: pp. 78-81; Henry Méchoulan, *Amsterdam au temps de Spinoza. Argent et liberté*. Paris 1990.
24 H.F. Wijnman, 'De Hebraicus Jan Theunisz. Barbarossa alias Johannes Antonides als lector in het Arabisch aan de Leidse universiteit (1612-1613). Een hoofdstuk Amsterdamse geleerdengeschiedenis' in *Studia Rosenthaliana*, 2, 1968, pp. 149-177.
25 On the teaching of navigation at Amsterdam, C.A. Davids, *Zeewezen en wetenschap. De wetenschap en de ontwikkeling van de navigatietechniek in Nederland tussen 1585 en 1815*. Amsterdam/Dieren 1986, p. 314.
26 H. Brugmans, 'De voorgeschiedenis van het Athenaeum' in H. Brugmans (ed.), *Gedenk-*

schools), there was no chartered institution of public education at a higher level in the town. The lack of such an institution was clearly considered a deficiency in the rapidly growing metropolis that reached 125,000 inhabitants around 1630 and virtually doubled this figure some decades later.[27] The big Dutch cities were not normally against the foundation of a university within their walls, as was the case in some other countries. On the contrary, a university or 'illustrious' school seems to have been considered a normal city institute in the Dutch Republic, and all the major cities made some effort to obtain such an institution. Leeuwarden, the capital of Friesland, even tried on several occasions to achieve the transfer of the provincial university that had been inaugurated at Franeker in 1585.[28]

In 1629 the city council of Amsterdam discussed the project to found at the city's expense a scholarly institution at a higher level than that of the existing grammar schools.[29] Apart from the prestige such a higher school would confer, the council advanced expressly two arguments of a practical nature: upon completion of their course at the grammar schools the pupils had not been sufficiently instructed in the principles of philosophy to embark upon an academic education. Secondly, they were frequently of an age (roughly between 15 and 18, as may be inferred from the matriculation registers at Leiden) that rendered it undesirable that they should be removed from parental control and abandoned to the rough environment of a university town abroad. This moral motive was in fact a common, indeed a stereotype argument in support of the foundation of new universities. Ironically, fifty years earlier the Estates of Holland had advanced the same motive to legitimate the foundation of Leiden university. The *privilegium fori*, that is, the privilege of its own jurisdiction, which the university of Leiden had obtained from the stadtholder as early as 2 June 1575, guaranteed not only the immunity of the university's *suppositi* from the regular jurisdictions, it also permitted, at least in theory, a closer control of student behaviour.[30]

boek van het Athenaeum en de Universiteit van Amsterdam 1632-1932. Amsterdam 1932, pp. 13-22; H.F. Wijnman, 'De beoefening der wetenschappen te Amsterdam vóór de oprichting van hat Athenaeum in 1632' in A.E. d'Ailly (ed.), *Zeven eeuwen Amsterdam*. Amsterdam 1947, vol. 2, pp. 435-461.

27 Hubert Nusteling, *Welvaart en werkgelegenheid in Amsterdam 1540-1860*. Amsterdam/Dieren 1985.

28 On urban rivalry with regard to university foundations in the Dutch Republic see: W. Frijhoff, 'Hooger onderwijs als inzet van stedelijke naijver in de vroegmoderne tijd' in P.B.M. Blaas & I. van Herwaarden (eds.), *Stelelijke naijver. De betekenis van interstedelijke conflicten in de geschiedenis. Enige beschouwingen en case-studies*. The Hague 1986, pp. 82-127.

29 For the Proceedings of the City Council see: Chr. L. Heesakker, 'Foundation and early development in the Athenaeum illustre at Amsterdam' in *Lias*, IX, 1, 1982, pp. 1-18.

30 P.C. Molhuysen, *De voorrechten der Leidsche universiteit*. Amsterdam 1924; on the activities of the university courts see: C.M. Ridderikhoff, 'De Franequer Los-Kop' in G. Th.

In fact, the University of Leiden, where at that time the proud and bellicose nobility of the German Empire, Poland, Scandinavia and even remoter countries congregated, always with a numerous train of armed servants (up to fifteen or twenty men in certain cases), had in recent years been the theatre of repeated student unrest. Understandably, the Amsterdam burghers were afraid that their offspring would be contaminated, although the assimilation of the standards of public conduct of the foreign aristocracy was precisely one of the aims of the grand tour of numerous Dutch burgher sons.[31] As Gerardus Johannes Vossius – one of the two chosen professors for the new college – wrote in the summer of 1631 to Archbishop William Laud, several students had been wounded at Leiden during the last months and a student from a high-born family in Zealand had recently been killed. He added that the specific problem of Leiden University was the absence of colleges: the students had to rent rooms in the houses of craftsmen ('apud cerdones') or, since Leiden was important for its woollen trade, in the houses of labourers, 'quos imperium exerceant ipsi, unde fit, ut nocte bene poli per plateas grassentur, non sine periculo et suo et alieno',[32] in other words, they terrorised the townspeople with their nightly debauchery.

The other argument, namely that of the inadequate preparation of the pupils for the university, does not sound very convincing, though it appears to have been a fairly widespread opinion at the time that *gymnasia* and 'illustrious' schools supplied better basic instruction than the fully-fledged universities. That was for example the opinion expressed in 1634 by the Harderwijk professor of theology Henricus van Diest: 'pro fundamentis vere jecendis potius Gymnasium quam Academiam eligeram', emphasizing the usefulness for young theologians of *peregrinatio academica* which involved attending several institutions.[33] In fact, the Amsterdam City Council's argument cast doubt upon the education given at the 'trivial' (grammar) schools. Yet only four years earlier, in 1625, the Estates of Holland had adopted a new school regulation for the grammar schools of the whole province. It prescribed very precisely what subjects had to be taught, in what way, and what books had to be used in the different classes from the *sexta* to the *prima* (or

---

Jensma, F.R.H. Smit & F. Westra (eds.), *Universiteit te Franeker 1585-1811. Bijdragen tot de geschiedenis van de Friese hogeschool.* Leeuwarden 1985, pp. 119-132; Marc Wingens, 'Deviant gedrag van studenten: verkrachters in de 17e en 18e eeuw' in *Batavia academica* VI/1, 1988, pp. 9-26 and Marc Wingens, 'Zur Vermeidung der Schande: Organisation und strafrechtliche Tätigkeit der Universitätsgerichte in der Republik der Niederlande (1575-1811)' in Heinz Mohnhaupt & Dieter Simon (eds.), *Vorträge zur Justizforschung: Geschichte und Theorie*, vol. I. Frankfurt-am-Main 1992, pp. 79-101.

31 A. Frank van Westrienen, *De Groote Tour. Tekening van de educatiereis de Nederlanders in de zeventiende eeuw.* Amsterdam 1983, chapter 6.
32 Paulus Colomesius (ed.), *Gerardi Joan Vossii et clarorum virorum ad eum epistolae.* London 1690, vol. 1, pp. 172-173.
33 Henricus van Diest, *De ratione studii theologiae.* Harderwijk 1634.

from the *octava* to the *tertia*, following the old numbering). The elementary skills (reading, writing, arithmetic) were supposed to have been achieved at the elementary school, the Latin school included rhetoric and some rudiments of logic, at any rate enough to start a normal university course.[34]

As a matter of fact, the city council's concern was not so much to educate adequately the young people as to provide the citizens with a centre of learning for all cultivated burghers. The new higher school of Amsterdam had to be a local instrument of civic culture (of civility), not an alternative to the university, which must of necessity be organized at a more comprehensive level and must recruit on a national scale. The famous title of Caspar Barlaeus's lecture, given at the inauguration of the Amsterdam 'illustrious' school in the first days of 1632, is quite eloquent in this respect: *Mercator sapiens*, the educated merchant.[35] Still more eloquent is Barlaeus's colleague, Vossius, in another of his letters to Archbishop Laud: Among the people from all the countries of the Christian world who come together at Amsterdam there are men 'egregiae eruditionis ... vel saltem doctrina paramentes. Horum igitur omnium votum fuit, ut et ipsi audire quotidie aliquem possint, qui vel antiquitates gentium, aut naturae arcana pandat'.[36]

Some weeks later, on 12 February 1631, he explained to the exiled Hugo Grotius (who was soon to be considered the most suitable candidate for a chair at Amsterdam) the exact difference between the university of Leiden and the planned 'illustrious' school: 'Aliud esse Academiam statuere, quam ad rem opus sit privilegiis et immunitatibus a suprema potestate concessis, aliud autem gymnasium erigere, in quo juventus et alii Musarum amantes, absque eiusmodi privilegiis, liberaliter imbuantur doctrina: quale jus penes singulas esse civitates';[37] in other words, the foundation of a chartered university with immunities and privileges was a sovereign right, quite different from the normal duty of every city to institute public lectures for the adequate education of the young and the instruction of the city's adult population. This new conception of a higher school as a civic enterprise for the explicit purpose of promoting civic culture and not merely to educate the youth, was not particular to Amsterdam. The same concern is found in Middelburg in Zealand, where merchants ('movitatis studiosi mercatores') were found among those who attended the public lectures held at the abbey church in the city centre.[38]

---

34 E.J. Kuiper, De Hollandse 'schoolordre' van 1625. *Een studie over het onderwijs op de Latijnse scholen in Nederland in de 17de en 18de eeuw*. Groningen 1958.
35 Caspar Barlaeus, *Mercator sapiens, sive oratio de conjungendis mercaturae et philosophiae studiis*. Amsterdam 1632; new ed. 1967.
36 Colomesius (as note 32), p. 168 (12 January 1631).
37 Colomesius (as note 32), pp. 173-175, quotation p. 174.
38 W. Frijhoff, 'Zeelands universiteit: hoe vaak het mislukte, en waarom' in *Archief, medelingen van het Koninklijk Zeeuwsch Genootschap der Wetenschappen*. 1987, pp. 7-41, footnote 66.

In fact, Amsterdam was not the first expanding metropolis to experience the need for other types of higher education, more closely linked to the realities of public life, the new ideals of a commercial society and the service of the modern state. As early as 1572, Sir Humphrey Gilbert had pointed out in his *Queene Elizabethe's Achademy* that England needed such institutions for a more adequate service of the state.[39] Marischal College at Aberdeen had been founded in 1593 as a rival to King's College for people who wished to learn new disciplines: chairs in Hebrew, Syriac, physiology, anatomy, astronomy, geography, history, moral philosophy and other matters made up for the deficiencies of traditional learning.[40] In 1612 Sir George Buck referred to the City of London as 'the thirde universitie of England', indeed a university where all arts and sciences could be learned or assimilated.[41] In his view, the Inns of Court, schools providing a more practical training in law but also a more general culture, were the most outstanding colleges of the capital. In the meantime Gresham College had been opened in London under the administration of the Mercers' Company and the Common Council of the City (1596). Lectures in the seven liberal arts were given in English, and Gresham College became a serious competitor to the traditional arts curriculum provided by Oxford and Cambridge. Since the students would be merchants and other common citizens, the lecturer was reminded not to read 'after the manner of the universities' but to 'cull out such heads of his subject as may best serve the good liking and capacity of the said auditory'.[42] However, the old universities adhered to their monopoly to award degrees.

The Amsterdam initiative seems to be the product of the importance of modern culture for the citizens. On the last day of 1629 (31 December) the city council of Amsterdam took the decision to look for a competent person to give lessons in philosophy and history. In fact, the negotiations were started with two famous scholars, Caspar Barlaeus (rhetoric) and Gerardus Johannes Vossius (eloquence) both professors of philosophy at – of all places – Leiden university. They accepted the proposal, but after the disclosure of their intentions they were confronted with an angry Leiden senate afraid of an intellectual haemorrhage. The concern of the Leiden senate was not without foundation: in recent years Leiden had lost the famous theologian Franciscus Gomarus, the godfather of orthodox Calvinism, to the 'illustrious' school of Middelburg and Johannes Meursius, professor of Greek language and history, to Sorø Academy in Denmark. Clearly, institutions of this type could entice famous scholars away from their old universities to alternatives

---

39 Joan Simon, *Education and Society in Tudor England*. Cambridge 1966, pp. 341-343; John M. Fletcher (as note 5), pp. 18-19.
40 Lubor J'lek (ed.), *Historical Compendium of European Universities*. Geneva 1984, p. 76.
41 Lubor J'lek (as note 40), p. 19.
42 Quoted after Joan Simon (as note 39), p. 388.

of the old universities. Moreover, on 2 June 1630 the Swiss Protestant academies, churches and clergy of Zurich, Bern, Basel, Schaffhausen and Geneva expressed in a public letter their concern that the 'new Amsterdam Academy' was likely to be a hotbed of Arminianism.[43] This accusation, still dangerous in the aftermath of the Synod of Dordrecht (1618-1619) and inspired, if not dictated, by a Dutch ghost-writer, may explain some of the secrecy with which the Amsterdam city council proceeded. The candidates who were approached to fill the chairs were indeed representatives of the Remonstrant faction, although it was never the purpose of the city council to establish a theological school at Amsterdam.

Only after the final decision had been taken at Amsterdam, in the last days of 1630, and the two newly appointed Amsterdam professors had notified the Leiden Senate of their imminent departure did Leiden take action. On 9 March 1631, the Academic senate decided to start a lawsuit against Amsterdam.[44] Some weeks later, however, the board of administrators of the university, less bellicose, proposed a compromise. Amsterdam could be allowed to found a school of history and philosophy outside the 'trivial' school, provided it was not called university, academy or high school ('hoge school') and that no public lectures were given, with the exception of some customary academic ceremonies of a purely symbolic nature.[45] According to this proposal the new school could only use such names as *acroama, auditorium* etc., that is, names referring to a space not an institution. This was unacceptable to Amsterdam. A teaching institution in the country's major city had to enjoy the prestige of a public school. On 6 June 1631 the conflict between Leiden and Amsterdam came before the Court of Holland and Zealand. At the request of the Estates both parties agreed to a short procedure. The memoranda and statements of the lawyers teach us a great deal about the self-perception of a university at that very moment and the institutional relations within the educational network.

To begin with, Leiden asked, on 13 June, for the immediate prohibition of all public higher instruction at Amsterdam.[46] Its foundation charter had stipulated, according to Leiden university, that 'no similar school may ever be founded in Holland and Zealand'. To the Leiden senate this implied an embargo on all higher instruction outside Leiden in these provinces, not only

---

43 *Missive van de Leerars ende Professoren der Ghereformeerde Kercken, Academien, ende Hooghe Scholen, der vier Steden in Switserland, als namentlijck Zurich, Bern, Basel, ende Schafhuysen, mitsgaders by die van Geneven, ghescreven aen de EES Heeren Professoren der H. Theologie tot Leyden.* s.l. 1630 [Royal Library, The Hague, Pamflet 4057]; H. Brugmans 'De stichting' in H. Brugmans (as note 26), pp. 23-32.
44 P.C. Molhuysen (as note 19), vol. 2, 1916, pp. 159-160. All the documents related to this conflict have been published by P.C. Molhuysen in vol. 2, pp. 153-164, 214*-289*.
45 P.C. Molhuysen (as note 19), vol. 2, p. 155 (6 April 1631).
46 P.C. Molhuysen (as note 19), vol. 2, p. 216*-219*.

on the university courses leading to degrees but on all public lectures. Leiden furthermore invoked the school regulations issued by the Estates of Holland in 1625. Indeed, this document prohibited all forms of 'trivial' instruction outside the lawfully founded and formally recognised Latin schools. Of course, the Estates had implicitly meant to put a ban on Catholic and Remonstrant (Armenian or even Socinian) schools and schoolmasters; the latter were rather common in the educated circles imbued with Christian humanism from which such schoolmasters were drawn; the Estates had not intended to prohibit civic initiatives as such. Yet, the prohibition could be extended in that sense. Arguing in favour of such an extension Leiden reduced higher education to a formal two-step system organized in two different, chartered or at least formally founded institutions: the Latin schools of the towns, clearly separated from but immediately followed by the university of the province, where not only higher instruction in arts and for the professions was given but also the intermediate level of propedeutics was provided. There was no place in this conception for autonomous intermediate forms of learning or for alternatives.

Amsterdam replied with a long document in which all the arguments presented by Leiden University were closely scrutinized.[47] In the first articles it launched an implicit attack on Leiden's appeal to the Estates of Holland's decision, challenging the assumption that sovereignty was vested in the Estates instead of the local authorities, as some law students argued.[48] The lawful Christian authorities, Amsterdam claimed, had been made 'custodes utriusque tabulae' by God himself. They had to provide everything that contributed to the welfare of its subjects. Nobody had the right to obstruct the authority in this essential care for the church and the whole Republic. Since public law admitted that cities had the duty to organize elementary and 'trivial' teaching of the young, they also had the right to continue the teaching of those who had progressed in the humanities, all the more so since the pupils were not yet mature enough to leave home for an uncontrolled and autonomous life in a university town replete with moral dangers. The planned courses in philosophy and history were thus – though not entirely in conformity with the real intentions of the magistrate – presented by the city council as a continuation of the 'trivial' school, of which they formed a superstructure of the kind the Sturmian formula had initiated at Stras-

---

47 P.C. Molhuysen (as note 19), vol. 2, pp. 219*-229*.
48 On the sovereignty of the Provincial Estates see: Theo Veen,'Van Vranck tot Kluit. Theorieën over de legitimatie van de soevereiniteit der Staten Provinciaal (1587-1795) 'in Ph. H. Breuker & M. Zeeman (eds.), *Freonen om Ds. J.J. Kalma hinne*. Ljouwert 1982, pp. 302-324. More generally on the sovereignty claims of the provinces and cities: J.V. Rijpperda Wierdsma, *Politie en justitie. Een studie over Hollandschen staatsbuouw tijdens de Republiek*. Zwolle 1937; J.L. Price, *Holland and the Dutch Republic in the Seventeenth Century. The Politics of Particularism*. Oxford 1994.

bourg.⁴⁹ Amsterdam might also have referred to the schools of the modern devotion at Zwolle, under its headmaster Johan Cele, and somewhat later at Deventer, under Alexander Hegius, the class system of which largely overlapped the arts faculty of the nearby universities; these schools were in fact the origin of the *modus parisiensis*.⁵⁰ The intermediate structure proposed by Amsterdam had, therefore, a threefold purpose: moral control, better instruction and lower costs to the parents, not to mention its added value for a flourishing civic culture.

A second series of arguments advanced by Amsterdam concerned the instruction itself. First of all, Amsterdam rejected the argument that the school regulation of 1625 prohibited any higher education outside Leiden. On the contrary, according to the school programme fixed by the Estates themselves, in the last half (i.e. the highest order) of the first class (that is, 'the highest' class, the *prima*) courses should be provided on physics (Magirus), ethics (Walaeus), arithmetics (Gemma Frisius), natural philosophy and geography (Sphaera Sacrobosci, Mela, Dodonaeus, Ortelius), Roman and universal history (Florus, Justinus and Sculpicius Severus). Amsterdam advanced the proposition that that was exactly what the two professors Vossius and Barlaeus had been recruited to teach; it is also quite clear that the representatives of the city council knew that such a proposition was far from the truth. At any rate, Leiden had nothing to fear from Amsterdam with regard to the faculty system: philosophy and history were not commonly called 'faculties', and Amsterdam did not claim any of the real faculties, i.e. theology, law and medicine (art. 66).

The third argument attacked Leiden's interpretation of its monopoly position, the socalled *privilegium exclusivum*. The foundation charter, Amsterdam argued, stipulated that no similar school should ever be founded. But what was the meaning of similar? Amsterdam insisted: 'Our school is not one hundredth part similar to the university of Leiden'; it was only a signpost ('wechwijser') to such a higher school as intended by the foundation charter of Leiden (art. 79-80). Besides, the Amsterdam lawyer Luchtenberg put forward the view that the Dutch language did not make any distinction between the terms university and high school ('een universiteyt ende een hooge schoole', art. 98). Both described the same institution; and if there were such a distinction, Leiden should have complained earlier, because in the past it never opposed the establishment of public lectures in two cities, Dordrecht and Middelburg, under the jurisdiction of the *privilegium exclusivum*.⁵¹ In the

---

49 Anton Schindling, Humanistische *Hochschule und Freie Reichsstadt: Gymnasium und Akademie in Straßburg, 1538-1621*. Wiesbaden 1977.
50 G. Codina Mir, *Aux sources de la pédagogie des Jesuites: le 'modus parisiensis'*. Rome 1968.
51 The same argument, namely that Leiden should have prevented the creation of 'illustrious' schools at Dordrecht, Middelburg and Amsterdam, resurfaces a century later, in 1757,

first instance at Dordrecht in the province of Holland, Nansius had given a series of public lectures in Greek, and then Adrianus Marcellus and Johannes Polyander (in 1630 a professor at Leiden!) had taught philosophy there (art. 146-147). In fact, a formal 'illustrious' school was erected at Dordrecht at the conclusion of the conflict under review, in 1636.[52] Secondly, at Middelburg in Zealand as early as 1595 public lectures were instituted on philosophy (by the Scotsman John Murdisson), on history (by Jacobus Groterus) and on theology (by Joannes Isenbach); Antonius Walaeus (at that moment a professor at Leiden) simultaneously taught ethics and physics in Middelburg in 1607; and a formal theological college was erected in 1611 with the help of the theologian Franciscus Gomarus, who for religious reasons left his Leiden chair in order to teach at the rival institution (art. 140-144).[53] In any case, Amsterdam did not wish to found such a higher school but only to provide for some public lectures, as was the privilege of every *magistratus politicus* to do. Friesland provided a clear example of such a solution, since the provincial university at Franeker did not prohibit the public lectures held at the province's capital Leeuwarden, two miles away, by Hermannus Renecherus (this was a dubious example indeed, since Renecherus had left Leeuwarden before the foundation of the University of Franeker) and Dr Nicolaus Mulerius, physician, headmaster of the Latin school and lecturer in Greek and Philosophy at Leeuwarden before his appointment to the new University of Groningen in 1614 (art. 138).

In support of this crucial argument the Amsterdam lawyer had collected a file of historical examples showing such a local juxtaposition of a fullyfledged university and public lectures held outside the university. He drew his examples from all over Christendom, beginning with Italy, where the public *gymnasium* of Venice (a reference to the college or to the rather dubious medical faculty created by the corporation of physicians in 1470 as an examining body?)[54] was tolerated notwithstanding the monopoly conferred upon the University of Padua by the signoria itself. Similarly at Rome (the Collegio Romano!), at Naples and in other cities, where, in spite of the existence of universities, public lectures and even disputations 'de omni re scibili' were given by individual scholars (art. 125-129). The same applied to the Southern Netherlands, where Louvain University suffered the existence

---

in the lawsuit between Leiden University and the City Council of Zealand where a fullyfledged university was to be founded according to the last will of Burgomaster Pieter Mogge (d.1756) who had left 420,000 guilders for that purpose. The documents are conserved in the Archives of the Leiden senate (University Library of Leiden), no. 522; see also Frijhoff (as note 28), pp. 120-127.
52 G.D.J. Schotel, *De illustre school te Dordrecht*. Utrecht 1857.
53 W. Frijhoff (as note 38), p. 9.
54 Richard Palmer, *The 'Studio' of Venice and its Graduates in the Sixteenth Century*. Trieste/Padova 1983.

of a public school at Antwerp (art. 136). Here the lawyer was apparently thinking of the Jesuit College in that town. It had an excellent reputation in Holland. Catholic parents frequently sent their sons to Antwerp in order that they should get the necessary education preparing them for further study at the University of Louvain. In France the colleges, gymnasia academica ('collèges de plain exercise'?) and seminaries were numerous, the lawyer argued, even in university towns like Paris, Toulouse and Valence. The same was the case at Oxford and Cambridge, where public lectures were held in many colleges. Here, however, the lawyer revealed his ignorance of the collegiate university formula. He did not realize that in Paris, Oxford and Cambridge the teaching colleges were founded within the university, or at least incorporated into it.

Better examples could be found in Germany, but evidently the lawyer's knowledge was mostly based on hearsay, not on any close scrutiny of documents. It is nevertheless interesting to note his observations, since they give us a fair idea of the common knowledge an ordinary Dutch student had of universities. He listed the following colleges for Germany: Bremen, Danzig (Gdansk), Herborn, Siegen, Hamburg, Cologne, Ingolstadt, Altdorf, Neustadt (an der Haardt), Düsseldorf, Dortmund and Wesel (art. 125). The point at issue in the lawyer's demonstration is not quite clear. Seemingly he wished to show that *gymnasia academica* did coexist with universities. This may have been the case in Cologne, where the famous *Gymnasium Tricoronatum*, run by the Jesuits, had, however, been incorporated into the university as early as 1556. Three institutions on the list were in fact fully-fledged universities: Cologne, Ingolstadt and Altdorf. We may add Neustadt, where the university of Heidelberg had been established in 1576-1583. Since many Calvinists went to study there, it may be considered a 'university in memory', although only a *gymnasium academicum* survived. All the other institutions listed by the lawyer were lawfully established *gymnasia academica* or 'illustrious' schools of the type Amsterdam planned to found and mostly of Calvinist orientation, but not in juxtaposition to a territorial university (*Landesuniversität*). They represent indeed the institutions of higher learning in the immediate vicinity of the Dutch Republic or frequented by Dutch students. As such they offer an example of the intellectual horizon of a cultivated Dutch citizen: not the world, but his country and its immediate surroundings.

Leiden presented its counter-plea a month later.[55] Of course, some errors in the Amsterdam lawyer's document were painstakingly dismantled. Besides, Leiden argued, the examples quoted by Amsterdam never concerned privileged institutions. In particular, Leiden pointed out that the Jesuits' claim to the right to found fully-fledged universities or even colleges next to existing universities had never materialised despite the pope's own privileges. The

---

55   P.C. Molhuysen, (as note 19), vol. 2, pp. 229*-241*.

Leiden lawyer was referring to some recent examples of Jesuit foundations intended as institutions of higher education which had failed to be realized as such due to the intervention of universities claiming their *privilegium exclusivum*: for example, at Cracow in Poland (1622), at Pontoise and later at Sens (under the jurisdiction of Paris University, 1614). At Tournon an attempt to create a fully-fledged Jesuit University in 1623 was successfully opposed by Valence, Toulouse and Cahors,[56] whereas the extension of the Jesuit colleges of Liège and Louvain as theological schools was prevented in 1612 and 1624 respectively by the University of Louvain.[57] This especially well documented case, extensively treated by Leiden and Amsterdam, conveys some of the impact which the Jesuit educational offensive had had during the first quarter of the seventeenth century, even in predominantly Protestant countries. It testifies also to the general feeling of uncertainty about the status and structure of university and semi-university level institutions.

Finally, two new arguments put forward by Leiden deserve our attention. The first is of a social character. Leiden argued that there was no need for an intermediate level of instruction since the 'trivial' school had always produced excellent ministers, administrators and judges (art. 18). This means that in the perception of the university itself, higher learning was not essential to enter the service of church and state. The lemma 'seminarium Ecclesiae ac Reipublicae' corresponding to these goals and frequently applied to the university, seems therefore more suitably applied to the lower level, i.e. that of the Latin schools. It was indeed commonly used for Latin schools throughout the Dutch Republic. With this sentence the university purposely profiled itself as a professional institution for lawyers and physicians in search of specialised knowledge and a degree, perhaps also for those aspiring to a doctor's degree in divinity and other learned scholars, but not for the common minister and the bulk of those looking for some applied knowledge or general education. The latter had to be provided by the grammar schools at the lower level for which the 1625 regulation had fixed a programme that would satisfy the normal needs of society at large. Thus, the conflict persuaded Leiden not only to advance a less ambiguous definition of its own goals, but also a distinction between two levels of knowledge: applied knowledge and true learning. Only the latter pertained to the university's mission. (Humboldt was not far off.)

The other interesting point concerned terminology. Leiden revised its previous sharp distinction between Latin schools and universities. It intro-

---

56 See the bibliography in Simone Guenée, *Bibliographie de l'Histoire des Universités françaises des origines à la Révolution*, vol. 2. Paris 1978, pp. 456-458. For a Dutch echo of this famous lawsuit: Nicolaes à Wassenaer, *Historisch verhael aller gedenckwaerdiger geschiedenissen*, XIII. Amsterdam 1629, p. 2.

57 F. Claeys Bouuaert, *Lancienne Université de Louvain, Études et documents*. Louvain 1956, pp. 128-154.

duced the notion of a 'higher school' ('hooge schoole') which, it claimed, was not the same as a university. It was a university level institution in that it provided public lectures in arts, but the difference between a university and a higher school is that universities are assumed to teach the whole range of arts and sciences whereas the higher schools teach only some of the arts and sciences. Examples of such higher schools were easy to find: nearby Harderwijk in Gelderland (which, in fact, had chairs in four faculties)[58] and Herborn in Germany, attended by many Dutch Calvinists.[59] Therefore, higher schools were not to be considered intermediate institutions with a propedeutic goal, as Amsterdam claimed, rather they were autonomous, non-privileged schools of the *studium particulare* type. The implicit message was, of course, that they should not act as a substitute for lower levels of university education.

At this point the discussion loses its interest, for Leiden had admitted in principle the correctness of the point made by Amsterdam, that is, the lawfulness of *alternative* forms of university level education. This compromise was acceptable to all concerned, provided that no attempt be made by the Amsterdam *Athenaeum* to substitute itself for Leiden university. It was not surprising that the court of Holland and Zealand on 22 December 1631, without formally permitting the foundation of an 'illustrious' school at Amsterdam (which could have been seen as contrary to the Leiden foundation charter), denied the University of Leiden the right to resist the 'foundation and realization of public lectures in philosophy and history' within the city of Amsterdam.[60] Through this debate the court must have realized that the academic landscape had gained new contours due to the new social needs and cultural requirements of the rising social strata and the new power relations; that instruction was not quite the same as learning; that learning should not be restricted to academics and professionals; that the 'republic of letters' would have to cope more and more with local forms of civic culture; that new sciences could be developed and promoted outside the university before being incorporated into the university's teaching system; that ancient and new forms of knowledge transfer could very well coexist; that burghers of a town could have interests other than those of citizens of a state; and that the state in conserving the principle of a single university in a single state, did not necessarily have to prohibit all other forms of learned communication and cultural transfer; in brief, that there were always legitimate alternatives to *greedy institutions* like universities.

---

58 M. Evers, 'The Illustre School at Harderwijk 1600-1647' in *Lias*, XII/1, 1985, pp. 81-113.
59 Gerhard Menk, *Die Hohe Schule Herborn in ihrer Frühzeit (1584-1660). Ein Beitrag zum Hochschulwesen des deutschen Kalvinismus im Zeitalter der Gegenreformation*. Wiesbaden 1981.
60 P.C. Molhuysen (as note 19), vol. 2, p. 287*.

Educational politics in the Austrian lands and the foundation of the Jesuit university of Graz, 1585*

Gernot Heiss

The founding of Latin schools, academies and universities in the early modern period is in two specific ways connected with the process of the formation of territorial states: in the first instance, the emerging territorial states required for their governmental and administrative purposes an ever increasing number of appropriately educated noble and bourgeois officials. Secondly, the sons of local families, for economic but especially for political reasons, were to stay in the country in order to be educated under the control of the state to become useful, dependable and patriotic subjects. For the development of schooling in Lower and Inner Austria (i.e. Austria below and above the River Enns, Styria, Carinthia and Carniola) these two aspirations were just as important as they were for other parts of Europe. However, what characterised these Habsburg hereditary lands more specifically – in contrast to other territories of the Holy Roman Empire – was the significance of political and 'confessional' conflict between the Estates and the territorial prince. This antagonism had a marked impact on the development of higher schools.

In Lower and Inner Austria in the second half of the sixteenth century the predominant section of the nobility of the Estates adhered to the Augsburg Confession although the territorial overlord was a Roman Catholic. The otherwise powerful Habsburg dynasty had found it impossible in these regions to determine the confession of its subjects. At the same time many German territorial princes – at the very latest as a result of the *cuius regio eius religio* principle adopted by the Augsburg Religious Peace of 1555 – had been highly successful in making their own confession that of their subjects as part of their claim to absolute authority over their centralising territorial

* An expanded and slightly altered version of this paper is scheduled to appear in German (and Czeck translation) under the title: 'Von der Autonomie zur stattlichen Kontrolle? Die Wiener und die Grazer Universität im 16. Jahrhundert' in Helmuth Grössing (ed.), *Probleme der Wissenschaftsgeschichte*. Vienna 1998 (= Wiener Beiträge zur Geschichte der Neuzeit 23).

state. The difference existed depite the fact that the legal and bureaucratic structural preconditions for a '*Verdichtung der Staatlichkeit*' were by no means less favourable in these parts of Austria than elsewhere; in some respects they may even be considered more favourable than in those areas where confessional absolutism could develop virtually unhindered in the sixteenth century.[1]

However, there were several other reasons why the Habsburg lands should have undergone such a retarded and slowed down development towards absolutism. The Habsburgs believed, at least until 1576, that they had to show some consideration for their own imperial policy framework within which they tried their best to achieve confessional unity by an agreement between the conflicting religious parties. Furthermore, the Habsburg rulers, as territorial lords, decided to humour the Estates who refused to contribute to the war effort unless religious and political concessions were made to them. In the precarious geo-political situation at the borders of the Empire close to the sphere of Ottoman influence they did not, even in the 1580s, dare to ignore the threatening posture of the Estates even though the role which the territorial Estates played in the territorial defence – a role that had since the fifteenth century enhanced their self confidence as Estates – rendered it quite absurd to voice such a threat. Guided by such political considerations, the Habsburgs granted the nobility of these regions for themselves and their subjects the right of free practice of the Augsburg Confession in 1568/1578. It is also essential to remember that the proximity of the somewhat refractory Bohemian and Hungarian Estates resulted in an upgrading of the Austrian Estates on several occasions from the twenties of the sixteenth century until the beginning of the Thirty Years' War.[2]

The confessional divergence was throughout essentially a political issue, although the potential to become explosive varied somewhat. The conflict intensified when the Habsburgs, as emperors, gave up their attempts to mediate between the Christian confessions. From then on they tried to enforce the Roman Catholic religion in their territories with considerable pressure. They interpreted every deviation of a subject in matters of religion

---

1 For a discussion of the separate development of the Babenberg/Habsburg lands since the Privilegium Minus of 1156 see Othmar Hageneder, 'Der Landbegriff bei Otto Brunner' in *Annali dell'Instituto storico italo-germanico in Trento – Jahrbuch des italienisch-deutschen historischen Istituts in Trient* 13, 1987, pp. 154-161.

2 In greater detail: Hans Sturmberger, 'Dualistischer Ständestaat und werdender Absolutismus' in *Die Entwicklung der Verfassung Oesterreichs vom Mittelalter bis zur Gegenwart*. Vienna 1963, pp. 24-49, especially pp. 31f. See also Herbert Hassinger, 'Ständische Vertretungen in althabsburgischen Ländern und in Salzburg' in Dietrich Gerhard (ed.), *Ständische Vertretungen in Europa im 17. und 18. Jahrhundert*. Göttinen 1969, pp. 245-285.

as resistance to princely authority. This corresponded to a general intensification of conflict between confessions.³

The political and confessional divergence of positions prompted the establishment of a dual administration: the bureaucracy of the princes promoting absolutist centralisation and the administration of the Estates of the individual regions.⁴ The magnificent buildings of the Estates in Graz, Linz and Klagenfurt remind us to this day of such activities of the Estates. In the same way as the territorial prince concerned himself with the organisation of the Post-Tridentine Roman Catholic Territorial Church, so also the Protestant Estates tried to establish Protestant territorial churches. And both parties promoted, in opposition to each other, their own schooling in order to satisfy the need for reliable officialdom in terms of religion and politics to serve the institutionalised churches of the two confessions. In what follows, the plans and attempts to assign to the Jesuits – even in the first decade of their presence in Austria – the reform of the University of Vienna, as well as the development of the school of the Protestant nobility in Graz and the founding of the University of Graz, are to serve as examples which characterise this early modern educational development in the context of the particular political conditions of the region.

I THE SUMMONING OF THE JESUITS AND THE REFORM OF THE UNIVERSITY OF VIENNA: TOWARDS A CATHOLIC TERRITORIAL UNIVERSITY

As early as the 1520s Roman Catholics attributed the successes of Protestants to the influence of Protestant printed tracts as well as to the popularity of their preachers, and conversely, to the lack of capable well-educated Catholic clergy. The traditional ecclesiastically directed education system had totally broken down with the onset of the Reformation. Nevertheless, it was rapidly reconstructed and even extended in Protestant as well as Catholic areas, simply because of the need for well-educated priests and secular officials.⁵

---

3   Concerning the periodisation of the confessional polarisation see Heinz Schilling, 'Die Konfessionalisierung im Reich. Religiöser und gesellschaftlicher Wandel in Deutschland zwischen 1555 und 1620' in *Historische Zeitschrift* 246, 1988, pp. 1-45, especially pp. 24f.
4   Against those historians who stress that the territorial lords were the exclusive prime movers in the process of the modernisation of the state, it must the stressed that, especially in the Inner Austrian development of the appropriate bureaucracy, the Estates were the driving force from the fifteenth century. This happened in the context of their organisation of the defence of the territory; cf. Winfried Schulze, *Landesdefension und Staatsbildung. Studien zum Kriegswesen des inneroesterreichischen Territorialstaates*. Vienna-Graz-Cologne 1973, *passim*.
5   In the years between 1450 and 1600 16 new universities were successfully founded in the German speaking area: Greifswald (1456), Freiburg im Breisgau (1457), Basel (1460),

Much more difficult to solve were the problems of the central European regions of the Habsburg lands: the University of Prague had become the educational institution for Utraquist clergy whereas the University of Vienna had been in perpetual crisis.[6] During the reign of Ferdinand I (1521-1564) several attempts were made to rescue the University of Vienna and especially to reform theological studies there. One relied largely on the following measures which were considered infallible: intensification of the overlord's influence and cleansing the institution of its Protestant teachers and students. However, such measures yielded only limited success. The students stayed away from the city which was threatened by the Turks and by pestilence,[7] and in any case, the studies offered by the university were no longer considered very attractive. Even when Ferdinand forbad his subjects to study in places other than Vienna, Freiburg-im-Breisgau or Ingolstadt,[8] and when he persuaded the Estates, in 1550, to agree to the funding of scholarships for theologians at the University of Vienna,[9] this made very little difference.[10]

The summoning of Jesuits to the University of Vienna in 1551 marked the ultimately decisive attempt to improve matters. With the help of the Jesuits in Vienna a new, learned and disciplined Catholic clergy was to be educated, and the education of secular leaders was not to be forgotten either. In addressing St Ignatius of Loyola Ferdinand I stressed the importance of inhibiting the spread of 'bad' and 'heretical' doctrine. This could be brought about by having the youth (male only, of course) educated by decidedly

---

Ingolstadt (1472), Trier (1473), Mainz (1477), Tübingen (1477), Wittenberg (1502), Frankfurt on Oder (1506), Marburg 1527), Königsberg (1544), Dillingen (1553), Jena (1558), Helmstedt (1576), Würzburg (1582), Graz (1585). The last seven of these belong to the era of the confessional confrontation; see Kurt Mühlberger, 'Zu den Krisen der Universität Wien im Zeitalter der konfessionellen Auseinandersetzungen' in *Bericht über den 18. oesterreichischen Historikertag in Linz 1990*. Vienna 1991, pp. 271f.

6 Arthur Goldmann (as note 6), pp. 1-14, and Kurt Mühlberger (as note 5), pp. 272f. cite the Turkish threat and the frequent plagues as reasons for the declining frequency of student attendance; this is obviously in addition to the Reformation and the competition of the newly founded universities.

7 Arthur Goldmann (as note 6), pp. 1-14, and Kurt Mühlberger (as note 5), pp. 272f. cite the Turkish threat and the frequent plagues as reasons for the declining frequency of student attendance; this is obviously in addition to the Reformation and the competition of the newly founded universities.

8 Decree, Ferdinand I, 5 April 1548; cf. Rudolf Kink, *Geschichte der kaiserlichen Universität zu Wien*. Vienna 1854, vol. 1, pp. 297f. and for the revocation of the decree through the intervention of the Estates see p. 300.

9 Josef Jaekel, 'Ferdinand I. und die Stipendiaten aus den Partikularschulen Oberoesterreichs 1551-1554' in *Beiträge zur oesterreichischen Erziehungs- und Schulgeschichte* 5, Vienna-Leipzig 1904, pp. 69f.

10 For matriculation figures see Franz Gall & Willy Szaivert (eds.), *Die Matrikel der Universität Wien*, vol. 3: 1518/II-1579/I. (=Publikationen des Vereins für Oesterreichische Geschichtsforschung, 6: Quellen zur Geschichte der Universität Wien, 1 Section: Die Matrikel der Universität Wien). Vienna-Cologne-Graz 1971.

Catholic men who acted as inspiring examples not only by their theological training but also by their moral purity. It was also envisaged that suitable young men should live in the College in Vienna in company with the Patres of the Society of Jesus, so that 'as from a nursery of virtues' capable men should come forth to be preachers, or, according to their inclination, pastors and ecclesiastical administrators or secular officials.[11]

In the history of the Jesuit College of Vienna, written some two decades later, we read that it was for the following reason that King Ferdinand called the Society of Jesus into the country: to prop up and support the university 'that was breaking down'.[12] However, already in the first decade of its existence the college developed from intended saviour into a dreaded rival of the university.

According to the reports sent by Jajus from Vienna Ferdinand I and those of his counsellors who were sponsors of the Jesuits declared themselves anxious to turn the college in Vienna into an institution which parallelled the arts faculty of the university, and from which confessionally reliable professors would emanate and replace the old guard at the university.[13] On 9 December 1551 Jajus wrote that there were quite competent professors of the Humanities at the University of Vienna,[14] that they taught Greek, Hebrew, philosophy,[15] medicine or law, but that some of them were suspected of heresy.

---

11 Ferdinand II to Loyola, 11 December 1550 in *Cartas de San Ignacio de Loyola*. Madrid 1875, vol. 2, pp. 548f. The same task, namely to educate spiritual and secular leaders, is also conferred upon the universities by the territorial lord; cf. Arthur Goldmann (as note 6) p. 24.

12 Historia Collegii SJ Viennensis ab anno 1550 usque ad annum 1567, auctore (secundum sententiam traditam) Laurentio Magio SJ, typescript of MSS 118.E.5 of the Monastery of Pannonhalma by Antonio Petruch SJ, f.25. For the very precise ideas see Jajus to Loyola, Vienna [21 July 1551] in *Epistolae PP. Paschasii Broeti, Claudii Jaji, Joannis Coduri et Simonis Rodericii SJ. Monumenta Historica SJ* [24]. Madrid 1903 p. 370. Firstly, in order to achieve the renewal of theological studies (including scholasticism) the Vienna Diet had set aside scholarships for theology students; secondly, the king was determined to make available before Christmas 30 scholarships for the upkeep of Jesuit scholars. The Jesuits set an example of good conduct and through them Vienna would resume the theological studies which involve 'disputations and other activities which are the practice at the University of Paris and in Spain'.

13 Polanco in the name of Loyola to Jajus, Rome, 8 August 1551 in *Monumenta de Ignatio Loyola SJ fundatoris Epistolae et Instructiones*, vols. 1-12 (=Monumenta Historica SJ [22, 26, 28, 29, 31, 34, 36, 37, 39, 40, 42], Madrid 1903-1911, serie I vol. 3, pp. 602-605. There is also to be found a record of the intention that the Jesuits should build up a course from the beginning of Latin studies to the higher faculty of Theology.

14 The Jesuits counted among these: Grammar, History and Poetry as well as Rhetoric, see Karl Hengst, *Jesuiten an Universitäten und Jesuitenuniversitäten. Zur Geschichte der Universitäten in der Oberdeutschen und Rheinischen Provinz der Gesellschaft Jesu im Zeitalter der konfessionellen Auseinandersetzung*. Paderborn-München-Vienna-Zürich 1981, p. 58.

15 The Jesuits counted among these: Logic, Physics, Metaphysics, Ethics and Mathematics, see Karl Hengst (as note 14).

However, because of their calibre as scholars neither the king nor the university authorities wished to dismiss them immediately, rather they wished to test their faith and then dismiss those – one after the other – who proved not to be true Catholics and who had no intention of conforming. In order to have suitable replacements for them and in order to 'encourage holy competition in having (as in Paris) the same classes taught at different colleges', they urged that the humanities and the arts should be offered at the Jesuit college, too.[16] From this perspective – and also in compliance with the 'modus Parisiensis' – the Jesuit College was perceived as a precondition for the renewal of the university. Even the founding of a complete, public course of lectures in the college was seen as promoting the overall interests of the university.[17]

In planning their colleges the Jesuits had, already ten years after their foundation, the fairly clearly formulated aims cited by Claudius Jajus. When German princes questioned him about the extent of teaching in Jesuit colleges in Augsburg in 1550, he replied that the colleges were to cover all areas of teaching with the exception of law and medicine (meaning, that the college was expected to be not only some kind of grammar school, but also a minor university with the faculties of arts and theology); and he confirmed that there should be full public access to all these exercises in the colleges.[18] In Vienna the rivalry was not a peaceful one, rather it developed very soon into conflict. The first of these issues of conflict concerned the awarding of university degrees to Jesuits and later also non-Jesuits who had only attended courses in dialectics and philosophy at the Jesuit college.[19] The other area

16 Jajus to Loyola, Vienna 9 October 1551 in: Ep ... Jaji (as note 12), p. 375; compare with this Jajus to Loyola, Vienna, 16 December 1551 in: Ep ... Jaji (as note 12), p. 377: attesting that Ferdinand I and those who had persuaded him in Augsburg to erect a college in Vienna (i.e. the Bishop, Urban Textor and the Vice Chancellor Dr Jacob Jonas) desired that there should be chairs for all subjects except Law and Medicine and that the Jesuits should open a school there offering unrestricted access.

17 See the instruction to Polanco in the name of Loyola for his mission to Germany, Rome 24 September 1549 in *Mon. Ignatinana I/12* (as note 13), pp. 245f.: arguing that it would be advantageous for the University of Ingolstadt if a college like that in Messina or Gandia could be erected there: '*ubi etiam linguae et philosophiae, non tantum theologia, cum exercitatione scholastica modo parisiensi tractaretur*'. In Vienna the two Jesuit Theology Professors were not only to instruct at the university but also at the college, admitting Jesuits and non-Jesuits, see Ferdinand I to Loyola, 11 December 1550 in *Loyola Cartas* (as note 11), II, pp. 548 f.; Jajus to Loyola, Augsburg, 12 September 1550 in Ep ... Jaji (as note 12), p. 358.

18 Jajus to Loyola, [Augsburg, end of 1550] in Ladislaus Lukács SJ (ed.), Monumenta paedagogica SJ, vol. 1 (1540-1572) (=*Monumenta Historica SJ* [92]). Rome 1965, p. 393; he also asked to have the printed index of lecturers and lectures of the College at Messina sent to him so that he might be able to present a full, public course of studies available at a Jesuit College. Messina became the model of the Jesuit University, see the discussion (below) of Graz University and especially Karl Hengst (as note 14), pp. 60f.

19 *Vita Ignatii Loyolae et rerum Societatis Jesu historia*, auctore Joanne Alphonso de Polanco, vols. 1-6, 1461-1556 (=Monumenta Historica SJ [1, 3, 5, 7, 9, 11]. Madrid 1891-1556, vol 3, p. 241f.

of conflict concerned the awarding of degrees by the Jesuits themselves. And finally, there was also the intention of the Jesuits – evident from 1555 onwards – to take over the theological faculty of the university itself. In 1555 it was the general of the Order and his counsellors who considered it essential to carry out the plan to 'unite' the study of languages, the arts and theology at the college with those of the university (which amounted to a takeover by the Jesuits) in order to check-mate the 'heretical' professors at the university.[20] The very active rector of the Jesuit college, Pater Johannes de Victoria, sought to implement such directives in the subsequent years, to capture all three chairs of theology and one or the other chair of philosophy for the Jesuit order.[21] He did this despite the fact that there were no suitable incumbents even of the two chairs of theology which had already been filled by the Society of Jesus. In 1563 Victoria was provided with a new opportunity to transfer the whole of theological studies together with the preceding studies at the arts faculty to the college and subsequently to parallel the university and compete with it. The chance arose when Ferdinand I confirmed the *ius promovendi* which had been newly given by the pope to the Society of Jesus.[22] On account of the danger that this confirmation of papal privileges of the order constituted for the continued existence of the University of Vienna, the territorial lord revoked them after only two months.[23]

As far as the university of Vienna was concerned the policies of the territorial lord and his advisors in preferring the Jesuit order only succeeded in 1623.[24] The Jesuits, however, had managed to start a school which taught the

20 Nadal to Loyola, Venice, 6 July 1555 in *Epistolae P. Hieronymi Nadal SJ ab anno 1546 ad 1577*, vol. 1 (= Monumenta Historica SJ [13]). Madrid 1898, p. 314; Polanco in the name of Loyola to Lanoy, Rome, 22 November 1554, in *Mon. Ignatiana* I/8, p. 69, Polanco, *Vita* (as note 19), vol. 5, p. 274.
21 Compare i.a. Victoria to Polanco, Vienna, 14 August 1557 in Archivum Romanum Societatis Jesu, Rome, Epistolae Germaniae, 185, fol. 171v-172r; Polanco in the name of Vicar General Lainez to Victoria, Rome, 4 September 1557 in *Lainii Monumenta. Epistolae et acta P. Jacobi Lainii secundi Praepositi Generalis SJ* II (=Monumanta Historica SJ [45]). Madrid 1912, p. 419; Victoria to Lainez, Vienna, 2/3 February 1558 in Archivum Romanum Societatis (as above), Epistolae Germaniae 186, fol. 21v-22v; Canisius to Lainez, Piotrcovia, 30 December 1558 in Otto Braunsberger (ed.), *B. Petri Canisii SJ – Epistulae et acta*. Freiburg im Breisgau 1898, vol. 2, pp. 348f.
22 Confirmation of the privilege by Ferdinand I, Vienna, 1 October 1563, inserted in the one by Maximilian II, 20 September 1568 in a copy of 24 December 1660 in Ernst Beck, 'Die Anfänge der Jesuiten in Wien und Niederoesterreich bis zum Tode Ferdinands I (1551-1564). Typescript Diss., Vienna 1928, fol. 192-196.
23 Decree Ferdinand I, 20 December 1563, quoted in Ernst Beck (as note 22), pp. 178; cf. Bernhard Duhr SJ, *Geschichte der Jesuiten in den Ländern deutscher Zunge. vol. 1: Geschichte der Jesuiten in den Ländern deutscher Zunge im XVI. Jahrhundert*. Freiburg im Breisgau 1907, p. 50.
24 Johann Wrba SJ, 'Der Orden der Gesellschaft Jesu im alten Universitätsviertel von Wien' in Günther Hamann, Kurt Mühlberger, Franz Skacel (eds.), *Das alte Universitätsviertel in Wien, 1385-1985*. Vienna 1985, pp. 52-56 and Johann Wrba SJ, 'In der Nähe des

arts and which received the sons of the Catholic nobility to prepare them for more or less intensive studies of law in one of the Northern Italian universities.[25] Even some Protestant nobles are said to have sent their sons to the Jesuit school in recognition of the high quality of instruction. As a rule, however, the Protestant nobles sent their sons to the socalled '*Landschaftsschulen*' [territorial schools]. I should like to devote the next section to a consideration of these schools of the Estates, before returning in a third section to the actual founding of the university of Graz, as an example of the territorial lords' school and university policy.

II THE NOBLE ESTATES AND THEIR SCHOOLS

The nobility of the early modern period felt it very necessary to acquire schooling and university training in order to satisfy the new demands of a 'professionalised' political administration and to retain its position as the political elite. The proper schooling of the young nobleman was perceived as the essential precondition to be able to serve the territorial lord or the Estates or even to be successful as a landlord administering one's own manorial domain. Skills in debating and dealing with authorities as well as knowledge of Roman Law were deemed essential requisites of the ruling elite. This was also in evidence in the careers of bourgeois 'learned lawyers' – a frequent profession in the service of the Habsburg territorial lords of the Austrian lands.[26]

In the second third of the sixteenth century the noble Estates of Styria, Carinthia, Carniola and Austria above and below the river Enns employed

Römischen Königs. Die Gründung des Jesuitenkollegs in Wien' in Andreas Falkner & Paul Imhof (eds.), *Ignatius von Loyola und die Gesellschaft Jesu, 1491-1556*. Würzburg 1990, p. 345.

25 For example, the sons of the Court Chamberlain and Master Provisioner for Hungary, Hieronymus Beck von Leopoldsdorf, see H.J. Zeibig (ed.), 'Die Familien-Chronik der Beck von Leopoldsdorf' in *Archiv für Kunde oesterreichischer Geschichts-Quellen* 8, 1859, p. 226. Concerning the study of noble youth with the Jesuits the following observation was made in the next century by Karl Eusebius von Liechtenstein: The young men of his house had to learn Latin in order to finish the *humaniora* as soon and as well as possible so as to be able to begin with logic at the age of 14. For *humaniora* and logic he recommended the schools of the Jesuits. He considered logic the 'science of all sciences ... and *clavis scientiarium*'; its study 'opened up human understanding'. By means of logic, he argued, it was possible to acquire a good understanding of law – the reason for the nobility to study at all, namely to be enabled to administer law in order to govern the land and people well. See the instruction by Karl Eusebius von Liechtenstein to his son concerning household administration [about 1680], copy in Vaduz Castle, Library.

26 Gernot Heiss, 'Standeserziehung und Schulunterricht. Zur Bildung der niederoesterreichischen Adeligen in der frühen Neuzeit' in: *Adel im Wandel. Politik -Kultur-Konfession 1500-1700* (=Katalog des Niederoesterreichischen Landesmuseums NF 251). Vienna 1990, pp. 392-394.

schoolmasters in Graz, Klagenfurt, Ljubljana, Linz and Vienna to further the educational and employment chances of their sons. In Graz, the schoolmaster retained by the Estates promised, as early as 1538, to instruct young lords in Greek, Latin, German, in writing and Arithmetic, singing, playing a musical instrument, acting as well as the Arts.[27] Throughout the records of the Estates there is frequent mention of subjects which really form part of the syllabus of the Faculty of Arts and provide preliminary courses in Law and Theology, at least as programmes and occasionally also in reality.

It is alleged that 'secular law' was taught in Graz already in the 1550s. When in 1573/1574 David Chytraeus [Kochhafe] compiled not only a Protestant Church Order but also a Directive for Schools at the request of the Styrian Estates, he envisaged a three-year primary education (*schola puerilem*) followed by three to four classes of secondary schooling (*schola classica*) to be rounded off by the '*classis*' or '*schola publica*'. The latter was to offer public lectures in philosophy, theology, law,[28] (as well as Greek, mathematics[29] and history), and it was obviously intended to bridge the gap into University studies.[30]

The aim of this type of school with classes in Latin, philological and philosophical as well as – in some instances – legal and theological lectures was the education of secular and spiritual leaders to safeguard the Protestant interests of the Estates in state and church. In the school of the Estates in Graz – thus the instruction of the rector in 1574 – it was the stated intention, not only to 'form' youth for 'the service of the Church of Christ and for the office of preacher, but also for the service of the common good in Christian government, to look after other people [the neighbour] in all manner of useful ways'; indeed it is the task of the school of the Estates 'to turn young men into truly beautiful shoots in whom the whole country can rejoice, especially when native born offspring is prepared for the government of the Fatherland to fill the most prominent offices in which it is necessary to be able to teach, counsel, adjudicate, speak and write so that they can be preferred to foreigners'.[31]

27 Johann Loserth, *Die protestantischen Schulen in der Steiermark im sechzehnten Jahrhundert*. Berlin 1916, p. 8.
28 The juridical section of the fifth class of these schools was almost exclusively attended by nobility; by comparison with the philosophical and the theological sections it was called '*schola procerum*', see Johann Loserth (as note 27), p. 35.
29 Johannes Kepler was teacher at the Graz school (1594-1599) and at the Linz school (1612-1626).
30 Johann Loserth (as note 27), p. 30; no original has survived, but it can be reconstructed from the reformed school order of 1594 and other sources, cf. Johann Loserth (as note 27), pp. 155-166.
31 Richard Peinlich, 'Zur Geschichte der freien Schulen zu Graz [1. Teil, zur evangelischen Stiftsschule]' in *Jahresberichte des k.k. Ober-Gymnasiums zu Graz 1866*, pp. 9f.

The Graz school is cited here as an example which represents the aspirations of the other schools of the Estates in Klagenfurt, Ljublijana, Vienna (or rather Lossdorf/Horn) and Linz which had been developed along the same lines.[32] The philological and rhetorical orientation of these schools owed a great deal to German humanists and especially to the influence of the Strasbourg praeceptor Johannes Sturm. The new demands that were now made on the secular and ecclesiastical officials were taken care of in the provision of legal[33] and theological instruction. The young Austrian nobles who had received their education at these 'Schools of Rhetoric'[34] and who had become acquainted with some basic principles of theology and law, had been trained in Roman virtues and in the rhetoric of Cicero were deemed to be fully equipped 'to continue with the steadfastness of their fathers with the defence of the Protestant Faith, the promotion of Justice and the protection of the Liberties of the Province (including the privileges of the Estates) to argue in favour of faith and law'.[35]

III THE FOUNDATION OF THE JESUIT UNIVERSITY OF GRAZ

In 1574 in an oration delivered on the occasion of the newly extended *'Landschaftsschule'* in Graz David Chytraeus celebrated Emperor Ferdinand I (who had died ten years before) as the patron of the school. Ferdinand had, he said, by fatherly admonition kindled in the Styrian nobility a great love

---

32   Extensively on this topic, see Gernot Heiss, 'Konfession, Politik und Erziehung. Die Landschaftsschulen in den nieder- und inneroesterreichischen Ländern vor dem Dreißigjährigen Krieg' in Grete Klingenstein, Heinrich Lutz, Gerhard Stourzh (eds.), *Bildung, Politik und Gesellschaft*. Vienna 1978, pp. 13-63 (*passim*); see also Gernot Heiss, 'Die innerösterreichischen "Landschaftsschulen": Ein Versuch ihrer Einordnung in das Schul- und Bildungssystem des 16. Jahrhunderts' in Rolf-Dieter Kluge (ed.), *Ein Leben zwischen Laibach und Tübingen. Primus Truber und seine Zeit. Intentionen, Verlauf und Folgen der Reformation in Württemberg und Innerösterreich*. Munich 1995, pp. 191-210.

33   The *Institutiones* of Justinian were treated there, see Johann Loserth (as note 27), p. 35; see also Gernot Heiss, 'Argumentation für Glauben und Recht. Zur rhetorisch-juridischen Ausbildung des Adels an den protestantischen "Landschaftsschulen" in den nieder- und inneroesterreichischen Ländern vor dem Dreißigjährigen Krieg' in Roman Schnur (ed.), *Die Rolle der Juristen bei der Entstehung des modernen Staates*. Berlin 1986, pp. 682f.

34   Anton Schindling, *Humanistische Hochschule und freie Reichsstadt. Gymnasium und Akademie in Strassburg, 1538-1621*. Wiesbaden 1977, p. 175; Schindling evaluates the method of Johannes Sturm in Strasbourg as precisely fulfilling the intention of the classical school of rhetoric.

35   Memorandum by Johannes Memhard, rector of the Linz school, on the occasion of the submission of the school order, s.d. (1578), see Ferdinand Khull (ed.), 'Schulordnung und Instructionen aus den Jahren 1577-1579 für die evangelische Schule der Landstände von Oberoesterreich zu Linz an der Donau' in *Beiträge zur Oesterreichischen Erziehungs- und Schulgeschichte* 3, Vienna 1901, p. 214.

of the study of religion and the humanities, whereas the Styrian nobility had previously, for the greater part, neglected the pursuit of knowledge.[36] In this oration there is not the slightest hint of the religious conflicts, and no mention of the rival institution which had been sponsored precisely in order to promote the renewed Roman Catholic religion, the Jesuit college. On such occasions one usually ignores conflicts, but it is possible that the by-passing of the conflict actually indicated that the conflict was then not being taken so seriously. It is quite conceivable that one wished to stress the common aims of educating noble youths to be versatile politicians, diplomats and landlords; that the confessional conflict was not yet a priority. It may well have indicated that the arrangement made possible a relatively tolerant co-existence. There are other indicators which permit such a conclusion. There was, for example, the mention of Protestant nobility sending their young men to the Jesuit college and thereby acknowledging that the high quality of this institution superceded everything else. It is also said that the Protestant nobility attended the festivities which marked the opening of the Jesuit University 14 April 1586.[37] However, in the arguments advanced by Archduke Charles of Inner Austria on the occasion of the establishment of the College and later of the Jesuit University, there is a significant shift of emphasis in favour of a decidedly confessional orientation.

The first indication of the archduke's intention to found a Jesuit institution is contained in the report by a Jesuit who had been sent to Graz as a Lenten preacher at the request of the archduke in 1570. He did not merely report on his somewhat cool reception in the town (no one was willing to show the Jesuit the way), on the beauty of the town and the wealth of its inhabitants, on the attendance at his sermons, despite the fact that the preacher of the Protestant Estates had warned against the Jesuits; he also reported that the latter had argued that the Jesuits were responsible for the pernicious corruption of the people.[38] The report also mentioned the wish of the archduke to found a Jesuit college in the country[39] as a means of improving the religious conditions of Catholicism. When negotiations started fourteen months later, the archduke was anxious to speed up the process, and he

---

36 David Chytraeus, 'De Ferdinando Caesare ... oratio a ... Sigismundo a Sauraw recitata in Schola Provincialium Graecae in Stiria' in David Chytraeus, *Oratio in Schola Provincialium Stiriae introductione habita a Davide Chytraeo etc.* Witenbergae, Iohannes Crato, 1575, unpaginated.
37 See the account of the festivities in *Litterae Societatis Jesu duorum annorum MDLXXXVI et MDLXXXVII*. Romae 1589, pp. 211ff.
38 Stephan Rimel to Emerich Forsler, Graz, 12 March 1570 in Archivum Romanum (as note 21), 151 fol. 8rv.; see also Bernhard Duhr, *Die Jesuiten an den deutschen Fürstenhöfen des sechszehnten Jahrhunderts*. Freiburg im Breisgau 1901, p. 24.
39 See note 38.

referred to the activities of the Protestant Estates as the reason for such a step.[40]

According to this report the Protestant Estates were in the process of establishing an important school at great expense. They are said to have recruited six learned masters in Tübingen. The negotiator adverted to the zeal of the Protestant Estates and to the success of the Protestant preachers as considerable arguments in favour of erecting a College of the Society of Jesus in Graz: to be passive in the face of such zeal would result in dire consequences for the Catholics. After all the archduke (i.e. the Catholic party) had control of only one insignificant school in the four provinces. This persuaded the young men to go abroad for their studies; they then either stayed abroad or they returned riddled with errors to the detriment of the Fatherlands. The archduke, the report maintained, was therefore without the assistance of learned men or was even attacked by those who had returned after their study tours abroad. Furthermore, there was a dearth of good pastors. The prelates, it said, were prepared to support a seminary financially, and they would also admit members of the nobility. The Jesuit reported that the population was of a rather more Catholic inclination, processions attracted many people although they were ridiculed.[41] In the opinion of the provincial of the Jesuits the archduke had no other means of preserving religion than to found this and several other Jesuit colleges. And the archduke's brother-in-law, Duke William of Bavaria, was of the same opinion.[42]

In the foundation charter of the Graz College at the end of 1573 archduke Charles set the Jesuits the task of preserving and spreading 'the true Catholic faith' by the education of youth and the formation of learned men – especially clergy.[43] In line with these assignments the school of the Jesuits in Graz was extended in the following years. A sixth class, that for rhetoric, was introduced, and the catalogue of books used in instruction in 1579 shows

---

40 Forsler to the General of the Society of Jesus, Franciscus Borgia, Graz, 22 May 1570 in Archivum Romanum (as note 21), 133 I fol. 202r-205r; see also Forsler to Borgia, Vienna, 20 September 1570 in Archivum Romanum (as note 21), 151, fol. 295r-298v (extensively on the role of Graz on the basis of the reports by Rimel).

41 Forsler to Borgia, Graz, 22 May 1571 in Archivum Romanum (as note 21), 133 I fol. 202r-205r. See also Bernhard Duhr (as note 39), pp. 24f. It is likely that the seminary was intended to overcome the problem of the badly educated counsellors. Almost identical phraseology arguing against the dangers of study in foreign countries as a reason for the founding of the university is used by Archduke Charles to Pope Gregory XIII, Graz, 20 December 1584 in Augustinus Theiner (ed.), *Annales Ecclesiastici* 3. Rome 1856, p. 533.

42 Maggio to Nadal, Vienna, 12 September 1571 in Archivum Romanum (as note 21) 133II, fol. 360r.

43 Charter of foundation, 12 November 1573 in Richard Peinlich (ed.), 'Geschichte des Gymnasiums in Graz. Zweite Periode. Collegium, Gymnasium und Universität unter den Jesuiten' in *Jahresbericht des k.k. Ober-Gymnasiums zu Graz* 1869, pp. 8-10.

that the higher classes were given instruction in (pastoral) theology, logic, Greek, rhetoric and poetry.[44]

The plan to found a university at Graz is likely to have been drawn up in the same year, 1579 (it was politically a very important year in which plans were made in Munich by the territorial lord to proceed against the Inner Austrian Protestant Estates).[45] It envisaged a full university which adopted as its model the University of Vienna founded in 1364, but under the control of the Jesuits.[46] The territorial lord seemed primarily concerned to establish a higher institute of education in the country not only for clergy but also for government officials and even for medical doctors. From a Catholic perspective it was essential to train the future court officials, princely counsellors, priests and medical doctors in the country not only for financial reasons (which would, of course, also have applied to the Protestant Estates) but also in order to avoid the danger of having the candidates, when abroad, influenced by Protestant doctrines.

Ultimately, Archduke Charles only founded the university of Graz on 1 January 1585 as *Studia* in the Arts and in Theology and with the possibility of aquiring academic degrees only in those two.[47] Although Archduke Charles referred to the privileges which the Jesuits had been given by the pope and the emperor to promote the establishment of universities, he presented an entirely personal argument stressing his duties as well as his legitimate interests as territorial lord. He said that he had endowed the university because he was obliged as overlord to lead his subjects to peace, harmony and obedience, and to preserve them in this order. He stressed that this was in argreement with the family tradition of the Habsburgs to maintain the rightful Catholic religion unadulterated and because his faithful subjects would in this way return to their former condition of faith and the glory of the Catholic religion.[48] He had watched in great pain how the souls of his sub-

---

44 'Index lectionum et scholasticarum exercitationum, quae hoc anno 1579 in Collegio Societatis Jesu Graetii studiosis praelegentur' in Richard Peinlich (ed.) (as note 43), pp. 18f.
45 Regarding the Munich conference between Archduke Charles, his father-in-law, Duke Albrecht V of Bavaria, and his brother, Archduke Ferdinand of Tirol, see Johann Loserth, *Acten und Correspondenzen zur Geschichte des Gegenreformation in Inneroesterreich unter Erzherzog Karl II., 1578-1590*. Vienna 1898, pp. 36-38.
46 Hermann Wiesflecker, 'Das Gründungsdatum der Universität Graz (Neue Beiträge zur Gründungsgeschichte)' in *Zeitschrift des Historischen Vereins für Steiermark*, Special Issue 16, 1968, pp. 54-58. The design of the privilege was modelled on the Vienna Charter of foundation issued by Duke Rudolf IV; see also Walter Höflechner, 'Zur Geschichte der Universität Graz' in Kurt Freisitzer et al. (eds.), *Tradition und Herausforderung. 400 Jahre Universität Graz*. Graz, 1985, pp. 4f.
47 Charter of foundation, Graz, 1 January 1585 in Richard Peinlich (as note 43), pp. 25-28.
48 The ideological interest of the territorial lord in the enforcement of order, obedience and unity of faith is even more clearly enunciated in the memorandum of Archduke Charles to Pope Gregory XIII, Graz, 20 December 1584, see Augustinus Theiner (ed.) (as note 41), p. 533.

jects had by the injustice of the times and the instigation of hateful and dangerous men been pushed from the highest throne of faith and that rather than being imbued with good manners they were poisoned by contrary opinions and heretical errors. These are the sentiments expressed by Archduke Charles in the foundation charter. Within the framework of the aspirations to restore the unity of faith in his territories – this was considered absolutely essential to internal peace and order at the time – the purpose of the foundation was to have learned men in the country who could serve the common good so that the Catholic religion could be preserved where it still existed and reconstructed where it had collapsed. Since even less important princes – thus went the argument of the archduke – when they considered the welfare of their subjects were persuaded to institute public *Studia* so that they could retain the sons of their subjects in the country, and provide themselves with sufficiently learned men, how much more was such a measure proper for him who possessed several countries with a diversity of populations and languages.[49]

The foundation charter also reveals the reason for the archduke's invitation to the Jesuits to direct this university. The document discloses that he had taken advice to find out how the dangerous sickness (heresy) could be combatted by an appropriate means. He had become acquainted with the Jesuits and thought them most appropriate. Their reputation as men of extraordinary piety, religion and doctrine, with great zeal for God and the care of souls had already spread the length and breadth of Germany. He had summoned them to Graz and had founded a college there in 1573, always with the intention of erecting a higher school and a publicly accessible university, and this had now come to fruition after some delay.[50]

The university of Graz was, therefore, from its inception one of those territorial universities of which several were founded in the course of the sixteenth century: in these instances the founders, the territorial lords or even imperial city governments, departed from the medieval model of the university and its freedoms in order to exercise firmer social control over their subjects. To stress this again, the strengthening of social control mechanisms was the prime target. In this general context Graz was also from the beginning a typical Jesuit university where some of the corporative rights of the univer-

---

49 See, very clearly formulated, Charles to Gregory XIII, Graz, 20 December 1584 in Augustinus Theiner (as note 41), p. 534. The size of the Inner-Austrian territory in the hands of the Habsburgs is 1564 amounted to 47.776 km²; the territory comprised Styria, Carinthia, Krain, Görz, Gradiska, Trieste, Istria, Fiume/Rijeka, Austrian Friuli. By comparison with this Bavaria was *c.*17.400 km²; see Walter Neunteufl, 'Die Entwicklung der inneroesterreichischen Länder' in *Inneroesterreich 1564-1619* (=Joannea 3), Graz, [1967], p. 522.

50 Charles to Gregory XIII, Graz, 20 December 1584 in Augustinus Theiner (as note 41), pp. 533 f.

sity (for instance, the election of the rector) were suspended in favour of the principles of the hierarchically directed order.[51] The plan to found a full university had been given up; besides financial considerations and the misgivings of the urban and territorial bureaucracy towards the privileged and undisciplined students,[52] the lack of interest of the Jesuits in law and medical faculties over which they would not exercise direct control may have been decisive. At the beginning of the seventeenth century they resisted the establishment of a law faculty in Graz although this had been recommended by the highly influential counter-reformation Bishops Martin Brenner and George Stobaeus.[53] The university of Graz was a Jesuit university in the narrower sense, of the type that had first come into existence – in line with the Messina model – in the German speaking parts of Europe in Dillingen. There, too, the development of a full university that had originally been envisaged had been suspended when the Jesuits took over in 1563/1564.[54] Given this restriction the Jesuits were unable completely to fulfil their task of educating the new elite, and the law students as well as the medical students continued to travel to Northern Italy.

CONCLUSION

My discussion has not merely been concerned with an attempt to reform the University of Vienna by the Jesuits and with the founding of the university of Graz, but has also reviewed the higher schools of the Protestant Estates and of the Jesuits in Graz as parallel examples of educational endeavour. I have tried to show how, for similar reasons, these schools offered university subjects. Archduke Charles, therefore, could persuade himself quite easily in 1584 that the school run by the Jesuits had been so much extended that it could be considered the equivalent of a university.[55] The schools of the Estates also gave introductions to legal studies in order, for financial reasons,

---

51 Peter Baumgart, 'Universitätsautonomie und landesherrliche Gewalt im späten 16. Jahrhundert' in *Zeitschrift für historische Forschung* 1, 1974, pp. 23-53.
52 Hermann Wiesflecker (as note 46), p. 58 maintains that already in the first plan for a full university the Jesuits would have appointed the rector; but in this first project there are still many privileges for the students missing in the 'realisation' of 1585 and there was envisaged in Graz – as indeed in the Vienna Privilege of 1365 – a separate city for students.
53 Johann Andritsch, 'Landesfürstliche Berater am Grazer Hof (1564-1619)' in *Inneroesterreich, 1564-1619* (=Joannea 3), Graz 1967, p. 91. See also Walter Höflechner (as note 46), p. 9.
54 Karl Hengst (as note 14), p. 176.
55 Charles to Gregory XIII, Graz, 20 December in Augustinus Theiner (as note 41), p. 534 asks for the confirmation of the studies as a full university: '*et nunc ... plane Universitatem similiter a me institutum ...*'.

to shorten young noblemen's stay abroad or to make it even unnecessary. These schools also offered theological studies in order to train capable students from bourgeois backgrounds to become accomplished pastors.

The two antagonistic parties who opposed each other politically and confessionally – the Catholic territorial lord who sought to establish his own sovereign rule and the Protestant Estates who, as representatives of the region sought to share power with him – promoted higher schooling for exactly the same reasons. Both required dependable officials for the political administration and educated theologians for the organisation of their churches. Both parties were actively involved in the modernisation process, that is, they both took steps which led to the formation of the modern state.

The schools of the provincial Estates were designed to serve the propagation of the faith by training preachers, by instructing children in the Protestant doctrine and piety (indoctrination)[56]; and the quality of their schools promoted in the eyes of the parents the good reputation of Protestant doctrine. In order to spread the Reformation the leaders of the Estates tried to influence nobility and magistrates and then to win over the lower orders of society through them. As far as Inner Austria was concerned this meant to serve several vernaculars, German and Slovenian, in the countryside,[57] to print religious tracts in the languages of the country and to offer instruction in these vernaculars in the lower classes of the schools.[58] One was convinced that through the spread of the 'true' faith it was possible to create the preconditions to end the Turkish threat and other 'punishments of God'.[59]

All these aims and aspirations can also be found among the Jesuits: *propaganda fide* had exactly the same function; cooperation of the Jesuits with landlords and magistrates was desirable, with the ordinary subjects as the ultimate target; heresy was seen as the cause of pestilence; and the Turkish threat was deemed to be God's punishment.[60] In this context it was thought

---

56 Gerald Strauss, *Luther's House of Learning. Indoctrination of the Young in the German Reformation*. Baltimore-London 1978, *passim*.
57 Miroslav Ostravsky, 'Reformation in Krain' in Miroslav Ostravsky, *Beiträge zur Kirchengeschichte im Patriarchate Aquileia*. Klagenfurt 1965, p. 53.
58 Compare with this Primus Truber's Schools' Programme in the Slovenian Church Order in Miroslav Ostravsky (as note 57), pp. 48f.
59 The argument that the spread of the 'true' faith was the precondition of victory over the Turks was advanced e.g. in the letter by the Protestant Styrian nobleman Hans Ungnad von Sonneck to the electors and princes, Urach, 14 September 1561, in Ivan Kostrencic, *Urkundliche Beiträge zur Geschichte der protestantischen Literatur der Südslaven*. Vienna 1874, p. 49.
60 For example, Canisius to Schweicker, Ingolstadt, 10 January 1556 in Otto Braunsberger (ed.), *Petri Canisii SJ – Epistulae et acta*, vol. 1. Freiburg im Breisgau 1896, p. 591: '*Turcas vincent, qui sectarum servi in Sathanae castris esse coeperunt*'. Nicolaus Lanoy to Loyola, Vienna, 3 November 1555 in *Epistolae Mixtae ex variis Europae locis* etc. 5 (=Monumenta Historica SJ [20]). Madrid 1901, p. 77.

absolutely necessary to educate children in the faith, to enhance the quality of this education so as to ensure the enactment of the faith[61] and the distribution of the message through printed tracts.[62]

If the social development of the second half of the sixteenth century is seen under the auspices of 'confessionalisation' (in accordance with Ernst Walter Zeeden, Wolfgang Reinhard, Heinz Schilling et al.) the parallels in the conduct of political and confessional opponents cannot surprise.[63] The schools' policy of the opponents, the Catholic territorial lord and the Protestant noble Estates, was similar: both opponents directed their schooling towards training with the aim of propaganda and indoctrination in order to form loyal officials for the new bureaucracy. The measures adopted rested on the same assessment of what was essential at the time of the formation of territorial administration and what the struggle for the enforcement of religious 'truth' demanded: literacy, eloquence and knowledge in encounters with the authorities, i.e. legal knowledge and awareness of the right faith. The polarisation of opponents, their aggressive confrontation, increased considerably in the course of this process. And this development also furthered the founding of universities as institutions which exercised control over the formation of elites and attempted their ideological indoctrination.

The question why the Inner Austrian Estates did not resist the dissolution of their schools (1598/1601) and the revocation of their religious concessions cannot be dealt with here. I should only like to allude to the dependence of these Estates on the ideological centres where Protestantism had been successful with the help of the prince. As just one example of what is meant here: the Tübingen Theologian Jakob Andreae when asked how the Inner Austrian Estates should conduct themselves in the face of counter-reformation measures adopted by the territorial lord, said (obviously on the basis of his own exprience at home) that the 'threatened Christians' should not undertake anything which might create the impression that the Gospel had led them to resistance and tumult against the lawful overlord.[64]

61 In this context it is worth mentioning the Jesuit Theatre and also the dramatised catecheticals for children, see Dawant to the Supreme General of the Order, Vienna, 27 April 1555 in *Litterae Quadrimestres ex universisis praeter Indiam et Brasiliam locis in quibus aliqui de Societate Jesu versabuntur Romam missae*, vol. 3 (= Monumenta Historica SJ [8]). Madrid 1899, pp. 388f; Hermann Duhr (as note 23), pp. 455f.

62 The Jesuits founded a printing press in Vienna at the end of the 1550s with this aim in mind, see Moritz Grolig, 'Die Buchdruckerei des Jesuitenkollegiums in Wien (1559-1565)' in *Mitteilungen des Oesterreichischen Vereins für Bibliothekswesen* 13, Vienna, 1910, pp. 105-120.

63 Gernot Heiss, 'Konfessionsbildung, Kirchenzucht und frühmoderner Staat. Die Durchsetzung des "rechten" Glaubens im "Zeitalter der Glaubensspaltung" am Beispiel des Wirkens der Jesuiten in den Ländern Ferdinands I' in Hubert Ch. Ehalt (ed.), *Volksfrömmigkeit. Von der Antike bis zum 18. Jahrhundert*. Vienna 1989, pp. 191-220.

64 Hermann Loserth (as note 27), p. 396; for similar memoranda relating to the Empire where the prince enforced 'his' confession, see Gernot Heiss (as note 32), p. 37 note 132.

Schooling, too, can be assumed to have conditioned the quiet conduct of the nobility. It played a central role in the 'spiritual-moral and pschycological structural change of the political, military and economic man'.[65] Gerhard Oestreich called this characteristic feature of the early modern period 'social discipline', Norbert Elias 'civilisation' and Max Weber 'occidental rationalisation'. The school was the place where the modern individual learned rational thinking, discipline and self control. In the process of civilisation education and its institutionalised form exercised a 'debarbarising' effect; a function which was explicitly mentioned as the reason for founding Trinity College, Dublin.[66] The secular elites, too, were 'civilised' in their schools,[67] which had previously only happened at the court and through courtly culture. In the sixteenth century in particular the nobleman learned in the schools the modern, individual and yet disciplined social conduct. Thus the Imperial Counsellor and Field Marshal Lazarus von Schwendi considered the disciplining and civilising of the German nobility through schooling and military training a tremendous achievement. Emperors, Popes and Councils had previously not managed to defend themselves against the barbarity of the feuds of the nobles. Yet now, all this had changed and resulted in good conduct over the last hundred years; and what had achieved this was the introduction of education and schools, especially the invention of the printing press and the distribution of books. By these means, altogether too harsh and provocative ways were tempered and everything brought to greater peace, better ordering and a properly regulated life.[68]

---

65 On 'social disciplining' as a 'fundamental process, see Gerhard Oestreich, 'Strukturprobleme des europäischen Absolutismus' in Gerhard Oestreich, *Geist und Gestalt des frühmodernen Staates. Ausgewählte Aufsätze*. Berlin 1969, pp. 187f. ; see also Winfried Schulze, 'Gerhard Oestreichs Begriff "Sozialdisziplinierung" in der frühen Neuzeit' in *Zeitschrift für historische Forschung* 14, 1987, pp. 265-302.
66 See article by Helga Robinson-Hammerstein in the present volume.
67 Almost all the documents, characterised as 'Argumenta', edited by Ferdinand Khull, 'Aus der alten Landschaftsschule in Graz' in *Mitteilungen des historischen Vereins für Steiermark* 45,[1897], pp. 21-35 are admonitions to better conduct and obedience.
68 Eugen von Frauenholz, *Des Lazarus von Schwendi Denkschrift über die politische Lage des deutschen Reiches von 1574*. Munich 1939, p. 8.

The Jesuits and universities in Italy

Gian Paolo Brizzi

The involvement of the Jesuits in public education dates back to the Society's foundation by Ignatius Loyola, but it was especially during the generalships of Claudio Aquaviva and Muzio Vitelleschi that the network of Jesuit colleges in Italy played an important role in education generally.[1] Thus, to understand and properly evaluate the historical development of Italian universities in the early modern period, the role of the Jesuits cannot be ignored.

This opinion, which serves as an epigraph to my article, is also the conclusion. This apparent reversal of rhetorical conventions is prompted by a desire on my part to contend with a historiographical tradition which, since the Risorgimento, has been conditioned by the political battles over public education. Consequently, the educational activities of certain religious orders and congregations have been either ignored or misrepresented. As regards university-level education, this historiographical tradition has seen the Jesuit colleges as insignificant phenomena, limited to a few geographically and culturally peripheral examples.

Such an opinion is essentially based on the failed attempt by the Jesuits to establish higher schools in the two most prestigious Italian university seats: Bologna and Padua. Both of these instances created a great deal of noise in university circles. In Padua the conflict between the Jesuit college and the University ended in 1591 with the closure of the Jesuit institution.[2] Later, in 1641, the University of Bologna obtained an order from Pope Urban VIII which prohibited the public activities of the Jesuit school; University and

---

[1] G.P. Brizzi, 'Les jésuites et l' école en Italie (XVI-XVIII siècles)' in L. Giard (ed.), *Les jésuites à la Renaissance. Système éducatif et production du savoir*. Paris 1995, pp. 46-48.

[2] About the conflict between the Jesuits and the Paduan University see A. Favaro, 'Lo Studio di Padova e la Compagnia di Gesù sul finire del secolo decimosesto. Narrazione documentata' in *Atti del r. Istituto veneto di scienze, lettere e arti*, s. V, 4 , 1877-1878, pp. 401-535; B. Brugi, *Gli scolari dello Studio di Padova nel Cinquecento. Seconda edizione riveduta*. Padova-Verona 1905; A. Favaro, 'Nuovi documenti sulla vertenza tra lo Studio di Padova e la Compagnia di Gesù sul finire del secolo decimosesto' in *Nuovo archivio veneto*, s. 3, I , 1911, pp. 89-100; R. Cessi, 'L' università giurista di Padova ed i gesuiti alla fine del Cinquecento' in *Atti del r. Istituto veneto di scienze, lettere e arti* 81, 2, 1921-1922, pp. 585-601; P. Pirri, *L' interdetto di Venezia del 1606 e i gesuiti. Silloge di documenti*. Roma 1959; A. Stella, 'Tentativi controriformistici nell' Università di Padova e il rettorato di Andrea Gostynski' in *Relazioni tra Padova e la Polonia. Studi in onore dell' Università di*

school had been quarrelling for years.[3] Based on these two failures a notion developed that in Italy the attempts by the Jesuits to challenge the role of the traditional universities were undermined by the strong reactions of the doctoral colleges, and of the university authorities so that the role the Jesuit colleges played in the development of the Italian university system was marginal.

This thesis can be revised by examining several factors. First, it is necessary to verify the legal status of the Society of Jesus' university-level schools, a status which was contested, for example, during the conflict with the University of Padua. Second, one needs to consider the characteristics of institutional structures and the form of didactics each adopted. Finally, one must evaluate the favour with which student populations regarded Jesuit institutions.

Many of the choices made by the Jesuits were necessarily shaped by the supranational character of the Society, but, on a practical level, these choices were applied with appropriate reference to the differing national contexts. Thus, to understand the subject properly it is necessary to look to a broader European context.

It is well known that the Society of Jesus, while not itself being a teaching order, did have a precise academic policy which integrated its widely-conceived apostolate; activities included everything from missionary work to preaching. In the colleges this policy had an operational unity; in the *ratio studiorum* it had an effective organisational and didactic base. In this regard there are several precedents in church history, and one need only recall that the growth of the medieval universities was intimately linked to the activities of the mendicant Franciscan and Dominican orders.[4]

Cracovia nel sesto centenario della sua fondazione. Padova 1964; W. Bouwsma, *Venice and the Defense of Republican Liberty*. Berkeley-Los Angeles 1968; G. Piaia, 'Aristotelismo, "heresia" e giurisdizionalismo nella polemica del P. Antonio Possevino contro lo Studio di Padova' in *Quaderni per la storia dell' Università di Padova* 6, 1973, pp. 125-143; S. De Bernardin, 'La politica culturale della Repubblica di Venezia e l'Università di Parma nel XVII secolo' in *Studi veneziani* 16, 1974, pp. 443-502; G.P. Brizzi, 'Educare il principe, formare le élites. I gesuiti e Ranuccio I Farnese' in G.P. Brizzi, A. D' Alessandro and A. Del Fante, *Università, principe, gesuiti. La politica farnesiana dell'istruzione a Parma e Piacenza (1545-1622)*. Roma 1980, pp. 141-145; J.P. Donnelly, 'The Jesuit College at Padua. Growth, suppression, attempts at restoration, 1552-1606' in *Archivum historicum Societatis Jesu* 51, 1982, pp. 45-79; U. Baldini, 'La scuola scientifica emiliana della Compagnia di Gesù, 1600-1660. Linee di una ricostruzione archivistica' in *Università e cultura a Ferrara e Bologna*. Firenze 1989, pp. 109-178; G.P. Brizzi 'Scuole e collegi dell' antica Provincia Veneta della Compagnia di Gesù (1542-1773)' in M. Zanardi (ed.), *I gesuiti e Venezia. Momenti e problemi di storia veneziana della Compagnia di Gesù*. Padova, 1994, pp. 481-489.

3   E. Costa, 'Contributi alla storia dello Studio bolognese durante il secolo XVII' in *Studi e memorie per la storia dell' Università di Bologna*. s. I, vol. 3, 1912, pp. 59-72; N. Fabrini, *Lo Studio pubblico di Bologna ed i Gesuiti*. Bologna 1941.

4   See in this regard *Le scuole degli ordini mendicanti (secc. XIII-XIV). Convegno del Centro di studi sulla spiritualità medievale*. Todi, *11-14 ottobre 1976*. Todi 1978.

From the outset the experience of the Jesuits in the field of education is distinguished by the modernity of its approaches. The general curia of the Society in Rome was, for nearly two centuries, a unique point for observing the state of education in the different countries of Europe. It was to these headquarters that reports and information on the state of the colleges were sent by college rectors and Provincial Generals. Every three years a scrupulous enquiry was made into the physical and intellectual condition of each of the Society's members, with a view to deploying human resources most efficiently.

After a century of activity the Society's infrastructure included 521 colleges, 49 seminaries, 280 residences and mission houses, 54 houses of probation, 24 professed houses, and nearly 16,000 members; it was all headed by one man – the provost general.[5] It was from the curia that the Society's activities were planned, including all the decisions governing organisation and the nomination of personnel. In the area of education the involvement of the Roman headquarters was extensive. The nomination of school heads, the devising of educational programmes, the publication of textbooks, the planning of research in Jesuit institutions, and the approval or censure of findings were all undertaken in the curia.

It is a matter of choice as to which particular circumstances one takes into account when looking at the Jesuits' work: individual countries had different effects on the Jesuit presence. Here is not the place to undertake such an analysis. I shall limit myself to discussing the extent to which the waves produced in the universities of the Empire by religious reforms determined the conditions favourable to the creation, or re-creation of university centres in catholic territories. These events largely favoured the Jesuits who, strengthened by the support of territorial princes and the papacy, took over the direction of certain universities, and in many others obtained control of chairs and even faculties.[6]

In Spain the society encountered difficulties primarily because of the fundamental stability of a university system over which the monarchy had exercised diligent control. In France there was a 'Gallican' reaction which counteracted any success the Society may have had. Until the middle of the seventeenth century only colleges at Bourges and Poitiers succeeded in integrating themselves into the local universities.

5   *Imago primi saeculi Societatis Jesu.* Antwerp 1640.
6   K. Hengst, *Jesuiten an Universitäten und Jesuitenuniversitäten.* Paderborn 1981; R.A. Müller, 'I gesuiti e le università cattoliche nell'impero tedesco' in G.P. Brizzi and J. Verger (eds.), Le università dell' Europa. Dal rinascimento alle riforme religiose. Milano 1992, pp. 197-217; R.A. Müller, '"Universitas et Societas Jesu". The Catholic Universities in Early Modern Germany' in A. Romano (ed.), *Università in Europa. Le istituzioni universitarie dal Medio Evo ai nostri giorni. Strutture, organizzazione, funzionamento.* Messina 1995, pp. 395-403.

If we concentrate on Italy, the idea of being involved in the intellectual life and education of the ruling elites was never abandoned by the Jesuits, even when circumstances forced them to adjust the form of their presence. Since their foundation, the Jesuits had paid particular attention to university towns; from 1538 onwards their most competent preachers had been sent to Siena, Padua, Ferrara and Bologna. For a long time the Society's establishments favoured not only political centres but also centres of cultural importance. In 1548, in Messina, they experimented with the first public school modelled in the *modus pariensis*, which was the basis of the *ratio studiorum*.[7] The *Collegio Romano* and the *Collegio Germanico* followed shortly after, and Loyola's initial reluctance to involve the Society in public education was overcome by the success of the new schools which proved to be an effective means of penetrating the social reality of Italian towns.

First at Messina, and then in Rome, the Jesuits competed in the creation of higher schools which completed an education in grammar with studies in the humanities, rhetoric, logic, physics, mathematics, metaphysics and theology. In this they undertook an educational programme all in all similar to that of the arts and theology faculties of the public universities. Their middle-level schools, that is to say the colleges which offered courses in grammar and rhetoric complete with a rudimentary course in moral theology intended for local clergy, were generally favoured by the ecclesiastical hierarchy and sovereigns. For their part, city councils encumbered by financial problems and the difficulty of giving their own schools a stable basis, welcomed the establishment of a Jesuit college. However, when it was a matter of moving from teaching elementary courses to more advanced studies in philosophy or theology, attitudes changed considerably. The professorial colleges, university authorities, student bodies and city leaders all closed ranks to defend their own privileges. These groups were ready to bring out their rhetoric of university liberties, as they had done in Bologna and Padua.

Nevertheless, the university system was not immovable, and it was beginning to manifest symptoms of the structural crisis which resulted in the progressive decline of universities as centres of scientific and cultural life in Italy. While in other countries the universities represented the most dynamic form of penetrating cultural life, a process which was an aspect of confessionalisation, in Italy the solidarity of the doctoral colleges tended to negate this dynamic intellectual role. These doctoral colleges, themselves part of the city oligarchies, showed an inability to renew the content and methods of the

---

7   G. Codina Mir, *Aux sources de la pédagogie des Jésuites. Le "modus parisiensis"*. Roma 1968, pp. 262ff.; G.P. Brizzi, ' "Studia humanitatis" und Organisation des Unterrichts in den ersten italienischen Kollegien der Gesellschaft Jesu', in W. Reinhard (ed.), *Humanismus im Bildungswesen des 15. und 16. Jahrhunderts*. Weinheim 1984, pp. 160-163; D. Novarese, *Istituzioni politiche e studi di diritto fra Cinque e Seicento. Il Messanense Studium generale tra politica gesuitica e istanze egemoniche cittadine*. Milano 1994.

traditional curricula, implicitly preferring that education and research be undertaken outside the universities, in scientific or literary academies, or in Jesuit colleges.

The breach that the Jesuit colleges made into this system was not small. Nearly a century after the opening of the college in Messina, the society had 117 colleges endowed with schools where, for 100 classes in the lower disciplines (grammar, humanities and rhetoric), 68 classes in philosophy and theology can be counted.[8] In certain cases their colleges mixed with the existing universities and entered into overt competition with them. This had negative results, as illustrated above, in Bologna and Padua, but elsewhere it brought about agreement as was the case in Rome, Naples and Turin. Conditions were most favourable in towns which lacked university establishments, or in those in which the Jesuits were called upon to re-launch defunct universities. The Society also played a role in universities which had encountered financial difficulties and in the capitals of territories which lacked a university of their own. In these instances the Jesuit projects benefitted from the ambitions of urban patricians and territorial sovereigns; moreover their foundations also changed the map of Italian universities. Towards the middle of the seventeenth century about 15 universities were in operation, and the Jesuits possessed fully functioning colleges which worked in an autonomous fashion or whose educational activities were linked to those of the local university, such as Parma, Palermo, Milan, Mantua, Genes, Brescia, Cremona, L'Aquila, Fermo, Macerata, Syracuse, Sassari, Messina and Cagliari.

Several questions are germane here. First, how was the expansion brought about, and what means were adopted to effect it? What was the context of the rapid spread of Jesuit schools? Finally, in what way did the Jesuit schools contribute to the modernisation of Italian university institutions?

The historico-political context in which this expansion came about was the *pax hispanica*, which characterised Italian political life following the Treaty of Cateau-Cambrésis. Certainly in the period looked at here the Spanish role was more than an occasional element. The Jesuits enjoyed a special relationship with Spain, if only because of the Spanish origins of the Society. They found solid support among the Spanish viceroys, governors and ambassadors who were favourable in a way that only the church hierarchy had been in earlier times. The ecclesiastical hierarchy, from Gabriele Paleotti to Carlo Borromeo, had considered the Jesuits to be docile instruments of their own pastoral effort, and consequently entrusted them with the direction of the diocesan seminaries. For the Peninsula's new Spanish leaders the involvement of the Jesuits in higher education was an element in the broader process of consolidating the new political order, because Jesuit

---

8   G.P. Brizzi (as note 1), p. 46.

schools contributed to the weakening of the doctoral colleges which were often part of the urban oligarchies opposing the Spanish.

The political practice which characterised the Jesuits is underlined by the preponderance of Spanish elements in the hierarchy – it is sufficient to note that the first five provosts general were all former subjects of the Spanish king. It was a matter of a quite explicit political orientation which, as Michel Certeau has noted, never failed to excite tensions at the heart of the order.[9] So close an association with the Spanish Crown often had drawbacks in Italian towns; for example, in Venice the anti-Spanish party often viewed the Jesuits as an internal enemy, partisans of the Spanish king ever ready to betray the Venetian *patria*.[10] Conversely, the Spanish link served the Jesuits favourably in several places, such as Modena, Parma and Mantua.

The legal standing of their colleges was recognised in 1547 through decrees of Pope Paul III granted for the college in Gandia and the following year for Messina.[11] The problem of conceding university status was solved between 1552 and 1578 by privileges granted by Julius III, Pius IV and Gregory XIII which reinforced the independence of the Society's colleges and curricula.

Thus a model was confirmed which clearly differed from that of the traditional university: the Jesuit rector, who was also the chancellor of the University, was nominated by the provost general of the Society. The Provost General also enjoyed other powers: the right to establish or reform the rules and statutes necessary for the functioning of the university; the right to determine the educational programme, the number of chairs, the choice of subjects; and the right to nominate both lecturers and university officials.

Based on a strong centralism, the focus of which was outside both the college and the immediate local context, the new schools acted with full autonomy in relation to matters such as, student bodies, the doctoral colleges, the city patricians, the ecclesiastical authorities and territorial governments, which elsewhere were sharing the management of the universities. Even the traditional hierarchy of university faculties was reversed: disciplines taught by the Jesuits in philosophy and theology courses prevailed over the medical and legal disciplines taught by laymen. Moreover, the Jesuits saw to it that their colleges could be seen as universities by adopting the formal, external signs proper to universities, including the preparation of a list of professors and courses to be posted at the beginning of each academic year, the adoption, in certain circumstances, of the term *gymnase* to indicate the higher schools in their colleges, and using a bell at the beginning of lessons to

9 M. De Certeau, Le *Mépris du monde*. Paris 1965, pp. 107-154.
10 G.P. Brizzi, 'Educare il principe' (as note 2), pp. 191-192.
11 P. García Trobat (ed.), *El naixement d'una universitat: Gandia s. XVII. Edició i estudi introductori de les seues constitucions*. Gandia 1989.

underline the public character of the education undertaken. Finally, they matriculated their students, or gave them confirmations of their attendance at courses which would permit them to qualify in the town college.

Disintegrating university institutions, 'nations' and student universities were banished from the heart of Jesuit colleges, with the notion of *libertas estudiantine* being supplanted by the principle of magisterial authority over students. To maintain discipline in their colleges, a notoriously difficult task in Italian universities, the Jesuits employed draconian measures including prison and starvation.[12]

Once any distinctions between collegial and noncollegial doctors were abolished, the professors found themselves in a modern hierarchical structure, which was headed by a rector and prefect of studies. It was the prefect of studies who controlled the educational activities of the professors and the students' results. The possibility of re-deploying personnel and resources from one college to another according to the needs of the moment represented an advantage to teaching staff which traditional universities could not provide. The traditional universities had, in effect, abandoned the practice of recruiting professors from outside their own corporate body.

The relationship between students and teachers was also placed on a new level with the creation of congregations which the Jesuits established in nearly all the university towns, congregations which sought to join *pietas* with *instructio*.[13] These congregations undertook several functions, such as the religious and moral formation of students, in addition to acting as centres for social activities. Moreover, they also undertook tasks which traditionally belonged to university bodies; in 1582 the Bologna congregation launched an enquiry into students' living conditions and presented a report to the senate advising that a survey be made of local accommodation.[14]

The regularity of courses, and the number of lessons given (which was at least two or three times as many as in traditional universities), met with the approval of students. Moreover, the Jesuit style of teaching – reading out the lecture – was favoured over the traditional style of exposition and commentary practised in the other universities.[15] The Jesuit schools also owed their success to the scholarly research undertaken in their own institutions. This is a little-known aspect of Jesuit educational history, but it is of crucial importance for understanding what differentiated their schools from tradi-

12 G.P. Brizzi, 'Educare il principe' (as note 2), p. 185.
13 L. Châtellier, *L'Europe des dévots*. Paris 1987; L. Châtellier, 'I gesuiti alla ricerca di una regola di vita per i laici: le congregazioni mariane' in P. Prodi (ed.), *Disciplina dell' anima, disciplina del corpo e disciplina della società tra medioevo ed età moderna*. Bologna 1994, pp. 383-393.
14 *Memoriale della Perseveranza ... per li signori scholari dello Studio di Bologna (1582)* in Bologna, Archivio di Stato, Assunteria di Studio, *Diversorum*, tomo IV, fasc. 6.
15 A. Favaro, 'Lo Studio di Padova' (as note 2).

tional ones. In the latter the dominant influence of the professorial colleges tended to favour conservative teaching methods and content. This in turn reinforced the principle according to which the task of the professors was limited to teaching, while research was undertaken by academicians, or was at least left to individual initiative without resources or support being provided on an institutional basis. In the Jesuit colleges, on the other hand, not only was research activity joined with teaching (staff were often undertaking both, either at the same time or alternately), but the Society's intellectuals enjoyed extremely advantageous conditions in contrast to their university colleagues.

In order to devote themselves full-time to research, professors were often excused from other functions, could make effective use of their students and fellow religious as assistants, and were released from their vow of poverty so as to profit from the financial aid of willing sponsors. The most important colleges were equipped with *cabinets scientifiques* and libraries, often with their own budgets. The international scale of the Society facilitated meetings and exchanges of research findings between various countries: for example, in Italy the Jesuits were among the first to know of Viete's algebra, Gassendi's astronomy and physics, of Descartes and the works of Tycho Brahe and Kepler. Finally, the cosmopolitan character of the order represented a decisive advantage for certain intellectual activities – especially in the physical and natural sciences – where data such as astronomical observations could be collected from outside Europe in Jesuit missions.[16]

The activities of Jesuit intellectuals were more structured than those of their lay counterparts, and could bear fruit in terms of the creation of schools of thought. This was the case with the school that developed between the sixteenth and seventeenth centuries at the heart of the network of Jesuit colleges in the Venetian province, which benefitted from the presence of such people as De Dominis, G. Biancani, N. Cabeo, N. Zucchi, B. Cesi, G.B. Riccioli, M. Bettini, F. Lana Terzi, G. Ferroni, and V.M. Grimaldi.[17] Here was a group working in a peripheral area, Emilia, but in continual and effective contact with other centres, especially Rome.

If we know a great deal about the results on a purely scientific level, it is more difficult to define the effects of this mastery on the students, as well as on the form and channels through which research activity influenced teaching. On the level of organisation, the *ratio* had envisaged the formation of academies within the colleges, and had fixed their structures. These acad-

---

16 J.L. Heilbron, *Electricity in the 17th and 18th Century*. Berkeley-Los Angeles-London 1979 (see in particular chapter 8).

17 U. Baldini, 'La scuola scientifica emiliana della Compagnia di Gesù, 1600-1660. Linee di una ricostruzione archivistica' in *Università e cultura a Ferrara e Bologna*. Florence 1989, pp. 109-178.

emies were intended to place the best students in close proximity to professors, but they were also open to students and scholars from outside, provided these were members of Jesuit congregations.

As well as the most celebrated, such as the one at the Collegio Romano, the academies were active in different colleges, and nearly all of the Society's boarding schools had an active academy within their walls. Their goal was not necessarily to promote research, but they certainly represented the meeting point between teaching and research. It is therefore not surprising to find in the work of Jesuit scholars evidence of the progress made by intellectuals. A study undertaken on the theses in natural philosophy prepared by the Society's students for public defence has shown that, in the first half of the seventeenth century, students knew and made use of the physical and mathematical studies of Lana Terza, Riccioli and Eschinardi, the anti-atomist epistemology of Bartolis and the *magi naturalis* of Kircher and Schott.[18]

On the other hand, alternating between research and teaching favoured a tendency to disclose findings, which can be found even in the texts addressed principally to schools, such as those published by Christoforo Calrio.

The combination of factors examined thus far has shown the original character of the Jesuit colleges as compared to the traditional universities. The great success with which they recruited students troubled the traditional universities. The alarm was first raised at Padua where the lecture halls of the university were emptied, to the profit of the Jesuit college and to the chagrin of the Paduan professors.[19] An examination of the evidence from the efforts of the Bolognese professors in 1634 to block the exodus of their students to the Jesuit colleges, shows the rootedness of the colleges in the sector of higher education from Palermo to Milan.[20]

The consequences were equally felt in terms of the distribution of students, which modified the traditional flows of students. In Rome at the beginning of the seventeenth century, the Jesuit college had around 2,000 students, compared to 100 at La Sapienza. The Jesuit colleges in Naples and Turin were also very attractive. The oldest universities faced competition from the minor university centres created or revitalised by the Jesuits: Bologna and Padua faced competition from the University of Parma, particularly its arts faculty which had been entrusted to the Jesuits. By the middle of the seventeenth century the faculty had one thousand students.[21] The

18 G. Baroncini, 'L'insegnamento della filosofia naturale nei collegi italiani dei Gesuiti (1610-1670): un esempio di nuovo aristotelismo' in G.P. Brizzi (ed.), *La 'Ratio studiorum'. Modelli culturali e pratiche educative dei Gesuiti in Italia tra Cinque e Seicento*. Rome 1981, pp. 163-215.
19 See the oration of Cesare Cremonino, delegate of Paduan University in Venice in *Monumenti veneti intorno i padri gesuiti* 1762, pp. 90-104.
20 See note 3.
21 G.P. Brizzi, 'Educare il principe' (as note 2), p. 151.

new universities of Cagliari and Sassari attracted Sardinian students away from Bologna and Pisa, where they had traditionally studied.[22] Even centres such as Fermo, Macerata, Syracuse, L'Aquila, Genes, Palermo and Mantua benefitted from the teaching in the new universities by reviewing their own educational roles.

More generally, the success of the curriculum proposed by the *ratio studiorum* brought about the closure of a level of schools, the propedeutic schools, which taught courses in grammar, humanities and rhetoric, the most popular courses in arts faculties. Students interested in these courses left the university lecture halls for the Jesuit schools. This phenomenon began in the later decades of the sixteenth century with important consequences for the composition and numbers of university students.

Even if the education practised by the Jesuits was limited to the faculties of arts and theology, and if their control was never over a whole university (with the case of Sassari being an exception), it should be remembered that the consequences of this limitation were modest during the period examined here. The demand of the new professionals came at a time of stagnation. Although they were not expecting from the curriculum professional openings or the acquisition of academic grades, there was a growing need for education among the privileged classes. These demands were seen to be met in the literary and philosophical model of instruction which characterised the curriculum of Jesuit colleges.

There is a great deal more to be extracted from examinations of the historico-institutional aspects of the Jesuits' teaching methods, and from what was taught, and from examining the clashes — religious, cultural, ideological — between the colleges and professors in the universities. I shall cite here the examples of the polemic unleashed against Averroist naturalism which was characteristic of the philosophy school at the University of Padua, and the attitudes adopted during the Galileo case.

The original contributions to education made by the Jesuits came to a sudden halt with the *Ordinatio* of 1651 and with new restrictions appearing in 1693 which affirmed that in the public teaching of logic, natural and moral philosophy it was wrong to contradict Aristotelian doctrines. The reaction that the Jesuits evinced from the middle of the seventeenth century to the scientific movement which was developing in the academies, and their negative attitudes towards Cartesianism brought about a decline in their schools at the very moment when the universities were opening themselves to the influence of the new sciences. Certainly, their attitudes had a profound influ-

---

22 See R. Turtas, *La nascita dell' università in Sardegna. La politica culturale dei sovrani spagnoli nella formazione degli Atenei di Sassari e Cagliari (1543-1632)*. Sassari 1988; R. Turtas, *Scuola e Università in Sardegna tra '500 e '600. L' organizzazione dell' istruzione durante i decenni formativi dell' Università di Sassari (1562-1635)*. Sassari 1995.

ence on the vigorous polemic arising against their schools during the eighteenth century. However, the originality of their organisation and educational techniques penetrated the Italian university system and contributed to the modelling of new universities, as these were envisaged in the reforming plans of the Enlightenment.

More research is required in a number of directions in order properly to evaluate the role played by the Jesuit institutions in the history of higher education in Italy. As regards the flows of students, we have only limited data; for the role played by individual institutions we have only a few studies which tend to be celebratory rather than critical, and we know too little about the original contributions made by individual teachers. Despite the limited data, we do have evidence that is more than mere lists upon which we can base further work. Clearly, as I asserted in my epigraph and do so again here in conclusion, we cannot meaningfully examine the history of university instruction in the early modern period if we do not pay attention to the role assumed by the Jesuit colleges.

Translated into English by Mark James Lilley

Index

Abravanal, Isaac, 93
Acquavira, Claudio, 187
Agricola, Rudolf, 86
Alvey, Provost, 76, 113, 122, 125, 133
Andreae, Jakob, 185
Andrews, Lancelot, 83
Anglo-Irish, 62-3, 64, 65, 66, 67, 69
Antonides, Johannes, 157
Apian, Peter, 80, 82
Aristotle, 135-48, 196
Arminianism, 126, 147
Arnold, Sir Arnold, 11, 14, 20

Bachury, Elijah, 93
Baduel, Claude, 150
Bagshaw, Edward, 139
Ball, William, 85
Bancroft, Richard, 32
Barclay, John, 146
Barlieus, Caspar, 160, 161, 164
Barnes, Thomas, 126
Barrington, Sir Thomas and Lady and Francis, 125, 126, 129
Basnet, Edward, Dean of St Patrick's, 7
Bathurst, Ralph, 140
Bayle, Pierre, 148
Baynes, Paul, 120
Bedell, William, 119, 121, 125, 128, 132, 134
Bedwell, William, 83
Bellarmine, Robert, 92, 99, 103, 104
Bernard, Richard, 122
Beza, Theodor, 91, 98, 99, 100
Birchinsewes, Ralph, 95
Blundeville, Thomas, 80, 81
Boethius, Hector, 95
Bohun, Ralph, 143
Borromeo, Carlo, 191
Bouchier, Henry, 109-10
Boyle, Robert, 136-7
Bradshaw, William, 118
Brady, Hugh, Bishop of Meath, 12, 13, 14-15, 15-16, 18, 20, 21, 22, 25, 27

Brahe, Tyco, 82, 194
Brenner, Bishop Martin, 183
Briggs, Henry, 85
Brightman, Thomas, 94
Brinckley, John, 91, 92
Broughton, Hugh, 94
Browne, George, Archbishop of Dublin, 2-11
Browne, Thomas, 137
Bruno, Giordano, 141
Buchanan, George, 95
Buck, George, 161
Burchardus, A. (Magdeburg), 151
Burnett, Gilbert, 143, 144
Butler, Charles, 87

Calvin, John/ Calvinist, 41, 66, 67, 93, 98, 99, 100-1, 112, 114, 126, 127, 130, 151-6, 161, 166, 168
Cambridge, 48
Carmemarius, 99
Campion, Sir Edmund, 22
Campion, Edward, 95
Cantebury, place of pilgrimage, 17
Cardanus, Hieronymous, 82
Cardinal, Sybrand, 157
Carion, Johannes, 95
Carpenter, Nathaniel, 138
Cartwright, Thomas, 43, 49, 96, 104, 105, 132
Cecil, Sir William, Lord Burghley, 2, 11-13, 15-16, 17, 20, 25, 26, 27, 28, 32, 37, 39, 42-3
Cele, Johan, 164
Ceporinus, 90
Chadderton, Mr., 123
Challoner, Luke, 75-115, 119, 122, 123, 125, 128
Chappell, William, Provost, 66, 121
Chapuis, Eustace, 154
Charles, Archduke of Inner Austria, 179-82, 183

Chauncey, Charles, 128
Cheke, John, 91
Chichester, Sir Arthur, 63
Cholinus, M. (Cologne), 151
Christ Church Cathedral, Dublin, 4, 5, 9
Christian humanism, 45, 47
Chytraeus, David, 95, 177, 178
Ciceronian Latin, viii
Cisneros de Jimenéz, 100
Civility, vii, viii, ix, 62, 186
Civilising influence, 15, 62
Clement VII, 99
Clenardus, Niclaus, 153
Cleonardus, 90
Clapton, Tamzin, (Thomasina), 127
Colet, John, 154
Collinson, Patrick, 41
Conring, Hermann (Helmstedt), 151
Conway, Brilliana, 129
Conway, Dr Robert, 30
Constantine, Emperor, 116
Cooke, Sir William, 105-6
Copernicus, Nicolaus, 81, 82, 141
Cotton, John, 121, 122, 125, 128
Court of Wards, 59
Creef, Thomas, Prebendary of St Patrick's, 30, 116-17
Culverwell, Ezekiel, 123-124, 127
Curwen, Archbishop Hugh, 15-16, 18, 19, 21, 30, 32, 45
Cusack, Sir Thomas, 14
Cuthbert, Michael, 129

Da Celpio, Ambrogio, 90
Daill, Jean, 147
Davies, Sir John, 106, 111
de Dieu, Ludovicus, 116
Dee, John, 82-83
De Lunoy, Jean (Hamburg), 151
Della Mirandola, Pico, 141
Descartes (see also neoterics), 194, 196
Despantarius, Johannes, 88-9
De Victoria, Johannes, 175
Digges, Leonard, 84, 85
Dillon, Sir Lucas, 1
Dillon, Sir Theobald, 59
Dod, John, 121, 123, 124
Donatus, 88, 89, 90

Dowdell, Henry, 145
Downing, Emannuel and Lucy, 116, 128
Drusius, John, 92, 94
Dunst, Henry, 85
Dury, John, 75
Drusius, Johannes, 146
Dyke, Daniel, 122-3, 125

Edward VI, king of England, 3, 4, 7-8, 9, 14, 27
Elias, Norbert, vii
Elizabeth I, queen of England, 13, 33, 36
Elyot, Charles, 88
English Civil War, 54
English Pale, 15, 22, 66
English Privy Council, 1, 10, 14, 18, 20, 25, 28, 30, 40, 63
Erasmus of Rotterdam, vii, 47, 48, 87
Estienne, Robert, 89, 97, 98, 100
Evelyn, John, 143
Eyre, William, 122

Farmer, William, 95
Fenner, Dudley, 86, 87
Ferdinand I, King of the Romans, 172, 173, 175, 178
Fitzsimon, Henry, 64, 65, 66, 67
Fitzwilliam, Sir William, 129
Fresius, Gemma, 80, 82, 164
Fulke, William, 85, 123

Gaelic Irish (people), ix, 19, 62, 64, 65, 66, 67, 69
Galen, 105
Gassendi, 194
Gataker, Thomas, the younger, 124, 134
Gesonides, 93
Gessner, Conrad, 106-107, 108
Gilbert, Sir Humphrey, ix, 161
Gilbert, William, 139
Gilbey, Anthony, 98, 100
Gomarus, Franciscus, 161, 165
Goodman, Cristopher, 43, 130
Gouge, William, 123, 124, 126
Gower, Stanley, 129
Grammar Schools, 8
Gray's Inn, 120

Gregory XIII, Pope, 192
Gresham College, London, ix
Groterus, Jacobus, 165
Grotius, Hugo, 160

Hagelganss, J.G. (Frankfurt-an-Main), 152
Hakluyt, Richard, 84
Hall, Jozeph, 106
Hampton Court Conference, 118
Hammer, Meredith, 36
Harding, John, 95
Harley, Robert, 129
Hartlib, Samuel, 140
Harvey, Sir Francis, 126
Harvey, William, 105
Hatton, Sir Christopher, 31-2
Hegius, Alexander, 164
Henrician Reformation, 4
Henry IV, King of England, 157
Henry VII, King of England, 37
Henry VIII, King of England, 6-7, 14, 20
Henry of Portugal, 153
Heyleyn, Peter, 130, 131
Hieron, Samuel, 125
Hildershem, Arthur, 124-125
Hill, John, 123
Holy Roman Empire of the German Nation, 47
Holzhalb, Leonard, 147
Hoode, Thomas, 81
Hooker, Thomas, 122, 126
Hübner, Joachim, 140

Illyricus, Matteus Flacius, 95, 96
St Ignatius of Loyala, 173, 187
Inns of Court, 54
Irish Articles of 1615, 130
Irish Colleges (on the continent), 55
Irish Parliament, 11
Irish Privy Council, 23, 25
Isenbach, Johannes, 165
Iunius, Franciscus (Heidleberg) 92, 98, 104, 151

Jajus, Cladius, 173, 174
James I, King of England, 62, 63
Jesuits, 46, 187-197

Jobst, W. (Justus) (Frankfurt-an-oder), 151
Johnson, Richard, 17
Julius III, Pope, 192

Keckermann, Bartholemew, 109, 142
Kepler, Johannes, 82, 194
Kimchi, David, 91, 93
Knight, William, 147

Larogue, Daniel, 148
Lascaris, Canstantine, 90
Laud, Archbishop William, 66, 159, 160
Lewkenor, Edward, 126
Lichtenberger, Johannes, 83
Lively, Edward, 94
Locke, John, 139-144, 146
Loftus, Adam, viii, 14-15, 16, 17, 18, 20, 21, 22, 26, 27, 30, 31-2, 34-52, 132-3
The Long Room, (Trinity College, Dublin), 52
Louis XIII, King of France, 157
Lubrianski, Bishop John, 153
Lucae, Franciscus (Frankfurt-an-Oder), 151
Luther, Martin, 93, 96
Lydiat, Thomas, 122

Maestlin, Mikael, 82
Mahaffy, J.P., 34-5, 132
Marcellus, Adrianus, 165
Marshall, Stephen, 126
Martinus, Petrus, 92, 94
Mary, Queen of England, 7, 16-17, 98
Maxwell, Constantia, 76
Meade, Joseph, 84, 120-1, 123, 127
Melancthon, Phillip, 47, 85, 86, 95
Mercator, Gerard, 83
Meursius, Johannes, 161
Middendorpius, J. (Cologne), 151
Mildmay, Walter, 127, 129
Monastic Cathedral, Bath, 4
Monastic Cathedral, Coventry, 4
Morton, Thomas, 104
Mulerius, Nicolaus, 165
Münster, Sebastian, 84, 92, 94, 97, 101
Murdersson, John, 165

Neoterics (Descartes, Hobbes and Locke), 140-1
The Nine Years War, 62, 63
Norris, John, 145
Nowel, Increase, 128

O'Gara, Fergal, 59, 60
Ortelius, Abraham, 83

Pagninus, Santes, 91, 92, 94
Paleotti, Gabrielle, 191
Parchitius, S. (Frankfurt-an-oder), 151
Pareus, David, 147
Parker, Matthew, 98, 99
Parker, Thomas and Robert, 128
Parr, Richard, 76, 102, 103, 131
The Particular Book (TCD), 57, 61, 108-9
Paul III, Pope, 192
Penton, Stephen, 144
Perne, Andrew, 83
Perkins, William, 86, 105
Perrot, Sir John, 2, 25-6, 27-9, 33
Phillip II, Kong of Spain, 156
Phillip of Hesse, 150
Pilgrim, Nicholas, 85
Pirckheimer, Wilibald, 84
Pius IV, Pope, 192
Plantin, Christopher, 97
Poliziano, Angelo Ambrogini, 47
Polyander, Johannes, 165
Possevino, Antonius, 107
Potter, Francis, 139
Presbyterianism, 43-4, 49-50, 116-17
Preston, John, 121, 123, 126
Puritanism, 41, 42, 49, 94, 96, 97, 98, 99, 104, 105, 111, 112, 116-17, 118, 120-34
Pym, Francis, 127

Rainold, John, 83, 85
Ramus, Petrus, 82, 84, 86, 87, 89, 111-12, 113, 114, 141
Recorde, Robert, 81, 82, 85
Reinhold, Erasmus, 81-2, 113
Renecherus, Hermannus, 165
Reuchlin, Johannes, 92-3, 94
Reynolds, Edward, 144-5

Rheticus, Georg Joachim, 81
Rich, Barnaby, 35-6, 39
Rich, Nathaniel, 127, 129
Rich, Richard, 126, 129
Rich, Robert, 126, 129
Rogers, Daniel, 121
Rogers, Ezekiel, 124, 125
Rogers, Richard, 126

Salignaci, Bernard, 91
Schwimmer, J.M. (Jena), 151
Secular Cathedrals, Lichfield and Wells, 4
Seton, Alexander, 86
Sherwood, Mr, 128
Schute, John, 85
Sibbs, Richard, 120, 121, 123, 126, 127
Sidney, Sir Henry, viii, 18, 22, 23-4, 25, 26, 37
Sixsmith, Thomas, 80
Sleidan, Johannes, 95
Smith, Thomas, 91
Snel, Rudolph, 87
Spanheim, Frederick, 116
Spenser, Edmund, viii
St John's College (Cambridge), 120
St Leger, Sir Anthony, 6, 7, 9, 10
St Patrick's Cathedral (Dublin), 1
Stabaeus, Bishop George, 183
Staneyhurst, Sir James, 22, 23-4
Staneyhurst, Richard, 87, 95, 100
Stapleton, 102, 103
Stone, Lawrence, 54
Sturm, Johannes, 87, 150, 163, 178
Sussex, Earl of, 37
Silburgius, 90-1

Talon, Omer, 87
Temple, Provost William, 60, 61, 65, 119, 134
Tirrel, Sir John, 110, 111
Travero, Walter, 49-52, 104, 132-3
Tremellius, Emanuel, 92, 97, 98
Twynne, Brian, 85

Ussher, James, 51, 75-115, 116-34
Ussher, John, 22, 30-1

Valla, Lorenzo, 88, 89, 90
Valleus, Antonius, 165
Van Diest, Henricus, 159
Vatable, François, 98
Vere, Lady Mary and Sir Horace, 128-9
Veronese, Guarino, 88
Viete, 194
Vitelleschi, Muzio, 187
Voetius, Gisbertus, 152-6
Von Schwendi, Field Marshall Lazarus, 186
Vossius, Gerard, 116, 159, 160, 161, 164

Walsingham, Sir Francis, 39, 43
Walsingham, place of pilgrimage, 17
Ward, Nathaniel, 127
Ward, Samuel, 94, 122, 124-5
Ward, Seth, 136-137, 138, 141, 142
Ware, Sir James, 128

Warren, Edward, 110
Waterhouse, Sir Edward, 1
Watts, William, 137
Webster, John, 136
Wellesley, Robert, Archdeacon of Dublin, 16, 17, 30
Weston, Dr Robert, Dean of the Arches, 21, 22, 23-4
White, Rowland, 22
Whitgift, John, 96, 99
Whittaker, William, 105, 123
Whittingham, William, 98
Wilkins, John, 138, 141
William, Duke of Bavaria, 180
William of Orange, 156
Winthrop, John, 127-8
Wroth, Sir Thomas, 11, 14, 20

Zwingli, Huldrych, 93